Full Circle

Full Circle

Log of the Navy's No. 1 Conscript

John Gritten

Cualann Press

ISBN 0 9535036 9 0

First Edition 2003

British Library Cataloguing in Publication Data. A catalogue record of this
book is available at the British Library.

Printed by
Bell & Bain Limited, Glasgow.

Published by
Cualann Press Limited, 6 Corpach Drive, Dunfermline, KY12 7XG, Scotland
Tel/Fax 01383 733724
Email: cualann@btinternet.com
Website: www.cualann-scottish-books.co.uk

Dedication

Full Circle is a small tribute to the men who died in the Allies' first 'Dunkirk', the evacuation from Central Norway. It is also a tribute to all those who were killed in actions in which I, one of the fortunate ones who survived six years without injury, was involved.

In particular, it is in memory of my cousin and Shotley Bridge playmate Arthur Grenfell Allen; schoolmates Geoffrey Askew; John Ashburner and Jan Fink, three who perished, and to any others who, unknown to me, suffered the same fate.

Edmund: *Thou hast spoken right, 'tis true,*
The wheel is come full circle, I am here.

King Lear, Act V, Sc iii

CONTENTS

Illustrations

Picture Section

Foreword

When a good journalist is on the trail of a good story one can expect a quality report. In *Full Circle* we have such a journalist with his very own good story: his wartime service at sea. Though it has its origins in the unpromising literary environment of the boiler and engine room as a stoker, John Gritten's early experience of action amidst the dramatic events of the Norwegian campaign are followed by the abundant interest of his service at sea and on land in different locations.

In due course he is commissioned—how fortuitously is a story in itself—and, armed with notebook and pen, fulfils his D-Day role in a tank landing craft bound for *King Red* beach in the *Gold* sector. His contemporary notes give a sense of immediacy to what has passed into history as a combined operation on a hitherto unprecedented scale. Just as graphic are some of the images of his final months of service in the Far East, observing the undiminished commitment of defeated Japanese sailors.

John Gritten's story is told with verve, humour, irony, illuminating context, insight and compassion. When he writes of what it feels to be below decks in a destroyer 'swaying and dipping, rolling, pitching, crashing and shuddering' as the vessel ploughs through turbulent seas, you feel identified with him. The smell and heat of the engine room are as well conveyed.

Relationships and duties, routine and action, are all here and we learn much as well. Of course we know that a 'Bunting Tosser' is a signals rating but do we know what a Sand-scratcher or Dab-toe is?

If you respond to close observation of those who face the challenge of the sea and of their wartime protagonists, this book is for you. It is also admirably illustrated. Gritten has a facility of communication which draws you into sharing his circumstances.

In the Second World War Experience Centre it is our mission to rescue from oblivion stories such as his and associated memorabilia. He has succeeded where so many have striven unavailingly. With warm congratulations to author and publisher, I commend this book.

Dr Peter Liddle
The Director
The Second World War Experience Centre
5 Feast Field
Horsforth
Leeds LS18 4TS

Preface

Nicholas Lezard, a Saturday *Guardian* books editor, once wrote: 'I have absolutely no problem in keeping the events of the Second World War intact in the communal memory. It gives ... 90 per cent of small boys a rudimentary grounding in the study of history.' Surely not only small boys: the communal memory is notoriously short. Eric Hobsbawm has recalled how he was once asked by 'an intelligent American student' whether the phrase 'Second World War' meant that there had been a First World War. This was, hopefully, an extreme example of communal amnesia.

These memoirs were originally written nearer the time when the events they recall took place, specifically for my sons who were no longer 'small boys' nor students, but adults. Now it is my eleven grand offspring and all of their generation who are inheritors of the 'communal memory' to which I am fortunate to be able to contribute my, in some respects unique, grams of input. But there is absolutely no intention to glorify war or to give the impression that something 'special' or 'manly' attaches to those who took part in it. Warfare is the antithesis of civilised behaviour and no aspect of it should be glamourised. I believe war memoirs should be regarded as contributions to history, in this case, about a war against the forcible imposition of totalitarian and racist regimes on whole populations.

In 1944 Joseph Mallalieu, the author and journalist who later became a Labour MP, wrote an entertaining book, *Very Ordinary Seaman*, about his wartime experiences as a Naval rating. In 1992 William Griffiths did likewise in *My Darling Children*: *War From The Lower Deck*. What these authors did so successfully for upper deck ratings I have attempted to do for the Navy's engine-room branch because, to the best of my knowledge, only men for whom the Royal Navy was a lifetime career have written about it. No other journalist, I believe, called up into the wartime Navy opted to be a stoker or, if he did, later wrote about it.

I would also bet my bottom euro that nothing has been written about that exclusive body of men, the permanent boiler-cleaning parties which were established at some shore bases during the war to relieve seagoing stokers of a vital but very insalubrious job and allow them more shore leave. They consisted of a mixture of a few young survivors from ships that had been sunk with three-badge 'stripeys', men who had done some twenty years' service in the regular Navy and had been called up from the RN Reserve. These unsung veterans surely deserve a niche in the historical annals, the majority of whom were in poor physical shape (I mention one man with one lung) who for six and a half days a week for years on end inhaled oil-fuel soot, powdered rust and black lead as their contribution to the war effort.

Nor has anything been written about the Press Division which was manned by a Commander RN in the Admiralty and by RNVR officers, all peacetime journalists, who had served first as ratings then as executive officers, before becoming Official Naval Reporters (ONRs), Photographers (ONPs) or sub-editors within the Admiralty. Exceptionally, I was commissioned to become an ONR directly from having been an engine-room branch rating for over three years. Each fleet—Home, Mediterranean, East Indies and Pacific—had its assignment of ONRs and ONPs who filed stories back to the Admiralty where they were sub-edited, censored and disseminated to the press and radio via the Ministry of Information. One would imagine that there was a host of ONR stories covering these fleet operations worth recalling, yet there seems to be no trace of them in official archives. Several stories I filed were blue-pencilled for security reasons and appear here for the first time, together with accounts of D-Day, the Walcheren assault and operations in South East Asia.

Some may be puzzled as to how dialogue can be quoted after this lapse of time. To have put in *oratio obliqua* the spontaneous verbal exchanges, badinage, and yarning of the men with whom I lived day and night for four years would have completely emasculated what was the colourful and often imaginative language of the Lower Deck. I vouch for the authenticity of the stokers' terminology and of the incidents in which they were involved. As to the exchanges with Cdr Rump and Captain Vian, they are close approximations to being verbatim but, again, would have sounded rather pedestrian in reported speech. All other quoted speech is as I noted it at the time and quoted it in my ONR stories.

Full Circle has one other claim to uniqueness. Almost exclusively, the numerous books published since the 1950s about the short-lived Norwegian campaign of 1940 have concentrated on its military and naval aspects. But what impact did the invasion, the Allied intervention and five years' Nazi occupation have on Norwegian *civilians*? Although I only set foot on a few square yards of Norwegian terra firma, I thought my own very limited view should be supplemented by an attempt to find out the reactions of the townsfolk on whose quayside I had spent those brief moments. It was a happy decision, resulting not only in being able to include in *Full Circle* a Norwegian civilian dimension but also a wholly unexpected spin-off: the establishing of a British memorial at Namsos, scene of the Second World War's first Allied evacuation and the setting up by the Norwegians of a Namsos British War Veterans' Committee which hosts the annual May visits to the memorial by its visitors from overseas.

Full Circle is a record of six wartime years, a narrative predicated on the wheel of fortune. It completes four turns …

John Gritten
November 2002

HMS *Afridi* during 1938 trials. Twice she heeled over 30° and stayed there for seconds. *(Photograph courtesy of the Imperial War Museum)*

FIRST TURN–*Afridi*

(Above) **This P&O liner had been converted into HM Armed Cruiser** *Rawalpindi* **but was no match for the huge guns of the battle-cruiser** *Scharnhorst (left).* **The engagement, in far northern waters in November 1939, was all over in fourteen minutes. Captain Kennedy went down with his ship but some survivors were rescued by** *Scharnhorst* **and spent the rest of the war as POWs.** *(Photographs courtesy of the Imperial War Museum)*

Chapter 1

Hooray and Up She Rises

*Hornblower hated the indignity of seasickness as much as he hated the misery
of it all. It was of no avail to tell himself, as he did, despairingly as he clutched
the rail, that Nelson was always seasick, too, at the beginning of a voyage.*

A Ship of the Line: C. S. Forrester

Just as a greyhound is sharp-nosed and sleek, so was this Tribal-class
destroyer, one of the greyhounds of the fleet. Slim of beam, she was
rolling through 90° arcs, her bows lifted to the leaden skies over
hillocks of solid water and all 1,850 tons of her pitched into each valley
bottom with a juddering thump that challenged the endurance of her
welded seams.

Inboard, everything that was not secured slid from one side to the
other. On the mess-decks, crockery clashed inside the lockers; on the
mess tables at mealtimes it would have tested a four-armed Vishnu to
wield and anchor simultaneously cutlery and plates, and stop tea
slopping over. Only a spontaneous muscular reaction stopped men from
toppling backwards off the benches. In the narrow passageways they
made headway, propelled like zigzagging pinballs, shoulders cannoning
off the sides. At night, objects skated with the regularity of a
metronome across the deck until they fetched up against something
immovable and slid back again, waiting for the next roll to take them on
the return journey.

In peacetime, seagoing exercises were cancelled in weather like this for fear of damage to ships' structures. Besides, in such boisterous seas a destroyer could yaw up to 140° off course. This was a new ship, the Royal Navy's largest destroyer, HMS *Afridi*, commissioned on 3 May 1938, a date of destiny. Tests had revealed that all the Tribals had 'rolling propensities' and, during her acceptance trials after she was built, *Afridi* had twice heeled over to 30° and stayed there for perilous seconds. It had been considered too dangerous for her to carry on and she had been ordered to return to port.

But now, this was into the eleventh week of the Second World War and though the BBC had announced it was the worst weather for forty years, peacetime precautions were on hold for the duration. Wild weather must not deter the Home Fleet's North Sea hunt for what was believed to be one of Hitler's pocket battleships.

~~

My seagoing nausea threshold depended on the size of the vessel. In peacetime I had experienced, without any abdominal qualms, a mid-Atlantic hurricane which had forced a 5,000-ton freighter to heave-to. On the other hand, rough seas and the stench of fish aboard a North Sea drifter had resulted in puking for the better part of eighteen hours afloat.

And now, as a result of circumstances part contrived, part unavoidable, Royal Naval Special Reservist No. 1, Stoker (Second Class) J. Gritten was aboard this seagoing bucking bronco spewing up his ring (the matelot's epithet for the human sphincter).

At precisely 04.00 hours on Friday 24 November 1939 I first felt *Afridi*'s swaying and dipping. The alarm rattlers had sounded exactly at this godforsaken hour of the morning. They woke me from a deep sleep, having joined my first RN ship the previous afternoon after a three-train haul from Portsmouth to HM Dockyard at Rosyth on the Firth of Forth and then the usual sub-surface tensions of accommodating to a new situation. I had catapulted out of my hammock onto the stokers' mess-deck even before the rattlers stopped and as a voice above us was shouting: 'All hands to action stations! Damage-control parties close up! Shut all watertight doors and hatches!'

Other naked legs—we slept in our vests and underpants—were sliding out of hammocks, some feet landing on the mess table beneath. Boiler suits were dragged on and men jostled up the ladder to 'close-up' at their action stations. I had been detailed the ammunition supply party beneath the for'ard 4.7 guns.

As I stood in the dim light 'tween decks, I became aware of a number of things in quick succession: the effort needed to keep balance on a swaying deck, the human chain I had joined, cradling and passing shells that had arrived by some, to me unseen, transmission from deep down in the ship, and which the last man in the chain was placing on a chute which ran at an angle to an opening in the upper deck. I was not prepared for the weight of the first of these 8-lb. shells, sagged at the knees and was relieved that the next rating in line was a brawny youth who lifted it out of my arms as if it were no heavier than a prize marrow. The last man lowered it onto the chute, heaved on a lever and sent it aloft where it was retrieved by the guns' crew. By the third or fourth shell I was no longer buckling under the weight. Still, I was glad when it was the turn of the much lighter copper cordite charges to be passed along the same route.

No guns were fired that first morning. The early hour had been chosen as an exercise in how swiftly the somnolent off-watch personnel could close-up at action stations. On subsequent mornings the same routine was carried out hours later, at dawn, when a U-boat might be spotted on the surface recharging its batteries and engaged. The next and following days, the guns were fired in anger, not at dawn and not at a submarine.

~~

Afridi's swaying and dipping, which I had first experienced at 04.00, gradually increased in proportion to a rising wind and swell—and so did my nausea. I had turned-to for my first boiler-room watch-keeping but that became no more than a figure of speech. Uncontrollable seasickness was compounded by incomprehension of this totally unfamiliar milieu.

In Portsmouth I had been given the Stokers' Manual and a rush course in what to expect in the Navy's engine-room branch. My applied mechanics had hitherto been confined to maintaining a bicycle (and I hadn't excelled even at that.) When the SPO (stoker petty officer) instructors used terms like super-heated steam, fan pressure, dirty cones, vaps or double-bottoms I had been completely baffled. I had no idea that simple words like trunk, glands, lips or shoes took on a different meaning down here in the bowels of a warship. The SPOs had blinded us with all this science with the aid of blackboard diagrams illustrating the digestive system of boilers and the anatomy of turbines. They had given instructions on how to brick a furnace and drummed into us 'leaky-tube drill'. This had nothing to do with urinary incontinence; it had everything to do with how to cope if one of hundreds of tubes burst, the tubes through which boiling water passed from a boiler's steel lower drums to the top drum where it was converted into steam to drive the turbines. It was impressed on us that without proficiency in leaky-tube drill (at least in theory) there was no hope of rising from second-class to first-class stoker, let alone upwards to leading stoker, the equivalent of promotion from private to corporal in the Army.

The trouble was that this was just theory. None of it was at all recognisable or relevant to what I saw on lifting the hatch, passing through the airlock doors and climbing down the near-perpendicular 15-foot steel ladder on the plates of boiler-room No. 1. All the pipes I had seen in neat diagrams in the Stokers' Manual or on the SPO's blackboards were here in reality sheathed in whitewashed asbestos lagging and quite unrecognisable. To my nauseous senses, above my head was a labyrinth of macaroni which disappeared into the dim recesses behind the boiler. On the macaroni—bizarre symbolism—were wheels of varying circumference. These were in fact valves, though for me they had no significance. Something I did recognise from my Pompey training was a four-sided gauge glass showing the water level in the top drum. 'Never keep your mince-pies off it for more than a second or two,' we had been adjured, 'or you'll get a burst tube, at least, and 350 lb. per square inch of steam on the loose.'

Fortunately for the efficient running of boiler-room No. 1 my presence was superfluous that day and for days to come as I clung to the rungs of the iron ladder or staggered across the canting plates to be sea-spew in the bilges. Control was maintained by the boiler-room's other two occupants: SPO 'Cock' Kent and Stoker Jimmy Robertson, both peacetime regulars, Navy professionals. Apart from the ship's erratic motions, all was calm, the speed and steam pressure steady. Cock—I never did learn his first name even after the many watches we were to keep together—had wedged himself against the oil-fuel pump and was keeping a wary eye on the gauge glass and the needle of the steam pressure gauge.

Jimmy Robertson paced back and forth across the boiler-room, at one moment straining forward as he went uphill, the next leaning backwards so as not to slip on the tilting steel plates. Every now and then he would turn one of the valves, in rows at each side of the furnace front, leap back to the centre, grab two handles and rapidly pull out and push back two rods, all in one coordinated movement. Or he would lift a little flap on the furnace front, peer inside, his face reflecting the inferno, and start jabbing with a poker at something I couldn't see. I neither understood what he was doing nor, for that matter, cared.

For three more days and nights *Afridi* rolled, pitched, crashed and shuddered. I kept my boiler-room watch-keeping because in the Navy seasickness is a non-sickness: it doesn't exist; one goes on 'working'. I gave up attempting to eat, retched only bile and grew progressively weaker. With the onset of split-second delirium I would see faces in the midst of the macaroni behind the boiler. On the third evening, down on the mess-deck, I just managed to heave my hammock out of the rack where it was wedged tight with all the others. Naval canvas hammocks contained a mattress and a thick woollen blanket. With its clews and rope it was a hefty piece of equipment. I reeled in my efforts to get the rope over one hook but was too weak to pull it up. 'Pusser' Reid, killick of the mess and a kindly disciplinarian, came to the rescue and secured it for me, earning my eternal gratitude.[1]

In rough weather the hammock was Jack's only consolation (apart from the daily tot), the only place which remained comparatively stationary while the world swung around it. But even this had its limitations: if your weight differed from your oppo's in the next hammock, things went bump all through the night. We all had our allotted hooks on which to sling our hammock and had to keep to them. Leading Stoker Roberts was next to me and was about four stones heavier. He probably didn't feel the impact with my hammock every time *Afridi* rolled; I did.

I would discover that, because of the limited space between decks, hammocks had to be slung at a height where the louvres in the ventilation trunk were about six inches from our faces. When they were open in northern waters, out came an icy blast. The alternative, to keep them closed, usually the one chosen in these latitudes, produced a fug that was scissile when over twenty men were sleeping, exhaling, farting in this confined space. Coming off watch in the early hours from the pure air pumped into the boiler-room by the giant fans, I would be struck by the

---

[1] For this and other 'Navalese' see Glossary p. 309.

stench on our mess-decks as I climbed into my hammock.

As Forrester's seasick Hornblower had felt 'the prospect of three days of this is just the same as the prospect of an eternity of it,' I was thinking 'for just how long can this go on?' Yet, sorry as I was for myself, by that third day at sea I realised how much worse conditions would have been if I hadn't chosen to be a stoker. As a seaman, my mess-deck would have been in the fo'c'sle, the forepart of the destroyer where the full lift of pitching bows shot the stomach up to the cranium, and left it there when they dropped. I also realised my good fortune in being in three watches. We worked below for four hours, having eight hours off-duty (providing we were not closed-up at action stations) and 'splitting the dogs' (doing a two-hour stint during the dog watches, 16.00–20.00). This meant that even in the roughest weather the stokers were able to keep some semblance of cleanliness and order on their mess-deck. The wretched seamen, on the other hand, had to work in two watches, four on, four off, and in such exposed conditions they were often exhausted when they came off watch. Few even bothered to sling their hammocks; they just lay down in their oilskins in the gangways or flats or on their mess-deck which, in consequence, never got a scrub-out until the ship returned to harbour. It became a dog's dinner of leftovers, vomit, dropped-off oilskins and broken crockery.

The hazards of being a seaman were also greater. During this bad spell *Afridi* lost two men overboard on the same night: a twenty-three-year-old south Londoner during the middle watch (midnight to 04.00) and a leading torpedo-man whom no one saw disappear. In the howling wind their cries would have been drowned as surely as were their bodies, snatched from the upper deck or a gun platform by the claws of the sea.

But during those first three or four days, if I did thank my lucky stars that I wasn't a seaman, there must have been moments, however fleeting, when I thought: 'God, why did I opt for the Navy at all? If I were a squaddy I'd be on terra firma, perhaps squatting with the French behind the Maginot Line or an erk manning a balloon barrage.'

The winter of 1939–40 was the period dubbed the 'Phoney War' when hardly a shot was fired on the Western Front and nothing heavier than leaflets dropped on the enemy from the air. But the war at sea had started from day one. How I joined the Navy even before that is the part contrived, part unavoidable phase of this history.

Chapter 2

First of the First 500

When I first put this uniform on
I said as I looked in the glass
It's one to a million
That any civilian
Your figure and form will surpass.

Patience: Sir W. S. Gilbert

The first surprise was that I had been summoned by a Commander Rump RN, not to the Admiralty in Whitehall, but to an office in Victoria Street within a whistle blow of the station. The second was that Cdr Rump turned out not to be in gold-braided uniform but in a tweed jacket and flannels. It occurred to me that perhaps the Silent Service wanted to keep this officer incognito for some reason, so some joker had come up with a pseudonym appropriate to a seafarer obliged to sit on his backside in a shore-based establishment. There was an economy of furniture in the large room I entered on that May morning in 1939 and the desk was almost bare. I wondered: had the Admiralty hired the office just for this purpose?

Cdr Rump, a man in mid to late thirties and above average height, greeted me genially with outstretched hand. I had not been expecting such informality. He signalled me to sit down but for the whole of the ensuing, mainly one-sided conversation, he stood, legs astride and hands clasped behind him.

~~

As a very junior reporter on the *Daily Mail* (based in Northcliffe House, which, although situated in nearby Tudor Street, had 'on Fleet Street' glamour in those days) I had written a story which appeared under the headline: 7,000 HUSBANDS ARE 'TWENTIES' with details about what was first dubbed the Conscription Bill, then the Militia Bill, and became, in May 1939, the National Service (Armed Forces) Act. This was history in the making. Conscription in Britain, the only European country that had hitherto entirely volunteer forces, had been introduced for the first time during the First World War. Then, at the end of the war to end all wars, it had been dropped. Now, for the first time, conscription was being introduced in peacetime. Men aged twenty were to serve six months and then one month annually. They would receive 1s. 6d (about 15p) a day, if married, their wives would get 17s (85p) a week, with 5s a week for their first child and 3s for the second. A sergeant-major who had joined the Army in the Great War gave me his opinion that 'these militiamen will be walking on velvet'. The pay for married couples seemed so attractive that there would be 'a rush to get married' among twenty-year-olds. Another piece of invaluable information I gave *Daily Mail* readers was that 'nearly 3,000 miles of khaki is now being woven in Yorkshire mills to clothe the new soldiers.'

Shortly afterwards it was announced that men choosing to serve in the Royal Navy would not be called up until they were twenty-one and only those who were passed as physically A1 would be accepted. My choice had immediately been for the Navy, principally for three reasons: my mother, unhappy in her second marriage, had regaled me as a boy with idyllic descriptions of her first one to an engineer commander RN; pictures and descriptions of First World War trench warfare and the film *All Quiet On The Western Front* had given me a horror of being in the PBI (Poor Bloody Infantry); and a voyage to the Baltic as a supernumerary in a Finnish tramp steamer and another in an old freighter up the Hudson to Albany NY had sealed my romantic notions about life on the ocean wave.

But there were two apparently insurmountable obstacles to joining the service of my choice: I would not be twenty-one for another nine months, so would be called up before then and an astigmatism would fail me in an eye test from being passed A1. I have never discovered how the process which led to the letter summoning me to Victoria Street was set in motion. It may have been the result of something I said to my news editor or, possibly, my often expressed preference to serve my six months in the Navy entered the Palace of Westminster grapevine via a familial initiative, even reaching the ear of the First Lord.

Certainly I had no foreknowledge of what Cdr Rump would tell me that spring morning.

~~

The commander launched into an explanation of why he had summoned me with a preamble which went something like this:

> The Army has been getting a lot of publicity over this national servicemen's call-up and I'm afraid the Admiralty has been dragging its anchor. We've got to keep a steady watch on the Estimates—every time they come up in Parliament we have to fight for the Navy's share. We must keep the Navy in the public eye and persist in reminding MPs of the Senior Service's paramount importance.

I was surprised at this frankness regarding the perennial inter-service wrangles over their respective shares of the defence cake. The Commander became more specific:

> As far as this call-up is concerned we mustn't miss the boat. But we can't call Naval National Servicemen Militiamen, so we have created the RN Special Reserve and the first 500 twenty-one year-olds will be called up on 16 August to do six months preliminary training and then for a month every year they will serve with the Fleet. And this is where you come into the picture: we will give you as your Official Number, RNSR No. 1, call you up with the others and expect you to write about it in your paper.

So, that was it: I was to age prematurely by a few months and, though Cdr Rump never mentioned it, I presumed a Nelsonic blind eye would be turned to any physical defects. In the event, I did attend a normal medical check-up along with other twenty-year-olds, including a perfunctory eye test, and passed. My Certificate of Service states that No. 1's 'date of enrolment' into the Royal Naval Special Reserve was 11 June.

R.N.S.R. 9.

CERTIFICATE of the Service of

SURNAME (IN BLOCK LETTERS).	OTHER NAMES.
GRITTEN	John.

In the Royal Naval Special Reserve.

Date of enrolment __11a June 1939__   Date of discharge _____

Man's Signature on discharge

Official No. S.R. __1__

Date of Birth __21st Feb 1919__

Where born { Town or Village __Ealing Middlesex__

County _____

Trade brought up to __Journalist__

Previous service in H.M. Forces { Corps or Force _____

From _____ to _____

Religious Denomination __Church of England.__

Nearest known Relative or Friend
(To be noted in pencil)

Relationship : __Wife__

Name : __Beatrice__

Address : __73 Rickenberio St__
__Newburn Rd__
__11/43__ __Hull__
__York__

Annual Training		**Swimming Qualifications**		
Commencement	Period	Date	Qualification	Signature
16th August, 1939	6 weeks disciplinary training	20-9-39.	P.P.T.	E. Joince

Description of Person	Stature		Chest, In.	Colour of			Marks, Wounds, and Scars
	Feet	In.		Hair	Eyes	Complexion	
On commencement of Training ... —							

Date	Wounds received in Action and Hurt Certificate; also any Meritorious Service, Special Recommendations, Prize or other Grants.	Captain's Signature
2 October 1939	Passed educationally for Leading Stoker.	H. Pole
22 apl 43	Qual FF	No. Hume

1939: No. 1's 'proof of existence'.

The Commander[2] was as good as his word. I was one of the 500 men who on 16 August 1939 got off the train at Plymouth and reported 'on board' HMS *Drake*, otherwise the Naval barracks at Devonport. All shore establishments in the Navy, we were quick to learn, were HM 'ships' which you 'boarded' or from which you 'went ashore.' According to Lower Deck mythology, West Country folk had a propensity for guzzling large quantities of Cornish pasties or tiddy-hoggies, hence Devonport was known throughout the service as 'Guzz'.

Once the 500 were assembled on the parade ground an officer prefaced his welcoming spiel by calling us 'Gentlemen of the Navy' without any manifest irony. Whether this was his own inspiration or a greeting hit upon in the course of lengthy discussion on how to deal with this influx of birds of six months' passage, it was certainly the last time we would be so addressed in the next few years. We were segregated in a different barrack block from the young lads who had recently joined, intending to make the Navy their full-time career. I suspect they were treated rather differently from us.

We were divided into classes and Chief Gunner's Mate 'Nobby' Clarke in charge of my Class 10 was a West Countryman in his mid-forties, stocky, blue-eyed, weather-tanned, whose hearing had been affected by the big guns roaring at the battle of Jutland in 1916. He combined a bluff exterior with a basic humanity and I never heard a critical word spoken by anyone about Nobby. In the limited time available he did his best not only to teach us the Naval version of square-bashing but to instruct us how to tie knots, splice rope and box a compass. He supervised our climb into the cross-trees of the 140 foot high mast which sprouted from the parade ground, rowing in a long-boat on the Tavy's estuary and swimming several lengths in a white drill suit. He introduced us to a totally new way of life and how to get in and out of a hammock without pitching onto the deck. We were inducted into the new parlance: lavatories, for instance, were henceforth 'heads', so-called according to cherished Naval tradition, because in the wooden-walls Navy, a plank was rigged outboard above the leeward bow wave at the head of the ship. The very thought of such hazardous natural functioning was enough to make one constipated. To my simple landlubberly mind

---

[2] Post-war research revealed that a Paymaster Lieut Commander R. H. Rump did exist and was based at HMS *President*, the RNVR (Voluntary Reserve) training ship that used to be moored alongside the Thames Embankment opposite Temple Gardens. Shortly after this interview he was posted to the boys' training ship HMS *Ganges*.

came a much less ingenious explanation: the heads of squatting men were all that was visible when the truncated swing doors, a manifestation of the Admiralty's homophobia, swung to. Before I got used to communal defecation I had nostalgia for the luxury of a locked loo.

To keep my side of the unspoken 'bargain' with Cdr Rump, on the first evening I wrote, on a mess table in Guzz, a feature story for the *Daily Mail* about the Gentlemen of the Navy. But we couldn't 'go ashore' that night and there was no public phone within the barracks. When I gave my screed to Nobby the next morning, impressing on him the urgency of getting it to my office, he said he would do his best but it would first have to be seen by an officer. It was over three weeks before he handed it back without a dot or comma altered. After that lapse of time, however, it was obviously hopelessly outdated for a national daily. In any case, by then there was an overriding and dramatic reason for it being totally irrelevant.

It was exactly three weeks after we had reported on board *Drake* that every man in the barracks was assembled on the parade ground and at one minute past 11 a.m. on that Sunday 3 September we heard the tired voice of the seventy-year-old Prime Minister, Neville Chamberlain, relayed over the speakers:

> This morning, the British ambassador in Berlin handed the German Government a final note stating that, unless the British Government heard from them by 11 o'clock that they were prepared at once to withdraw their troops from Poland, a state of war would exist between us. I have to tell you now that no such undertaking has been received and that consequently this country is at war with Germany.

He had hardly finished speaking when the banshee wails of Britain's first air raid warning rose and fell repeatedly. We streaked at the double for the entrances to the shelters under the parade ground. As I ran down a few concrete steps I was struck by how absurdly shallow the shelter was.

We would soon see for ourselves what the Poles had already discovered: that war was more than dodging in and out of shelters on account of a false alarm because a French aircraft had arrived from across the Channel ahead of schedule. At sea, within hours of Chamberlain's declaration of war, 119 civilians (including twenty-two Americans) and eighteen crew had lost their lives when a German submarine, a U-boat (*Unterseebot*), sank the British liner *Athenia,* 250 miles north-west of Ireland. Now, barely a fortnight later, we recalled what we had read and heard about that tragedy as we witnessed a long cordon of blanketed, unshaven, grey-faced men shuffling through the parade ground on the way to *Drake*'s sickbay. Some were borne on stretchers. It was with shock and foreboding that we learned that our aircraft carrier, *Courageous*, had been tin-fished (torpedoed) in the Irish Sea and these men were survivors who had been landed at Plymouth from Captain Louis Mountbatten's destroyer, *Kelly*. The details were only made public after the war: the 22,500-ton carrier had sunk a quarter of an hour after being struck; 518 men had died. *Kelly* and two cargo ships had risked themselves being tin-fished to pull 742 survivors out of the foul, heaving mass that was the ocean covered with oil-fuel and aviation spirit. Apparently, *Courageous* had turned into the wind to allow her Fleet Air Arm pilots to land their machines on her flight deck and this had presented the U-boat commander with a target he successfully exploited.

Only a few days later we witnessed a similar scene: more men wrapped in blankets trailing towards the sickbay from an 'own goal' on this occasion. At night one of our destroyers had sliced through a sister ship. The day would come when I would be working alongside one of the survivors, a stoker who had heard men screaming behind a bulkhead watertight door that had been slammed shut, dooming them to a watery grave in a vain effort to save the ship.

~~

But those early days in the Merry Andrew also had their lighter side. One morning we were lined up on the parade ground with Nobby explaining some of the more esoteric aspects of Naval routine. He always quietly explained what he wanted us to do before snapping out his orders without making us feel he was dealing with a bunch of morons. He realised he was dealing with men who came from all walks of life and despite living on an island, a surprising number in the economic depression years of the 1930s, when holidays for so many were unaffordable, had never even seen the sea, let alone a warship. He got around to initiating us into the routine of 'Off caps!'—the command Jack had to obey when standing at the table to receive his pay, when facing a disciplinary charge or cheering the monarch inspecting the fleet. To the mere civilian, the lifting of a cap would be accomplished without a second thought; but for the ingenious inventors of Naval discipline, that was too straightforward. The circumference of the cap's flat crown being larger than that of its peakless rim, it is the only part that can be grasped between thumb and forefinger, but it would have been too simple for Jack just to grab the front and pull it off his loaf. Instead, Naval routine insisted that he must stretch his right forearm across his face, grasp the crown-rim above his left ear and only then lift off. If he were simultaneously giving three cheers for the monarch, he continued the movement skywards; if in front of the paymaster, he had to place the cap, flat top uppermost, on the table for his pay to be placed on it by the supply assistant. He then removed the cash, replaced the cap on his head, saluted and retired. Inside the cap was a lining with pleats radiating from a hole in the middle, large enough to tuck something underneath. This was often Jack's receptacle for his pay book and it was a handy place to keep what barbers ashore would be referring to when they whispered conspiratorially: 'Anything else you require, Jack?' Personally, at that time I was keeping a few sheets of loo paper in mine: I had probably found a shortage in the 'heads' one day.

Having carefully explained this routine and after we had gone through the 'Off caps!' procedure by numbers, Nobby considered we were ready for a rehearsal. 'Off caps!' he ordered briskly and in one smooth, non-stop, curvilinear movement, off came twenty-five caps which were duly hoisted at arm's length above our heads. It was lucky for me that Nobby's eyes were focusing at that moment on one of my chums at the other end of the rank; the breeze helped too. For as I raised my arm there issued from the cap a stream of pusser's coarse, brown loo paper which fluttered merrily across the parade ground.

~~

We felt self-conscious in this strange uniform during our first runs ashore in Plymouth. The shapeless serge jumper was too thick for comfort on a summer's day and the serge bell-bottom trousers were prickly. We felt like walking sacks. Even worse for our self-esteem, we didn't look like sailors (a term, incidentally, only used by landlubberly civvies and which Jack rarely applied to himself.)

The 'regular' matelots 'Western Ocean rolling' the streets or thronging the bars had almost Mediterranean blue collars compared with our newly issued dark blue ones. That showed their years in the service compared with us sprogs [3] as a result of years of dhobeying [4] those collars until they had acquired this enviable faded hue. They also had better-fitting suits than those with which we had been issued and many sported gold instead of red badges (denoting the branch of the service in which they were serving) and chevrons or stripes (years of service) on their jumpers. At the moment we were conspicuous in having neither. This well-fitting rig, we would discover, had been bought by Jack at his own expense from so-called naval tailors who were in reality civilian men's outfitters thriving on Jack's narcissism. Many a matelot had got himself into serious debt to the naval tailors. The fact that no self-respecting matelot would go ashore in his pusser-issued uniform and would kit himself out in 14-inch instead of the pusser 12-inch bell-bottoms and in a jersey which showed to advantage his broad shoulders and slim waist, was really an ongoing 'mutiny' which was tolerated within limits. Only when Jack's sartorial whims went beyond these—some tried sporting 16-inch bell-bottoms—did authority pounce. All 'liberty men' were inspected by the Officer of the Watch before going ashore and such offenders had to fall out and stay on board.

If the Admiralty tolerance had extended thus far, argued the barrack-room lawyers, why did it not reform the uniform and issue the same style of tiddley suits that Jack favoured, thus cutting out the naval tailor 'sharks'?

~~

Our preliminary training was drawing to an end and the 500 were asked individually whether they had made up their minds on which branch of the service they wanted to join. We were now at war and our decision had far greater significance than if we had just been Special Reservists to be called up for a month once a year. Some in Class 10 chose the Fleet Air Arm, others wanted to be torpedo, ASDIC (anti-submarine) or supply ratings (looking after a ship's stores), or become cooks or officers' stewards. Those who had had some kind of clerical job in Civvy Street chose to be writers, usually working in the ship's pay office. My particular chum had worked in a Boots the Chemist pharmaceutical laboratory in Nottingham and so chose to be a sick berth tiffy (attendant),

---

[3] See Glossary p. 309.
[4] Dhobeying was a Hindi word of imperial Indian origin. A *dhobey wallah* used to be a servant who did the sahib's or mem-sahib's washing.

resigned henceforth to being dubbed a 'poultice walloper'.

Some may have opted for the engine-room department as engine-room artificers (ERAs) or electrical artificers (EAs) but I do not recall any of my classmates choosing to become stokers and Nobby Clarke was surprised when I made this my preference. 'Why not a writer?' was his anticipated rejoinder. It was a question I have had to answer many times. Had I chosen to be a seaman or opted for almost any other branch it would not have occurred to anybody to ask why. In the lay mind a stoker was a creature more ape than human, hairy, sweaty with a muscled torso glistening in the glow of a furnace. My short answer has always been that, for a change, I wanted to do something as far removed from a desk job as possible. If my interlocutor was not satisfied with that I would add that I had done some stoking 'outside', withholding the fact that this had been confined to having kept a single watch helping to trim coal on a transatlantic cargo ship. But this had not the slightest relevance to stoking in the RN since oil had taken the place of coal-fired boilers ever since the First Lord of the Admiralty, Winston Churchill, decided on the change in 1912. I never regretted that decision.

In over four years on the Lower Deck I never came across another stoker who had had an office job in Civvy Street. Professionals called up into the wartime Navy were considered 'officer material', did their six months obligatory Lower Deck service, usually as seamen, before joining HMS *King Alfred*, the officer-training establishment. The most colourful example I came across in this category was in HMS *Beaver*, Immingham Barracks at the mouth of the Humber: Trevor, a Welshman who had been training as an opera singer. One day at tot time, it might have been Trevor's birthday when he would have been offered 'sippers' by his oppos, he was persuaded to demonstrate his vocal talent. His fine baritone filled the big dining hall with Figaro's *Non piu andrei:*

> Say goodbye to pastime and play, lad,
> Say goodbye to your laces
> To your airs and your graces.

This was an apt choice since it was a catalogue of the pleasures and luxuries which the disgraced page, Cherubino, would have to give up when he joined the army. Mozart's impish humour would have been tickled by the storm of appreciative clapping, stamping, whistling and thumping with plates on the wooden tables from men who labelled any classical performance as 'pisspot music' even if it did not remotely resemble chamber music.

~~

After a passing-out ceremony marching-past an admiral, the first 500 dispersed to their various bases to begin training for whichever branch of the service they had chosen. My draft chit was for HMS *Victory*, another stone frigate, the Naval barracks in Portsmouth, and I became a 'Pompey' rating henceforth. It was obvious that *Victory* derived its name from its famous namesake on which Nelson died at the battle of Trafalgar and which is preserved for posterity in a Portsmouth harbour dry dock. What was puzzling, however, was why the town was known to every matelot as Pompey. I have since learned that out of various explanations the most plausible is that it derived from a French vessel, the *Pompée*, captured in the Napoleonic Wars and permanently moored in Portsmouth harbour where it was used as temporary accommodation for men press-ganged into the Navy and awaiting draft to seagoing ships.

It was the end of the RN Special Reserve, at least for the duration of the war. There would be post-war National Service Acts and a resuscitated RNSR was still functioning in 1950 with men between the ages of eighteen and twenty-six doing twenty-four months 'whole-time service'. National Service in general virtually ceased in 1958, the National Service Act was repealed in 1960 and the last group of National Servicemen was disbanded in 1962.

Post-war research into who was my counterpart in the Army revealed a Private Rupert Alexander who had been given the number 10000001. He apparently joined the Middlesex Regiment in 1939 as the first National Serviceman (although its Regimental Association informed me it had no trace of him). From other sources I discovered Alexander survived the war as a captain in the Royal Lincolnshire Regiment but, unfortunately, did not survive the hazards of the road: he became a car salesman in Spilsby, Lincolnshire, and died in a car accident in the early Sixties.

My counterpart in the RAF, No. 701000, Wallace Richard Weatherall, was called up in July 1939 just before his twenty-first birthday, not only survived the war, returning to his Windsor home in October 1945, but fifty-six years later gave me a run-down of his wartime service. This included helping to maintain three Wellington bombers at a

Suffolk base, being seconded to a secret site guarded by the Home Guard where our aircraft were guided home from operations over enemy territory, checking Hurricane fighters imported from Canada, and training glider pilots. His peacetime work was electrical maintenance and installation until he retired in 1980.

Although there was now no RN Special Reserve, the No. 1 stayed with me as my official number throughout my time on the Lower Deck. I never discovered whether there had been an RNSR 2 or anybody else among our 500 with a single digit. Having that one-off official number certainly brought no benefits; it led to confusion and the initial assumption by some chiefs and petty officers that I was more than a trifle dim-witted. For, in addition to the official number given to every rating, he also received, on joining a ship, a Ship's Book Number. Except on 'big ships' with complements of over 1,000—battleships, aircraft carriers, even cruisers—the Ship's Book Number would never be more than two or three digits. On the occasions when I was requested to declare my official number, by a Jaunty (Master-at-Arms) for example, I would reply: 'One, chief', to which would come the exasperated retort: 'Not your Ship's Book Number—I said your OFFICIAL Number.' With the bland air of someone who couldn't understand why he was being shouted at, I would repeat: 'One, chief', at which he would then demand to see my pay book with that marked effort at self-control reserved for dealing with someone with learning difficulties. But, of course, the pay book confirmed my one-ness. Once a CPO handed it back with the quip: 'Very *singular* indeed. Never seen anything like it, a perishin' once-er!' which was confirmation that a lot of odd things were happening in his peacetime caretaker Navy now that it was being flooded with H/O (hostilities only) personnel.

~~

At the end of my stokers' training course in the Pompey Grammar School, I was deemed fit to watch-keep in a ship's boiler-room although there had been no test to see what I had absorbed. My initiation in *Afridi*'s No. 1 boiler-room, as I have shown, revealed that it had been minimal. In Pompey barracks, all day long at intervals, men's names would be called over the Tannoy to report to the drafting office where they would receive, together with a rail warrant, a draft chit to join a certain ship by a specified time. I did not have to wait long. My chit said I was to report to HMS *Afridi* on 23 November.

Back in the stokers' mess, knowledgeable regulars informed me that she was the biggest destroyer in the Navy, the latest of the Tribal class, and that there were over a dozen other Tribals including *Maori*, *Nubian*, *Somali*, *Mohawk*, *Cossack*, *Eskimo* and *Tartar*. *Afridi* had eight 4.7 guns in twin turrets fore and aft and carried four torpedoes midships. Someone said he had seen her recently in Valetta Harbour, Malta. Further details I would learn anon: that she was 1,850 tons, had a maximum speed of over 36 knots and a wartime complement of approximately 250.

All of this told me as much about *Afridi* as being given a woman's vital statistics would tell me about her temperament or character.

Chapter 3

Vain Pursuit

*The departure of the German ships had not been detected, they had been
wrongly identified twice, the shadowing cruiser had been unable to make
contact, and then finally the last chance of correct identification had been
thrown away by ham-fisted interrogation of a survivor.*

Very Special Intelligence: Patrick Beesly

Although 23 November 1939 was for me personally a significant
day, the day I joined my first RN ship, it also happened to
correspond with two events. One of these would have
consequences of paramount importance for all Allied shipping: the other
would result in a foredoomed act of heroism and a will-o'-the-wisp chase
over miles of ocean. Both were taking place far from Rosyth where I had
joined the *Afridi*.

That night, a machine-gun post on Southend pier opened fire on a
German seaplane. Two bundles at the end of a parachute dropped onto the
Shoeburyness mudflats at the mouth of the Thames. A team from HMS
Vernon mine and torpedo base at Portsmouth were rushed to the spot and,
shedding all metal objects such as keys and cigarette cases, went to work
dismantling the first German magnetic mine to fall into our hands. These
mines, which detonated when a vessel passed over them, had had a
devastating effect on our east-coast shipping. Only that morning I had
seen in the Firth of Forth the gaping wound surrounded by jagged metal

inflicted on the cruiser *Belfast* [5] which had struck a mine two days before and broken her back. Anyone on her quarterdeck, wardroom or officers' cabins must surely have become a victim of the magnetic mine. Now, our experts were able to dismantle one and discover its secrets. This led to the degaussing [6] of our ships, encircling them with a current-carrying conductor which neutralised the magnetism in the mines.

The second event must have been taking place just after I had gone aboard *Afridi* and she was preparing for sea. Over 1,000 miles to the north-west, between the Faroes and Iceland, Captain E. C. Kennedy, commanding the former liner, HM Armed Cruiser *Rawalpindi*, was sending out his first ominous signal to the Admiralty: 'Enemy battle-cruiser sighted'. *Rawalpindi* was on the Northern Patrol which consisted of cruisers and lightly armed merchant cruisers. Their task was to patrol the huge stretches of water between Scotland and Greenland with the dual purpose of intercepting German vessels trying to get home from the Atlantic and to detect German pocket battleships trying to break out into the Atlantic to harry our shipping.

What the Admiralty did not know was that, just before the war started, two pocket battleships, the *Deutschland* and *Admiral Graf Spee*, had managed to slip into the Atlantic undetected. It was not until mid-October that our Operational Intelligence Centre (OIC) realised from signals sent out by doomed merchantmen and survivors' reports that there were two surface raiders sinking our shipping. The *Graf Spee* had steamed around the Cape into the Indian Ocean, seeking out and sinking merchant shipping. (What happened to some of the survivors of those merchantmen will be a dramatic story for a later telling. As to the *Graf Spee* herself, in December she would be pluckily engaged in the South Atlantic by three of our cruisers, would take refuge in the neutral Uruguayan waters of the River Plate and scuttle herself on orders from Germany, her captain shooting himself. For us it would be the first piece of good news since war was declared.) The *Deutschland* had also sunk three ships before being recalled at Hitler's request and, on 15 November, had reached Kiel where she was renamed the *Lutzow*. But because our Admiralty did not know this, Captain Kennedy's signal about sighting a battle-cruiser, though correct, caused confusion.

This was compounded when *Rawalpindi* sent another signal altering 'battle-cruiser' to 'pocket battleship' which the Admiralty took as

---

[5] Then a brand new cruiser, now the Naval Museum moored near London Bridge.
[6] Named after the German mathematician Karl Friedrich Gauss (1777–1855).

confirmation of its view that the pocket battleship *Deutschland* was returning to Germany (which she had already done eight days before). Kennedy had been right the first time: what had been sighted was indeed a battle-cruiser, the *Scharnhorst*. It was not returning from, but attempting to break into, the Atlantic from Wilhelmshaven together with her sister ship *Gneisenau*. Never before in wartime had German capital ships succeeded in getting thus far from their home base.

The error was understandable in the early evening gloom in those far northern waters and because the silhouettes of the German battle-cruisers and pocket battleships were similar. Although, according to German sources, *Gneisenau* was in company with *Scharnhorst* throughout, it was the latter which sighted and engaged the *Rawalpindi* and Captain Kennedy's signal only referred to one ship. In fact, the Admiralty did not realise until the middle of the following month that *Gneisenau* had been involved.

Kennedy gallantly engaged his mighty antagonist who carried nine 11-inch guns, and scored a hit on *Scharnhorst* with his comparatively puny 6-inch. But the engagement was all over in fourteen minutes. The cruiser *Newcastle* steamed to the scene, spotted *Scharnhorst* as she was picking up *Rawalpindi* survivors from a boat but lost contact in a rain squall. (This was before our ships were fitted with radar.) Even *Newcastle* erroneously identified the *Scharnhorst* as a pocket battleship. The German battle-cruisers made their escape down the Norwegian coast into the Baltic.

To the extent that these formidable surface raiders had been detected and for the time foiled in their attempt to make further depredations in the Atlantic, Captain Kennedy's signals and his and his men's sacrifice had not been in vain.

~~

Soon after putting to sea from Rosyth, *Afridi*'s Jimmy the One (First Lieutenant), Lt-Cdr M. D. C. Meyrick, told us over the intercom that the pocket battleship *Deutschland* had been spotted somewhere near the Faroe Islands and the whole of the Home Fleet under the command of Admiral Sir Charles Forbes was steaming north at full speed in search of her. It was not, of course, the *Deutschland* but the *Scharnhorst* and *Gneisenau*.

Whenever I was not on watch down below in the daytime I would stay outside on the heaving upper deck for as long as possible in the hope that the fresh air would relieve my nausea. It was then that I could see we were in the company of a number of wallowing grey shapes, destroyers and three cruisers. Experienced regulars explained that these were the *Southampton*, *Edinburgh* and *Aurora*, the Second Cruiser Squadron.

On the third day out from Rosyth, Saturday 25 November, our section of the fleet was attacked by German aircraft. This was the first time that I heard guns fired in anger and the dull crump of bombs that had missed their targets and were exploding in the water. It was not a new experience for my shipmates, however. About six weeks earlier, the *Gneisenau* with a cruiser and nine destroyers had been spotted by one of our reconnaissance aircraft off the coast of south-west Norway and Admiral Forbes had ordered the Home Fleet to intercept her. It was feared that she was trying to break out into the Atlantic to join the two pocket battleships already preying on British and neutral vessels. (It was one of Admiral Raeder's intentions to draw our ships to the Skagerrak, the 'sleeve' between southern Norway and Denmark, so that they could be attacked by U-boats and come well within range of German bombers.) On 9 October *Afridi* had been part of the force which had been subjected to air attacks all day long, with an estimated 100 bombs aimed ineffectually at the ships. On that occasion, too, contact had been lost and the *Gneisenau* and her escorts had doubled back to Kiel.

Now, our Humber Force, as it was called, was again hunting the enemy in the Norwegian Sea (including, though we were unaware of it, the *Gneisenau*) and again a barrage of anti-aircraft fire was put up by each ship whenever the Luftwaffe came within what was hoped would be the range of her guns. Despite these deterrents the raiders persisted in their attacks showing, as I witnessed when taking a brief spell topsides before going on watch below, a particular interest in the cruiser *Aurora*. One near-miss threw up such a gout of water that for seconds she was completely hidden from view. In breath-taking slow motion, the water fell back, revealing the cruiser still steaming ahead apparently unscathed.

In the boiler-room we had to guess what was going on up top from the sounds around us of our guns firing and sometimes bombs exploding in the sea, or from the orders for fluctuations in speed relayed over the bridge telegraph to the engine-room. Whenever an enemy plane seemed to show us unwelcome attention, Captain G. H. Creswell RN, DSC on the bridge took evasive action.

Afridi had three boiler-rooms which provided and controlled the steam needed to turn the turbines, making the twin propeller shafts rotate and drive the ship through the sea. If more speed was ordered from the bridge, the chief engine-room artificer standing by the engine-room throttles would open them up to allow more steam to the turbines. The team in the regulating boiler-room would then have to make more steam by turning on more sprayers to jet oil-fuel into the furnace and, if necessary, relay the order to the other two boiler-rooms. Conversely, if a reduction in speed was ordered, less steam needed to be generated and some sprayers in the boiler-rooms would have to be turned off. If this was not done speedily enough, steam, with the shutting off of the throttles, would rapidly build up in the boilers which had no outlet except the main steam safety valve. If that lifted there would be a dramatic reduction of power accompanied by the ear-splitting shriek of escaping steam that could be heard miles away. There would come a time when that would happen.

Jimmy Robertson was no longer pacing back and forth over the boiler-room plates. He was springing from one side of the boiler front to the other, turning the sprayers on or off, leaping to the appropriate handles of the air-flaps, jerking them in and out. This was to allow more air into the furnace to be consumed with the oil-fuel. The air came from two giant fans which roared overhead. Jimmy was performing these actions in one continuous, perfectly coordinated parabolic movement, all the while darting glances at the needle on the steam pressure gauge as it crept nearer to the red line of 350 lb. per square inch. If the needle were to go over that fateful red line, the main steam valve was in imminent danger of lifting. Or, if it started dropping back, it meant the steam was being used up faster than it was being made.

If *Afridi* increased speed beyond 30 knots, the lungs of the furnace craved more air and the huge fans revved up with a roar which drowned most other sounds. If there was a call from the bridge, Stoker Petty Officer Cock Kent had to put a finger in the ear that was not glued to the voice pipe. Then, because it was useless to shout, he would mouth at Jimmy: 'Up one!' simultaneously holding up a finger. Or: 'Up two!' holding up two digits at which Jimmy would repeat his balletic leaps to turn on the appropriate number of sprayers. But the duffle-coated figure on the bridge, who we knew was pitting his skill against that of the Nazi pilots and bomb-aimers by trying to anticipate their moves, might suddenly order SLOW or even DEAD SLOW on the telegraph when *Afridi* was straining at FULL AHEAD. That was the real test in the boiler-room: how speedily could those sprayers be turned off and steam reduced after the turbine throttles had been shut down? It was a race against the needle.

The only sounds audible above the roar of the fans when *Afridi* was at speed would be her 4.7s barking at the raiders or the measured bursts of the pom-poms and staccato yapping of the point-fives pumping tracer at our antagonists or the sub-marine explosions of near-misses. Whenever these sounds ceased we knew our evading manoeuvres had been successful and our former speed would probably be resumed.

There were no casualties in any of our sister ships that day and, as far as I know, the enemy went unscathed. Cock Kent gave Jimmy Robertson a recommend [7] to the engineer commander, Commander (E) Halliwell, for his cool and energetic performance.

It was that night that we lost the two men overboard,[8] tragedies that heightened our awareness of the hazards when *Afridi* was 'shipping 'em green' or passing from boiler-room to engine-room (there was no below-decks connection) or to the stokers' mess, and we gripped all the harder the rope that slid along the lifeline which was secured the length of the upper deck. There were no chest-high bulwarks on a destroyer and it was all too common for men to be washed overboard. We would hear that two men on our sister Tribal, *Cossack*, had met the same fate.

The foul weather continued into the next week with the Force 7 nor'-westerly ensuring that our upper deck was almost perpetually awash. Articles like a lifebuoy, a smoke-float igniter and tools—anything that was not firmly secured or thoughtlessly laid down for a minute—were lost overboard. But by then at least calm had been restored to my personal intestinal engine-room.

~~

Admiral Forbes's sweep in search of whoever had dispatched *Rawalpindi* had so far proved abortive. The dirty weather was a boon to a cunning enemy who took full advantage of it. Vice-Admiral Marschall in *Gneisenau*, with the advantages of scouting flying boats and an intelligence service that had decrypted our codes so that he was aware of our ships' movements, managed to give us the slip down the Norwegian coast and steam back to base.

---

[7] Naval semi-formal commendation.
[8] See p. 24.

Afridi's fuel, consumed unstintingly, not only in the distance covered, but in the evasive manoeuvring during air raids, was getting dangerously low and we cut short our southern sweep on the Tuesday morning to return to Scapa Flow, the Home Fleet's base in the Orkneys, where we tied up alongside an oiler.

Oiling ship was an operation involving all hands, stokers and seamen alike, as heavy flexible oil-fuel pipes had to be manhandled, hauled and connected from the Blue Ens'n auxiliary's tanks to our own. Over 380 tons of fuel were taken aboard and shortly after 20.00 we slipped past Lamb Holm into the open sea again.

By the next day, Wednesday 29 November, the swell had slightly abated but in the evening our steering gear broke down and we had to revert to steering from the forebridge. *Afridi* reduced speed to 12 knots which was not a healthy situation with possible U-boats lurking, as every man aboard realised. With the boiler-room fans barely turning and the turbines just ticking over, the ship was unusually quiet. This exaggerated any sudden, sharp sound like someone dropping something, and instantly reminded us of the possible underwater presence of an enemy listening for just such a giveaway indication of our position. We would learn that by coincidence the battleship *Rodney* also developed a serious rudder defect on the same day.

We were still at sea on the last day of November, our maximum speed now down to a mere 10 knots, when Admiral Forbes finally gave up trying to track down his elusive enemy and ordered all units of the Home Fleet to return to their normal duties.

It would be a long time before nemesis would catch up with the ship that blew *Rawalpindi* out of the water and not before *Scharnhorst* and *Gneisenau* again made a monkey out of the Navy—at least in the opinion of the media-susceptible British public. In 1942 they made a successful dash for home from the French port of Brest through the English Channel in daylight. At least the daring of the Germans was matched by many brave acts by those who belatedly tried to intercept them, including one for which a posthumous Victoria Cross was awarded.

Eventually, in 1943, *Scharnhorst* was sunk in those far northern waters, which, by a stroke of poetic justice, also were *Rawalpindi*'s grave. It was the guns of the battleship *Duke of York* and accompanying cruisers and the torpedoes of destroyers that prevented her from preying on our convoys to Russia.

Gneisenau's retribution was prolonged: she would be hit three times in April 1940 by *Renown*'s gunfire, damaged the following month by a torpedo in the destroyer *Ardent*'s heroic attack on her, tin-fished again by the submarine *Clyde* in June, severely damaged in April 1941 by yet another torpedo from a Beaufort of Coastal Command while lying in Brest, hit four times by RAF bombers five days later, and was again damaged by bombers in December 1941. After the daring escape through the Channel she struck a mine off Holland and when undergoing repairs in dry dock was bombed by the RAF and put out of action for the duration. She was, what Jack would call, 'an unlucky ship.'

Chapter 4

A Month of Mysteries

The new year (1940) was but a few days old when a prolonged spell of very severe cold set in. It lasted for nearly two months and added no little burden to the cares and the strain on their crews to whom the Arctic conditions brought much discomfort. In February all classes of ship actually kept to the seas for more days than ever before since the advent of steam. The average time spent at sea by all ships of the fleet totalled twenty-three days during the month.

The War At Sea: Captain Stephen Roskill DSC, RN

The normal duties to which Admiral Forbes had ordered us to return after the Fleet's abortive attempt to avenge the sinking of the *Rawalpindi* were, mainly, escorting convoys to and from neutral Norway. Severe storms persisted right up to the end of 1939 but, after those initial four days, I was no longer seasick.

For the brief moments we were not at sea, either in Rosyth or swinging around a buoy in Scapa, we felt we deserved the break. There was therefore understandable resentment on the stokers' mess-deck when we were hauled from our deep slumbers by a tugging at the strings of our hammocks and a whining voice persisted with the refrain: 'Wakey, wakey. Rise an' shine, the mornin's fine! Arses to the wind, cocks to the sun!' There would be groans from under the blankets and a muffled voice would be heard from a hammock: 'Shit in it, Chiefy!' to which the Chief Stoker would retort belligerently: ''Oo's that?' Compared with even the senior hands, like Pusser Reid, he was ancient, probably a three-badge man called back from the Reserve after doing full-time service. I never saw him in the boiler-rooms or engine-room and the only time he materialised was during these morning forays onto our mess-deck, always with that same plaintive whine.

Unable to pinpoint the protest, he would resume: 'I'm tellin' yer: 'Ands off cocks, on socks! Cummon, m'earties you've 'ad yer time by the dockyard clock! Lash up and stow! Lash up and stow!'

This was the accompaniment to his tugging at our hammock clews. He would then clump up the ladder and disappear through the hatch. If he had to come down a second time and found a hammock still slung with a body in it, he would tilt it violently until the beautiful dreamer half fell, half stumbled onto the deck or the mess table. If we were not at sea by then, the scene would be re-enacted at 07.30 the next morning, practically word for word.

Apart from those blissful hours in the hammock, I was quick to learn (as soon as my nausea had become just a bad dream) that there was another moment in the daily routine which every matelot with a G (for grog) in his pay book looked forward to with the eagerness of a wino. And if the Chief Stoker's daily refrain gave us the pyackers, in contrast, the bo'sun's pipe at 11.30 hours thrilled us with the joy of anticipation.

The rising two notes of the whistle would be followed by the shout: 'Up spirits!' and some wag could be relied upon to cap that with: 'Stand fast the Holy Ghost!'

Cups had already been laid out in lines on the mess table for G-takers. Navy rum had been called grog since Admiral Edward Vernon introduced the rum-and-water ration in his West Indies Fleet during the War of Jenkins Ear around 1740. He had been nicknamed 'Old Grog' because of his habit, considered eccentric even before officers wore uniform, of wearing a cloak of corded silk called *gros grain* by the French. Jack Tar transposed this into grogram, then grog. Now, Pusser Reid took the mess 'fanny' to the upper deck to queue up, with the leading hands of other messes, where pusser's rum was being meted out under the lynx eye of an officer. Petty officers and chiefs were allowed theirs neat; ours was diluted with two-parts water but still seemed more potent than any rum obtainable ashore. It was diluted so that Jack would not consider it worth putting his tot in a bottle and saving it up for when he went on leave or 'up-homers' (that is, to his lady-friend's home in port). Connoisseurs claimed rum went 'flat' forty-five minutes after it was diluted. The chiefs and POs were on trust not to do any such thing with their tots which is why they were given them neat. It was an open secret, however, that those willing to run the gauntlet of the Customs Officers at the dockyard gates did just that and I suspect there were not a few lockers in the chiefs' and POs' mess which contained a concealed bottle of neaters.

The ritual which took place when Pusser Reid returned with the fanny began with the solemnity accorded Holy Communion. There would be an air of religious intensity as at least twenty pairs of eyes—that is if we were not at sea and only a few men were on watch—homed-in on those rows of cups and didn't blink until the last drop in the fanny was poured into the last cup. Next, a kind of volunteer referee would stoop to cup-rim level and run his eye along the line, making absolutely certain that not one had a fraction of a dram more grog than another. Only when Pusser Reid got agreement that none overlapped the hypothetical Plimsoll line were we allowed to pick up the cups.

Any veteran tot-drinker would sluice it down in one gulp with the aplomb of a Russian tossing back a vodka. But it was at this stage that the tot performed its role as currency. Payment was usually in the form of 'sippers'. This meant offering one's tot to someone in settlement of a good turn he had performed. For instance, going ashore would be in two watches, so, if a man in the port watch had a date with a long-haired chum ashore on the night he should be on duty on board, he would offer his oppo in the starboard watch sippers to stay on board in his stead. It was like MPs pairing for a division in the House of Commons. If the attraction ashore was so impelling that a man wanted to catch the liberty boat several times in succession, he would offer 'gulpers'. However, it was unwritten protocol that even if 'gulpers' was his due, the recipient should not drain the cup to the dregs. A token sip should be left at the bottom for the donor. Any man who drained another's tot completely would be considered so low he could crawl under a snake's belly with a top hat on.

There has been no 'Up spirits!' in the RN since 1 August 1970 except when the mainbrace is spliced on ceremonial occasions. It is surprising that the tradition lasted for over 230 years since such strong alcohol, 'the opiate of the messes', must have inevitably impaired, however temporarily, Jack's alertness. It was abolished, according to the Admiralty Board, 'in the interests of safety and efficiency' with the modern Jack having to deal with 'complex and often delicate machinery and systems'. In corroboration, I can vouch that, after downing my tot followed by dinner and if there was no afternoon watch to keep, I would lie on the mess-deck table or a locker, crashing my swede in Jackspeak [9] and float off immediately into the realms of Morpheus.

Jack's conditions today have so improved that there is probably no excuse for such escapism. For us it was a highly prized boon. My only regret is that, with the Andrew's fixation on the victor at Trafalgar, the dark brown liquid was dubbed Nelson's Blood. Since his body was not pickled in neat rum, as commonly believed, I have always thought the description unfair to Old Grog. Why not Vernon's Blood? [10]

~~

It was after we had just returned to the Firth of Forth from a patrol that *Afridi* was ordered to sea again almost immediately. A U-boat had been reported off the Scottish eastern seaboard. We raced northward to the position we had been given. After steaming in the vicinity for some time, our 'pinger' (ASDIC rating), a Portland-trained expert, detected the characteristic echo of a submarine. A U-boat was apparently lurking in the depths.

In these early months of the war, the Navy still had an ambiguous anti-U-boat policy, despite the success of escorted convoys in the last year of the First World War. Although as early as September 1939 there had been recommendations in the highest quarters that the place for attacking U-boats was close to the convoys to which they would obviously be attracted, another policy also found favour, namely, to hunt for them in the vast expanses of the ocean. Since our number of anti-submarine vessels was severely limited, particularly destroyers, many of our convoys were insufficiently protected, with the inevitable consequence of a mounting toll of our merchant ships. One of the reasons for this shortage was the Admiralty's pre-war faith in the efficacy of ASDIC (so-named from the Anti-submarine Detection Investigation Committee set up in 1917). Few ships had been fitted with ASDIC and the officers in charge of their operation, and no doubt the Submarine

---

[9] See Acknowledgements and Sources, p. 306.
[10] In 1979 the Admiralty approved the re-blending of *Pusser's Rum* for sale to the public with the imprimatur 'The Official Rum of the Royal Naval Association' and a substantial donation from the sale of each bottle goes to the RN Sailors' Fund. A history of the tot will be found in *Nelson's Blood—The Story of Naval Rum* by the late Captain James Pack OBE RN (Royal Naval Museum Publications).

Service itself, were all too well aware of its limitations. Nevertheless, the Admiralty had been so convinced that ASDIC was the answer to any future U-boat threat that, in a period when there were cuts in defence expenditure, it believed that fewer destroyers would be needed, provided that they were equipped with ASDIC.

All that I knew about ASDIC when *Afridi* started searching for a U-boat was that part of the apparatus was a copper dome on the bottom of the ship and there was an ASDIC office, a Holy of Holies I never entered. Here (and on the bridge to where they were relayed), interpretations were made of the electrical impulses which were sent through the sea and bounced off anything solid in their path, creating an echo—the ping. The maximum range of these impulses was just over a mile and a half and they operated only when the ship was going slowly. The operator had to be highly trained: he needed all the skill and practice of playing the harp, as one anti-submarine commander put it, and with acute aural perception to be able to distinguish the slight variations in the ping according to whether the sound waves were reflecting off seabed rocks, a shoal of fish, differences in the water's density, or a submerged submarine. Later on in the war, I would hear the continuous, measured 'ping ... ping ... ping ... of the ASDIC as heard on a destroyer's bridge, like water dripping in a huge cavern. And sometimes I would hear the 'ping-ding ... ping-ding ... ping-ding ... ' which would indicate that we were getting an echo from some kind of submerged object.

Now, down in the boiler-room we had been told we were hunting for a suspected U-boat. As we circled around the area, we had cut down the speed to less than eight knots, the maximum at which ASDIC was effective. Instinctively, we entered into the spirit of the first act in a drama that would be played out over at least the next twenty-four hours. The forced draught fans were at low pressure and almost silent and we found ourselves talking more softly than usual as if our voices could be heard by our antagonists. I was acutely aware that here were two bodies of men, probably in close proximity but mutually invisible, the one on the surface intent on the other's destruction, the submerged prey equally determined to escape. Perhaps being ourselves beneath the surface made us that degree more aware of the feelings of the players from whom we were separated only by a thin wall of steel and a volume of opaque water.

The stillness was suddenly broken by a call over the voice-pipe from the engine-room and hardly had Cock Kent answered than the telegraph clanged 'FULL AHEAD'.

By this time I had become familiar with the machinery in the boiler-room. The Stoker Petty Officers, and especially Cock Kent, had encouraged me first to assist in, then to take over on my own the functions which I had admired Jimmy Robertson performing. I was now the one who jumped to and fro turning on all the sprayers and opening the air flaps into the furnace while Cock set the fans going at full pressure again. *Afridi* must have been leaping out of the water. Cock had already shouted to me the information he got from the engine-room: 'Depth- charges!'

I was surprised at the force of the underwater explosions that followed within seconds, as felt down below in the boiler-room. The steel plates on which we stood seemed to lift. One detonation after another followed in quick succession before we reduced speed and calm was restored.

Cock explained that a diamond pattern, probably as many as ten of these 250 lb. drums packed with explosive, had been launched. In all likelihood, they had been set to explode at different depths. A U-boat at this time could safely dive to more than 300 feet[11] and 'ideally' this one would be in the centre of the diamond. He went on:

> But if she were under way, say doin' eight to nine knots, she could've got out of range of our depth-charges because they take some time to sink to the extreme depth before explodin'. You've got to be bloody wary of those things. It's been known for the shock waves to damage a destroyer's engines, especially in shallow waters. It can upset the ASDIC as well. As soon as they're hurled overboard the ship's got to get away p.d.q. or she gets her arse blown off. Wouldn't be the first time that's 'appened.

Whenever I witnessed depth-charge attacks from topsides, I would see, after they exploded, a 100-yard stretch of sea flattened out and foaming white for a minute or two. Hundreds of dead fish would then float to the surface. On this occasion, as I learned afterwards, there was a slight discolouration of the surface which could have been a patch of oil but no air bubbles were sighted. It was an old trick of a U-boat under attack to release a little oil which it was hoped would fox the hunters into thinking she had been hit or worse and then lie with engines stopped on the seabed if the depth permitted. But now there was nothing that could be

---

[11] In another couple of years U-boats could dive to over 650 feet, well out of the range a depth-charge could be set to explode.

interpreted as wreckage. A marker buoy with a red flag was dropped over the side and all through the night we circled around it.

For the four eerie hours of the middle watch it was not possible to keep up a continuous conversation with Cock Kent, my sole watch companion, and each would turn inwards to thinking his own thoughts.

Cock smoked his pipe propped up against one of the pumps and I would resume pacing the plates back and forth. It was in such idle moments that the thought would pass through my mind: supposing, in sheer desperation, the U-boat captain decided to sneak up to periscope depth and take a pot shot at us with a tin-fish? It was a fleeting notion and, in fact, though our warships were certainly torpedoed, it is doubtful whether there is any record of a U-boat under attack doing anything other than lying doggo or trying to escape submerged.

Came the dawn and there was nothing visible on the surface although the pingers were confident that there was still something lurking below. We continued our circular prowl. At noon, another pattern of depth-charges was launched but still without any visible result. Eventually we turned south and returned to port.

A few days later I got chatting to Leading Seaman Coan, the three-badge senior ASDIC operator who had spent most of his adult life with ASDIC during its development at Portland. Shortly after this episode he received the Distinguished Service Medal. He was quite certain there had been a U-boat at the spot where the ASDIC had made contact. A minesweeper had been sent to investigate and, Coan claimed, an examination of its grappling hooks showed that paint had been scraped off the U-boat's hull. He conjectured that when she first spotted us approaching she had dived. At this precise spot in the North Sea, he said, there was a fissure in the seabed. She might have dived too deep and got stuck in the fissure; alternatively, she might have been blown into it by our depth-charges. Only after the war did we learn that U-boat crews called their vessels 'iron coffins'.

There was no doubt about Coan's sincerity, though he did fail to point out one of ASDIC's weaknesses: it could not indicate the depth of a target so that gauging the depth at which depth-charges should be set to explode was largely guesswork. However, all of us were only too willing to be convinced that our efforts had not been in vain. Yet I heard no expression that could be described as gloating. The thought of gradual suffocation, even of a crew that might have sent our own merchant seamen to their deaths, produced only the comment: 'Poor bastards!'

Our pity may have been unfounded: a cautious Admiralty needed definite proof and never credited *Afridi* with a kill. She was certainly not the first to make such an unsubstantiated claim. Lord Mountbatten's official biographer records that in the first days of the war, his destroyer, *Kelly*, after dropping depth-charges and seeing what appeared to be oil and debris on the surface, claimed a U-boat kill. But it was not logged by an Admiralty which preferred accuracy to propaganda, a policy which one day would cost the Director of Anti-submarine Warfare his job because his estimate of U-boat sinkings was less than the claims Winston Churchill as First Lord was making.

That was the first of three 'mysteries' that puzzled us in that month of January 1940. For those who believed Leading Seaman Coan DSM it was unsolved. However, the following month, our sister Tribal, *Gurkha*, did definitely sink *U-53* off the Farøes.

~~

Apart from our phantom U-boat, we had a *Marie Celeste* mystery for which we had a choice of three explanations. But circumstances would not permit a solution to that one either.

One bright day on the North Sea we discovered a Finnish freighter, crewless, gutted, yet floating with hardly a list. What had happened to make her crew abandon ship and where were they?

She may have been set ablaze by a bomb, torpedo or mine. She was a 'neutral'. The Finnish flag, a blue cross on a white background, one moment hung limply from her stern, the next was brought to life by a gust of wind. I couldn't see her stern and never learned her name. She had probably been bringing food and other cargo to Britain where rationing had begun in January 1940. The dearth of essentials would become critical as the U-boats applied their tourniquet. How many of her crew had been killed, I wondered? If picked up, where had they been landed and how long would it be before they would be able to return to their anxious loved ones?

We would never know the answers and I would only learn from dry post-war statistics that this freighter was part of the total of 755,000 tons of British, Allied and neutral merchant shipping sunk by enemy action of one kind or another in the first four months of the war. By February, the losses would be at the rate of nearly a quarter of a million tons in one month. U-boats alone would sink 274 merchant ships between the following June and October.

But for now, the Finn was a floating menace to shipping, especially at night or in a fog. *Afridi* had no alternative but to administer the *coup de grâce*. Round after round from our 4.7s were pumped into the hulk until the sea finally closed over her. Action such as this would be re-enacted a few months later at Scapa Flow in far grimmer circumstances.

~~

There was another wreck which remained afloat and which became a familiar if dismal sight during our frequent visits to Scapa Flow. This was the old battleship *Iron Duke*, lying on her side half on shore. She had been damaged below the waterline during a raid by Junkers 88s in October and had beached. Wagner's countrymen must have appreciated the *Götterdämmerung* touch about *Iron Duke* sharing the grave of some of her old enemies: the remainder of the Kaiser's fleet which, after being led into captivity at Scapa in 1918, had scuttled themselves. *Iron Duke* was only being used as a base ship and for coastal defence and it had apparently been the only available target on that particular October day in 1939. However, it was depressing and reminded us of what was at the time also a mystery: the sinking in Scapa of another veteran battleship, the *Royal Oak*, only three days before the attack on the *Iron Duke*. Though superannuated, she had still been operational and had been in the hunt for the *Gneisenau* earlier in the month.

All that we had heard was that in the early hours of one morning when the *Royal Oak* was lying close inshore, there had been a explosion on board and, after an interval of about twenty minutes, further terrific explosions, one of which had ripped her open and sent her to the bottom in about ten minutes with the loss of 833 men.

The 'explanation' on our mess-deck was an amalgam of misplaced confidence in Scapa's defences, underestimation of the enemy's daring and capabilities, scepticism regarding any claim coming from 'Lord Haw-Haw',[12] and anti-Irish prejudice.

Lord Haw-Haw had jubilantly announced that a U-boat commander named Gunther Prien had penetrated Scapa and torpedoed the *Royal Oak*. 'Bullshit', said our stokers. As far as subs were concerned, Scapa was

---

[12] The name given to Irish-American Berlin broadcaster, William Joyce, because of his affected la-di-da 'Mayfair' accent. Captured in 1945, he was tried for treason and hanged.

impregnable; they couldn't possibly get through the nets, booms, sunken blockships and patrol vessels which guarded the many entrances between the islands that ring this natural haven. The argument went:

> If the first explosion had been caused by a tin-fish, can you imagine a U-boat hanging around for twenty minutes before it fired more of them? Besides, with every vessel alerted after the explosions, how could any U-boat escape the surface craft hunting her and get through the same obstacles again to the open hogwash? Haw Haw is talking a load of bollocks! More likely it was those Irish dockers who loaded the *Royal Oak*'s stores …

I knew what had fuelled this speculation: the previous year there had been a few letterbox bombs in London. As a reporter, I had covered the first appearance at Bow Street magistrates' court of the alleged IRA perpetrators.

In the event, Lord Haw Haw had been right. The plan was sparked, according to one account, by intelligence provided by a German watch repairer who had worked in Kirkwall for years in peacetime. It had been carefully prepared by Admiral Dönitz, German C-in-C Submarines (later also Admiral of the Fleet and, for one week, Hitler's successor) and Captain Prien.[13] He carried out the operation on the surface throughout by slipping through on the night before the final blockship was to have been sunk to close the one remaining gap in the defences. Prien had accomplished what the Dutch Admiral de Ruyter achieved 272 years before, when he penetrated the Medway which was also protected by a boom and sunken ships. On that occasion the *Royal Oak* was sent to the bottom with other ships of Charles II's navy.

Captain Roskill, in the official Naval history, instanced February 1940 as the month when our ships were kept at sea 'for more days than ever since the advent of steam'. In fact, this had been the case for some time. He was certainly right about the 'Arctic conditions' and there were times, especially when the fans were going full belt, when we wore our duffel coats down in the boiler-room. Our crossing and re-crossing of the Norwegian Sea, escorting convoys, seemed never-ending. There was only time to pick up ammo and stores or to go alongside the oiler before we were at sea again. There was no shore leave and, on 4 January, I wrote

---

[13] Prien and the crew of *U-47* died in March 1941 when depth-charged by HMS *Wolverine*.

home that I had already been at sea for twenty days. In retrospect, I am surprised that whichever officer censored the letter allowed that piece of information, along with my description of an incident which had occurred on New Year's Day, to pass.

Afridi was anchored close to the Town-class anti-aircraft cruiser *Cairo* in the Shetlands oiling base of Sullom Voe, surrounded by bleak, snow-capped hills. I was, in fact, writing a letter on the mess table, just before tot time, when there was an unheralded burst of gunfire, followed almost instantly by the regular thump-thump of two-pounder pom-poms and the chatter of our point-fives.[14] The alarm rattlers sounded-off 'action stations' and we scrambled up the ladder as quickly as one man at a time could get through the narrow hatch. I reached my supply party at the double and joined in passing up the cordite to the guns' crews above. But the 'cease fire' sounded before our 4.7s went into action.

Over the hills had suddenly appeared two bombers which swooped like Highland eagles straight for *Afridi* and *Cairo*. One dived within fifty feet of our smoke stacks, firing with his machine gun. A couple of bombs fell astern as he skimmed on towards *Cairo*. Our gunners on the pom-pom and point-fives had fired bursts without scoring a hit, but *Cairo*'s fire was more accurate and the gunners claimed that both planes had been hit, were losing altitude and had black smoke pouring from their fuselages as they disappeared over the rim of the hills. We later received confirmation that one had come down on land and that a search party had set out to look for it. We immediately put to sea in case either plane had ditched in the drink and there might be survivors. But nothing was found.

At 18.30 that evening we had the satisfaction of hearing the incident reported on the BBC news, the announcer recording that three sheep had been killed when the planes jettisoned their remaining bombs over the hills. (In my letter home of 4 January I wrote: 'What a waste of good mutton!') There were cheers on the mess-deck when he added: 'A destroyer went in search of the bomber.'

It was the first time we had heard, albeit anonymously, *Afridi* given an honourable mention over the air. Later, we convinced ourselves that the little lyric, *Run, Rabbit, Run*, which was soon being sung and played all over the country was inspired by this incident, the writer substituting a bunny for a baa-lamb. If so, at least it was more down to earth than that other daft ditty spawned during the 'Phoney War': *We're Going To Hang*

---

[14] Multiple 0.5-inch Vickers machine-guns.

Out the Washing On The Siegfried Line.[15] We resumed escorting convoys of merchant ships between the Firth of Forth and Norway. Sometimes as many as fifty vessels, many of them neutrals, would gather off Methil in the Firth and *Afridi* and other Fleet units, including *Cairo* and another anti-aircraft cruiser, *Calcutta*, would escort them across the North Sea to the offshore limits of Norwegian territorial waters where we would pick up a returning convoy.

When one morning there was a dense mist off the Norwegian coast and the convoy was not at the rendezvous, ignoring scruples about Norwegian neutrality, *Afridi* not only crossed the invisible seaward frontier but nosed her way up Bergen Fjord until we found our flock and led it out of the fjord into the open, but still shrouded, sea.

Even on the stokers' mess-deck we knew that this was a breach of a non-belligerent's sovereignty, though no one doubted that, from the strictly naval point of view, it was the right action in the circumstances. It had been impossible to tell how soon the mist would have lifted and it was evident that we could not wait indefinitely for the convoy in waters so accessible to enemy bombers, U-boats and surface warships. Lower Deck thinking was straightforward and not troubled by the complexities of statesmanship or protocol. These ships were bringing much-needed supplies to our country; they had to be protected from enemy attempts to sink them. If they would not leave the fjord for fear of us not finding each other in the fog, then certainly, it was argued, it was the right thing to do to go in to collect them.

I doubt whether it ever crossed anyone's mind on the Lower Deck that the Norwegians might have had a different point of view.

---

[15] The German equivalent of France's Maginot Line of fortifications (by-passed by the Wehrmacht in its May 1940 Blitzkrieg).

Chapter 5

Up 'The Smoke'

Young newcomers on board might scoff at the queer matelots and try to do a big butch number about it, but that didn't last long. The moment they started trouble with someone just because he was homosexual (there were very few of them) then the troublemaker himself was in deep trouble, especially with the older hands, who understood such matters far better than the ODs [Ordinary Seamen].

Heart of Oak: Tristan Jones

The domestic kitchen is no better a place for cooking up rumours than any other room in the home, unlike its naval equivalent, the galley, which is supposed to have this additional function. It is particularly true of the officers' galley, to which the Lower Deck customarily attributes the source of a buzz or rumour. If a matelot sees in a 'galley buzz' something to his advantage, it will spread through the ship like a fire in an oil tanker.

Jack, to bolster his belief in the authenticity of galley buzzes, would tell you how even classified information had sometimes trickled through to the messes via the officers' galley. Any buzz which meant shore leave was in the offing was bound to gain credence. This could stem from a suggestion that some new device had to be fitted in the ship, a serious defect in the engines had to be put right, a boiler clean was overdue (in peacetime that would have been about every 900 hours' steaming; now in wartime there were no such certainties), or, even better, the ship was in imminent need of going into dry dock for a refit.

The last buzz was going the rounds of *Afridi* in January 1940. A refit would mean long leave. Spirits soared. The majority of the ship's company had had no leave since she was in the 'Med' and had perhaps only managed a weekend 'up-homers' when she was based on the Humber. Even when we had put into Rosyth, Edinburgh had been out-of-bounds and there were no fleshpots that I discovered in the grey little village of Inverkeithing or even in Dunfermline. By 18.00 hours we had to be inside Rosyth dockyard where swilling beer in the huge canteen could be curtailed at a moment's notice if it was announced that one's ship was suddenly under steaming orders.

Sure enough, before the month was out, we were steaming past Hartlepool lighthouse and docking in a West Hartlepool dry dock. Lower deck was cleared.[16] *Afridi* was to have a refit. Long leave would be granted: twenty-one days for each watch with one half of the crew remaining aboard for care and maintenance. I was part of the port watch which at first remained on board.

~~

Maintenance as far as the stokers were concerned turned out to be cleaning out the oil-fuel tanks. We were quick to gather from the precautions that had to be taken before entering the tanks that this was not the most salubrious of jobs.

First, the covers had to be removed and the tanks left open to give the accumulated gasses time to escape. A miner's Davy lamp was then lowered into the murky depths to test for gas. If the flame stayed white and strong, it was considered safe to descend; if it went blue or was extinguished, evidently gas was present and the exercise was postponed until further tests signalled the all-clear. We were also given sulphur pills which were supposed to afford protection against dermatitis. Being completely stripped, except for our underpants and a white linen cap-cover over our heads (our normal headgear in the boiler or engine-room), there was plenty of bare skin for contamination.

We were given a final order with a graphic explanation from Stoker Petty Officer Sam Hardy, another Londoner, which went like this:

---

[16] Order for the ship's company to assemble on the quarterdeck, usually for the captain to make an important announcement.

Sing for all yer fuckin' worth, lads, or at least keep natterin'. If yer run out of dirty ditties, just keep bletherin'—it don't matter about what. It's yer voices we want to 'ear, topsides. If we note anyone of yers not singin' or talkin' we'll 'oller down to the others to see if 'e's flaked out. Gas 'as a nasty 'abit of lurkin' undetected—pockets of it. I've known poor sods brought up, out for the count. So, watch it, lads. Keep bawlin' and jabberin'…

Caged electric light bulbs at the end of wandering leads (rubber-insulated electric cables) were lowered into the dark cavern and we climbed down the oil-slippery perpendicular iron ladder, its lowest rung beneath the oil, and waded ankle-deep through the evil-smelling, chocolate-coloured stuff. Buckets with cotton waste were lowered and we started soaking up the oil and wringing out the waste into the buckets.

To Sam, ever alert up top, crouching at the hatch opening, we must have presented a phantasmagoric image, our glistening, black-smeared bodies darting in and out of the pools of light from the lamps as we slid from one compartment of the tank to another, working with all despatch so as not to spend a minute more than we had to in the foul atmosphere. The tank's metallic emptiness resounded to our version of the Salvation Army hymn *This Is My Story*:

> This is my story,
> This is my song,
> Been in the Andrew too fucking long!
> So roll on the *Rodney,*
> The *Nelson,* the *Hood* [17]
> For this four-funnelled bastard
> Is no fucking good.

Our swabbing and squeezing falling into the rhythm of the ditty, we carried on:

> She's a tiddley ship,
> Through the ocean she slips,
> She's steaming by night and by day.
> And when she's in motion,

---

[17] Three battleships.

> She's the pride of the ocean,
> You can't see her arsehole for spray.

And we bawled out the chorus with gusto:

> Side, side, *Afridi*'s ship's side,
> Jimmy [18] looks on her with pride.
> He'd have a blue fit if he saw any shit
> On the side of the *Afridi*'s ship's side.

By the time we had rounded off our concert with a rollicking rendition of *Nellie Dean*, the job was done; the last bucketful of oily waste was hauled aloft and we followed.

~~

When it was the port watch's turn for leave, I went 'up The Smoke'. London by day in those first months of the war had not changed very much. The anticipated air raids hadn't happened and it seemed that the evacuation of children to the countryside had been unnecessary. The only addition in daylight to this first-impression was the barrage balloons gently swaying at the end of arcing cables that were supposed to sheer off the wings of any low-flying attacking aircraft. Even the central lawn of Ladbroke Square, my playground as a kid, had become a barrage balloon anchorage.

London by night, however, was transformed. The blackout regulations imposed a uniform Stygian gloom through which traffic crawled, only the minimum of light coming through cut-outs in the masked headlamps of vehicles. Air raid wardens patrolled the streets to make sure not a glimmer was exposed through carelessly pulled curtains.

One evening, a stroll up Campden Hill brought me to the tall square water tower which in those days dominated it, a feature in G. K. Chesterton's *Napoleon of Notting Hill*. In March 1941 the reservoir beneath it would be hit by a bomb and in April a Luftwaffe bomber would crash in the nearby grounds of what later became Queen Elizabeth College. Opposite was (and still is) a pub, the Windsor Castle, which I had never been in and on the spur of the moment I decided to have jug. I opened the door, pushed through the blackout curtain and blinked in the

---

[18] Jimmy the One: see First Lieutenant in Glossary p. 309.

light. A moderate-sized bar was patronised by a fairly full house of obviously well-to-do South Kensingtonians. There didn't seem to be anyone in uniform and I felt conspicuous and self-conscious. I wanted to back out, but it was too late. Several heads had turned as I entered and interest focused on what, at this early stage of the war, was as yet an uncommon sight. Jack Tar or a sailor (as they no doubt would have described me) was the embodiment of the matelot on a packet of Players but without the beard and whiskers known in the Jolly Andrew as a 'full set'.

I went to the bar and ordered a pint of bitter. As I started pulling up my jumper to get at my belt purse, there was more than one spontaneous offer to pay for it and the money was slapped on the counter. I was immediately engaged in conversations, the reluctant cynosure of all within hearing distance. This was still the period of the 'Phoney War', so dubbed by an American correspondent who, like all the rest of his tribe in France, was desperately scratching around to find something to write about. The public must have got the impression that at least the war at sea was for real and hence the interest in anyone involved in it. Whatever limited information the Admiralty had given the media they must have known about the sinking of the *Athenia*, the *Courageous*, the *Rawalpindi*, the *Jervis Bay* (whose captain received a posthumous Victoria Cross for engaging the pocket battleship *Admiral Scheer* in a valiant attempt to protect his convoy), the *Iron Duke*, the *Royal Oak* and our success in bringing about the scuttling of the *Admiral Graf Spee*.

It was assumed that Lord Haw Haw and his master might have their spies anywhere and there were reminders on pub walls not to indulge in 'careless talk' which 'cost lives' accompanying a cartoon of Hitler with an outsize ear. My cap tally gave no indication of the name of my ship; it simply read HM DESTROYER. The pints of bitter kept lining up in front of me without me having ordered any of them. At a certain stage they began to be laced with rum. Though I remained security conscious, inevitably my tongue loosened.

The principal donor of all this liquid bounty was a genial gentleman, probably in his mid-thirties, who encouraged me to give my opinions about life aboard a destroyer. This I did (from my veteran's experience of less than a couple of months) but without exposing any vital secrets (which I didn't have anyway) or of giving comfort to the enemy. Nevertheless, I did voice what I considered was the unjustifiable difference in living conditions ratings had to endure compared with those of officers. Here we were, I expanded, all on the same small ship, sharing equally the dangers, yet on the one hand, especially at sea, we had to live … and I described the conditions, especially on the seamen's mess-decks. On the other hand, each officer had a cabin to himself and even a servant, a rating whose job it was to keep clean and tidy his 'master's' cabin and clothes—a naval Jeeves.

My new drinking acquaintance listened intently, with evident interest. As for our captain, I said, I would not recognise him ashore since I had never even seen his face. A duffle-coated figure and muffled against the intense cold, he would be glimpsed occasionally as he climbed the ladder to the bridge.

'Time' was eventually called and the Windsor Castle's clientele gradually thinned out, wishing me cheery farewells and 'Good luck, Jack!' The lady I presumed to be the landlord's wife locked the door behind the last one—except for my companion and me. We still had our glasses to empty and the lady seemed in no hurry to get rid of us.

But even Tam o'Shanter found after his glorious booze-up 'nae man can tether time nor tide' and my time came at last to brave the cold outside. To my amazement I found my legs had a will of their own quite independent of the signals my brain was sending them. Beer, rum and the shock of a frosty night had drastically impaired communications. I had to steer a course, first down the steep hill on which the Windsor Castle was perched, up Ladbroke Grove's south-facing hill and down the other side. Luckily, the iron railings separating the pavement from basement areas, many of which would later be removed to be melted down for the war effort, were still there. Just as *Afridi* would zigzag when under attack from the air, I now followed a similar tack except that the ship's movements were controlled; mine were rudderless. I yawed from railings to the nearest lamppost, to which I clung like a red-nosed reveller on a comic postcard. Then rubber-legged steps took me a few yards downhill and again back to the railings. In spite of assuring myself that I was perfectly compos mentis, my self-esteem took a plunge.

An additional embarrassment was the echo of the parting words of my drinking companion in whom I had confided my Bolshie views on the injustices of rank and privilege. Like the others, he had bid me a fond farewell, adding before his final 'God bless' as the lady unlocked the door: 'By the way, I was particularly interested in what you had to say about the officers. I'm also on a destroyer—a lieutenant-commander.'

~~

On a subsequent leave about a year later, I had another encounter as a direct result of being in matelot's uniform. One afternoon near the Queen's Hall, the concert hall destroyed by enemy action, I had stopped to gawp at what remained of the Langham Hotel opposite Broadcasting House. A bomb had sliced off a corner, revealing some of its suites suspended over rubble.

'Terrible isn't it?' remarked a dapper, silver-haired gentleman who had joined me in surveying the ruin. Although there had been isolated raids before the London blitz proper had started in September 1940, to see the destruction of familiar sites never ceased to shock. There was nothing extraordinary about two strangers commenting about a bombed building and we exchanged comments on the barbarity of war in general and in particular about what the Nazis were perpetrating. Then I began to realise that this gentleman was paying more attention to me as a person than to anything I was saying. So, I was not taken by surprise when he said, quite conversationally and apparently confident that he would not be misunderstood: 'Would you like to come up to my place for tea? I live quite close.'

I have never been homophobic but his assumption that I, too, was gay (an epithet that would be invented decades later) presented a problem. I shook my head but, as if an explanation for his invitation were needed, he added: 'I was in the Royal New Zealand Navy myself in the last lot. Does much of that sort of thing go on still in the Navy?'

I was still thinking how to cope with the situation and, to gain time, played along with his misconception. I replied: 'I can't be sure. I'm on small ships … not much opportunity.'

His response was sympathetic. 'Ah, of course, I don't suppose there is. But are you sure you can't come up to my place? It's only around the corner. I'd make it well worth your while.'

'I'm sure you would,' I said, assuming a tone of regret for a lost opportunity. I was thinking desperately what excuse I could make for not 'having tea' with him. I came up with 'Afraid I've got a date in Shepherds Bush and I'm late already.'

'Oh, what a pity!' replied Silver Hair. 'Anyhow, the very best of luck and keep safe. And next time you're on leave, here's my card and do be sure and look me up.' As he handed me his card, we shook hands and I was turning to go when he added: 'Oh, and being a friend. As I said I'll make it well worth while.'

On turning into Mortimer Street to visit my hairdresser girlfriend I glanced at the visiting card. Engraved in copperplate was an Iberian-sounding name like Da Costa or Spinoza with his work title and business address. He was the director of a very well-known Bond Street art gallery. I pondered what a risk the poor man had taken. Apart from blackmail, many of his inclination had been victims of brutal attacks by matelots.

~~

In the Sixties (it was revealed forty years later) the Admiralty ordered a secret crackdown on homosexuality after it claimed that half of all sailors had practised same-sex acts and, according to a report in the *Times*, 'no ship was immune from the threat of blackmail.'

As to the art gallery director's query: 'Does much of that sort of thing still go on?', I can only record that in six years in the wartime Navy there was only one example I came across of apparently proven homosexual practice on board a ship. I had just joined the cruiser HMS *London* in Alexandria to take passage to the UK when 'Clear Lower Deck' was piped and the ship's company assembled on the quarterdeck to hear sentences pronounced on a cook and chief petty officer, who had to stand facing all of us, guarded by white-belted and gaitered seamen as sentences were pronounced. I cannot remember what the sentences were but under King's Rules and Admiralty Regulations the minimum for sodomy was seven years hard labour with almost certain dismissal from the service. Having recently witnessed the harsh treatment meted out to Naval prisoners, I could well imagine how these two unfortunates would be treated.

There's many a true word said in jest and Winston Churchill was historically close to the mark with his 'Don't talk to me about naval tradition. It's nothing but rum, sodomy and the lash.' No tradition dies harder than the association of sodomy with seafaring, dating from the days when continuous sea-time would run into months and men had no opportunities for contact with the opposite sex. Though all that is in the distant past, Jack's reputation lingered on. Paradoxically, he helped to maintain it himself by splicing so much of his badinage with anal allusions and there was an inexhaustible supply of epithets for those who, today, would simply, some would say inappropriately, be described as gay. Without malice or thought for their literal derivation, those in daily circulation in the mess or shore canteen included hatters or brown-hatters, beef-bandits, curp-hounds, knob-stranglers, sword-swallowers and so on, seemingly *ad infinitum*. If Jack called a messmate a brownhatting bastard, there would be no intentional allusion either to his sexuality or his parental origin. It was probably just light-hearted banter.

Some of the youngest members of *Afridi*'s stokers' mess who, like the rest, had signed-on in peacetime to make the Navy their career, hailed from densely populated, poor inner-city areas or North East pit villages. In our manifestly stratified society, my background was professional middle class. There is arguably a greater divide between classes of the same nationality than between similar classes across frontiers. With the 'frontier' that exists between the north and south of Britain, a middle-class Londoner was inevitably the odd man out in this milieu. Mutual accommodation and tolerance was called for and would take time to achieve among thirty-odd men from very different habitats now living in close proximity. For some of those in my age group, the combination of middle-class and Londoner meant that I had a 'soft' life 'outside' compared with theirs. Soft was mentally equated with effeminate, and, axiomatically, effeminate meant homosexual.

A common expression of dissent was 'Up your arse!' or the more nautical: 'Up your big-sea jacksie!' usually accompanied by a prodding of the air by an upward jerk of two fingers, their hypothetical goal implicit. When I was going up the mess-deck ladder one day a young Geordie made the gesture explicit. I have never been quick to take offence. Nevertheless, I must have registered some audible reaction because the killick of the mess, Pusser [19] Reid, who had witnessed the gesture, sternly rebuked the offender and followed it up with a fatherly lecture along these lines:

> You've got to understand that Hostilities Only ratings like him (with a nod at me) volunteered *(sic)* to fight Hitler and his shower of bastards. You should respect him for that, not take the piss. We joined the service in peacetime and what perks there were to be had, we had 'em. For the HOs there's no perks, just a hard slog at what they're not use to. So, just use your loaf, you young sprog and treat him as your 'oppo. If I catch any of you doing anything like that again I'll put him in the rattle. [20]

---

[19] See Glossary p. 309.

[20] That is: report him, probably to the Jaunty (Master at Arms) which would result in punishment.

Poor Geordie! The only touching-up he would be doing in a few short months' time would be gilding harps for St Peter. Until then, I don't think he bore me any ill will and, thanks again to Pusser Reid, a small blow had been struck for tolerance.

But in my naïvety I remained ignorant all the time I was on *Afridi* of the connotation of Nutty, the nickname which SPO Cock Kent gave me and which stuck. In Lower Deck parlance, nutty neither means 'nuts' nor off his rocker, nor toffee-nosed. Nutty is chocolate (fruit and nut?) and to apply it to someone infers that he would be the object of the invitation by the fabled lecherous chief stoker to come with him into the dark recesses behind the boiler to search for the phantom Golden Rivet in the ship's plating. Apart from giving me this nickname, Cock showed me the same respect as he would any other shipmate. It was just his little joke and, in retrospect, I am surprised I never asked him why he had bestowed this moniker on me. If I had done, Cock would have had to resort to his native Bow Bells ingenuity to avoid causing mutual embarrassment.

For all their ribald lingo, the majority of my messmates were a sober (at least while on board) and friendly lot. Some had been on 'big ships' where an excess of what they would term 'bullshit' prevailed, such as obligatory changing into different rigs at various times of the day and where the observance of pusser routine was strictly enforced. I gathered they regarded this as pettifogging, irrelevant to the fighting efficiency of a warship. The engine-room branch was not as constantly harassed 'from arsehole to breakfast time' on these big ships as were the seamen. Nevertheless, I gathered these stokers were glad they had been drafted to a 'small ship' where bullshit was minimal.

As one would expect, it was the married men who were among the more responsible members of the mess. The pay on which to keep a family was meagre enough and any opportunity was taken to supplement it. 'Knocker' White, for instance, ran a dhobey firm, that is, he did the washing when he was off-watch for those of his messmates who found this chore a bind. Even when leave was piped, Knocker never went ashore, preferring to save up the bobs [21] earned from his dhobeying labours and take the kitty home to his wife. In consequence, his pallor matched his name. Another dhobey firm which was not a competitor because there was enough washing for both of them was run by a Geordie twosome, Lofty Ford, one of the mess's older generation, and his 'oppo,

---

[21] The pre-metric shilling or 12*d*.

'Daisy' Adams. Daisy was short, with a pronounced lisp and the creased tragi-comic face of a Grock. Because of their difference in stature we called them 'The long and the short and the tall.'

Another man who seldom went ashore was Leading Stoker Roberts whose hammock bumped at night against mine when *Afridi* was rolling. Robbo was a well-built man, a dab hand at ballroom dancing. He and his wife had won prizes for shaking a wicked hip in competitions back home in Pompey.

A townie of Robbo was Franky Rattue who was given to sudden bursts of animated but good-humoured cursing of his lot at having joined the Jolly Andrew. Though unmarried, he too was saving up his pay to take home to his mother. I was not aware of that at the time but later will be recounted the mystery surrounding how those savings never reached their intended destination.

Other messmates included 'Wiggy' Bennett, a handsome, fair-haired youth who went ashore at every (infrequent) opportunity. There was Leading Stoker 'Pincher' Martin, swarthy, brusque and gold-toothed; Bernie Armstrong, a friendly good-humoured Midlander; the engineer's writer, Leading Stoker Jimmy Marden from Horsham, reserved but not aloof, whom I sensed concealed his disapproval of the boisterous obscenities of some of our young messmates behind a mask of resigned and amiable tolerance; and an Irishman, Achilles Daunt, the only one of my age group with whom I could have a serious conversation about the progress and broader issues of the war. Apart from Pusser Reid and a handful of older men, nobody bothered even to listen to the BBC news bulletins unless there was the possibility of a reference to some action in which *Afridi* or one of her sister ships had been involved. The only literature which got any attention were children's comics, though a copy of *Picture Post*, which somehow found its way into the mess with its pictures of the Russo-Finnish war, did get scanned.

Convinced of the future prowess of their infant, proud parents had given Achilles, twenty-three years earlier, the name of the Greek hero of the Trojan war. He had certainly grown into a strapping youth, tall and with a Palmolive complexion, fully capable of rebuffing with withering scorn and a flow of lucid and well-chosen invective, the inevitable leg-pulling of his Anglo-Saxon messmates. Before going home on leave to his non-belligerent Free State, Achilles had to purchase a complete civvy outfit to avoid internment. To have turned up in Dublin or Rosslare in His Majesty's uniform would have meant the Royal Navy would not have had the services of Stoker Achilles Daunt again for the duration. But, on his return on board, he vowed he would never set foot in Éire again. Perhaps this was because his relatives and friends disapproved of him having joined the navy of a foreign power and for fighting a war on its behalf. After all, his countrymen had taken up arms against the English for 800 years. Whatever the reason, Achilles was now at odds with his homeland and had decided to sell his newly acquired civvies to his messmates, preferring the ready cash to preserving them for when he could again wear them. That would not be until the end of the twelve years for which he had signed on.

For me it would be another six years before I would be able to wear the green porkpie felt hat I had bought off Achilles, with his A.D. initials on the band inside in Olde English lettering.

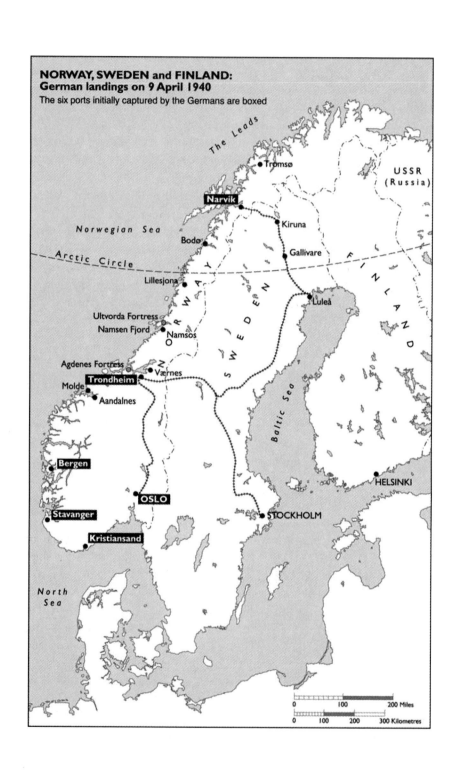

NORWAY, SWEDEN and FINLAND:
German landings on 9 April 1940
The six ports initially captured by the Germans are boxed

The Leads

Tromsø

USSR
(Russia)

Norwegian Sea

Narvik

Kiruna

Bodø

Arctic Circle

Gallivare

FINLAND

Lillesjona

SWEDEN

NORWAY

Luleå

Ultvorda Fortress
Namsen Fjord
Namsos

Agdenes Fortress
Værnes

Baltic Sea

Trondheim
Molde
Aandalnes

Bergen

HELSINKI

OSLO

Stavanger

STOCKHOLM

Kristiansand

North
Sea

| 0 | | 100 | | 200 Miles |
| 0 | 100 | 200 | | 300 Kilometres |

Chapter 6

Unhappy Weeks

The unswerving constancy of purpose of the young men who bore the brunt of the sea and air fighting during these unhappy weeks shines in strong contrast to the indecision and mismanagement at home which marred the whole [Norwegian] campaign.

The War At Sea: Captain Stephen Roskill DSC, RN

The scale of air attack that would be developed against our military forces on shore and our Naval forces off the Norwegian coast was grievously underestimated when the operations were undertaken.

Home Fleet Narrative: Admiral Sir Charles Forbes

While *Afridi*'s ship's company had been either 'up-homers' or on board during the West Hartlepool refit, our sister ship, *Cossack*, had been winning world fame, or notoriety, for points of view differed either side of the Norwegian and North Seas.

There were three principal factors which contributed to the importance of Sweden and Norway to the belligerents: Swedish iron ore; the Norwegian port of Narvik through which it was exported; and Norway's coastal waters through which shipping could slip the 1,200 miles to and from Germany. The Swedish iron-ore-producing towns of Gallivare and Kiruna were linked by a railway running north-west through the Norwegian mountains to the port of Narvik which, though about 160 miles north of the Arctic Circle, is ice-free all the year around.

Another rail link existed between these towns and the Swedish port of Lulea in the Gulf of Bothnia but this was ice-bound in winter. In 1938, Nazi Germany was getting an estimated nine million of its total twenty-two million tons of high grade ore from Sweden.

Since Norway was still neutral, its government continued to allow German ships to load the ore at Narvik and steam back through its island- strewn territorial waters, known to navigators as The Leads. In keeping with international law, these civilian-crewed merchant ships were exercising their 'right of innocent passage'. Furthermore, German ships that had escaped our blockade in the Atlantic also used The Leads to get back home. Conversely, because they were passing through the territorial waters of a neutral country, our warships could not legally intercept them.

As early as sixteen days after our declaration of war, the First Lord of the Admiralty, Winston Churchill, advocated mining The Leads. By November, irked by this obvious leak in our blockade of Germany and also wanting to prevent U-boats and surface warships from entering the Atlantic, he was proposing to the Cabinet an Admiralty plan for a mine barrage from the Orkneys to Norway to seal off the Norwegian Sea (as had been done in the First World War). At first the Cabinet approved of this 'Northern Barrage,' until the Foreign Office pointed out that the Norwegians certainly would not. In fact, when the Norwegians and Swedes were quietly informed of our intention to stop German sea traffic, such was their reaction that the scheme was deferred.

The next episode in The Leads saga was the encounter on 16 February 1940 in Jössingfjord, in the far south-west of Norway, between *Cossack* (commanded temporarily by our Captain Philip Vian), and the armed German supply ship, the tanker *Altmark*, to which 303 British merchant seamen had been transferred after their ships had been sunk in the South Atlantic by the *Admiral Graf Spee*. After *Graf Spee* was scuttled outside Montevideo, *Altmark* managed to evade pursuit and get to The Leads undetected. She was south of Bergen, escorted by Norwegian destroyers, before the Admiralty got wind of her. The Norwegians were genuinely ignorant of the presence of the prisoners because, whenever their officials went aboard, *Altmark*'s captain ordered the winches to be started up and hoses were played on the prisoners in the hold to drown their shouts. On the appearance of British warships, *Altmark* took refuge in Jössingfjord. Diplomatically it was a very tricky situation. Without knowing for certain whether there were any prisoners on board, Churchill gave direct orders to Vian to board the supply ship. *Cossack*'s boarding party removed the hatch covers and shouted 'The Navy's here!' down to the prisoners. The British media made the most of this episode and thrilled the nation. Vian, who had temporarily transferred to *Cossack* with his staff during *Afridi*'s refit in Hartlepool, was awarded the DSO and the DSM was awarded to our Signalman 'Dickey' Davies, who was in the boarding party and was wounded in the shoot-out. Six of *Altmark*'s crew were killed and six wounded but the ship herself was not sunk. She changed her name, continued her role as supply ship to the *Scharnhorst* and the *Gneisenau* and finally blew up in Yokahama, Japan, in 1942. The British seamen were brought back to Rosyth.

'Vian of the *Cossack*' as he was henceforth universally known, would give this laconic postscript to the affair in his memoirs: 'It provided clear evidence that the Norwegian interpretation of neutrality worked wholly to the advantage of the Germans.' True as that was, the elation the *Altmark* incident caused in Britain was not immediately apparent in Norway. At the British embassy in Oslo a young assistant press attaché called Cecil Parrott [22] who was married to a Norwegian and well versed in the language, recorded:

> The Norwegians were outraged by our action because they feared that it would instantly provoke countermeasures from the German side. They were right, since it was in fact only after the *Altmark* episode that Hitler finally gave his agreement to the plan for occupying Norway and thus forestalling the British invasion.

As early as December 1939 Hitler had given the go-ahead for the planning of an invasion of Norway, whether or not a coup could be arranged with the traitor Vidkun Quisling. But if there were at the time criticisms of the British action, the generally pro-British mood of the Norwegians seems to have been restored soon after the Nazi occupation and, whereas the tiny pro-German minority was dubbed 'Quislings', those who courageously supported the British were known as 'Jössings' after the fjord where the *Altmark* had been intercepted.

~~

---

[22] He would have a distinguished diplomatic career, becoming minister in Moscow (1954–57) and ambassador in Prague (1960–64). He was knighted in 1984.

When our refit was near completion Captain Vian returned to *Afridi*, the 4th destroyer Flotilla leader, bringing with him the *Altmark's* ship's cat, presumably after being debriefed, quarantined and de-Nazified.

For men who had formed the watch on board, there had been plenty of all-night shore leave. Inevitably, romances flourished and a few West Hartlepool lasses had heard Jack plight his troth before *Afridi*, after trial runs to test the engines, finally steamed into the North Sea in the last week of March. There must have been some heart-rending farewells as each party knew, however brave a face was put on it, the dangers that must be faced and the possibility of never seeing each other again. In a short while, for some, that would become a certainty.

We steamed slam into a tearing nor'easter which buffeted us for days with only an occasional respite. After such a long spell ashore I had the perverse satisfaction of finding that I was no longer the odd man out in one respect: for a couple of days most of the ship's company were throwing up. One night, about minutes into the middle watch, I was awakened from a deep sleep by a shuddering crash, momentarily convinced we had struck a rock or a mine. Heads shot up from many of the hammocks and one man leapt out of his, so conditioned were we to react to a sudden emergency. It was nothing worse than *Afridi* falling into an extra deep trough and her underside fetching up against the unyielding mass of water at the bottom. But with only an eighth of an inch of steel plating between us and the constricting pressure of the sea, 'protection' that could be torn apart by explosives in a fraction of the time it takes to say 'sardine tin', it is not surprising that the instinct for self-preservation made some overreact. There were guffaws at the expense of the unfortunate who had leapt out of his hammock and a neighbour who was less amused growled: 'You're shit keen on turnin'-to for the mornin' watch, aren't yer, Shiner? For fuck's sake get turned-in and crash yer swede!'

We were back to the old routine: the flotsam waltzing to and fro across the mess-deck; involuntary zigzagging when trying to walk straight ahead, our shoulders cushioning the impact as we cannoned off the walls of the passages; and wading through the miniature Severn Bore that swirled ankle-deep through the washroom. But we did have an unexpected rest for a few days when our mess-deck was put in quarantine after a stoker was carried ashore on a stretcher suffering from cerebro-spinal-meningitis.

~~

One of the ironies of working down below was that sometimes we only learned the details of some action in which our ship had been involved by listening later to the BBC. For example, on 12 April, we heard that two Heinkels had attacked us and the convoy we were escorting until our gunfire drove them off. But down below we could only hear the bombs detonating in the sea and it was from the radio that we learned that ten bombs had been aimed at us.

During this raid I had my only experience of a flashback, not a memory recall but an experience of the kind that every stoker had been warned about. By now I was considered reliable enough to function on my own in the regulating boiler-room, together with Cock Kent or any of the other Stoker Petty Officers. Of the three boiler-rooms, this was the one which received orders directly from the engine-room, mainly about the ship's speed, so that it had the main responsibility for regulating the steam pressure. It must have been when the Heinkels were spotted that our speed accelerated and this necessitated opening up the maximum number of oil-fuel sprayers in the minimum amount of time. Having now become a proficient acrobatic performer, I was, once again, leaping from one side of the boiler to the middle, then from the other side to the middle, turning on sprayers and pulling in and out the handles that operated the air intakes. However, on this occasion, because of a combination of the excess of forced draught and perhaps something cack-handed on my part, when I pulled out the two handles of one of the inlets, my head was illuminated by a halo of fire for a split second. Apart from surprise, the only effect was singed eyebrows.

~~

The first time I recall seeing our CO, 'Vian of the *Cossack*', apart from the duffle-wrapped anonymous figure climbing up to the bridge, was when he addressed us in Rosyth Dockyard on 7 April after Sunday divisions. The inspection in our Number Ones[23] was usually followed by a religious service. The men from other destroyers in our flotilla were assembled on the quay alongside *Afridi*. A buzz had already been going the rounds that troops had been seen boarding the cruisers.

In fact, much had been happening of which at the time we were entirely ignorant and most of it only came to light after the war.

---

[23] Best uniform with gold badges—probably our 'tiddley suit'.

Churchill, thwarted in his 'Northern Barrage' plan, nevertheless persisted in pressing for the mining of The Leads to force German ships into the open sea where we could attack them. With the Russian invasion of Finland on 30 November 1939, the Anglo-French allies felt they had an additional motive for breaching Scandinavian neutrality. The Russians, taken aback by the swift success of the German invasion of Poland, wanted to redefine their frontier with Finland. They feared for the vulnerability of Leningrad should Hitler attack the Soviet Union despite the Nazi-Soviet Non-Aggression Pact, as would happen in June 1941. The Finns rejected the Soviet demands: hence the invasion.

It was the French who came up with the idea of invading Norway, occupying the Swedish iron-ore mines and giving an Anglo-French expeditionary force the opportunity of passing through the two countries to help the Finns. It was envisaged that a simultaneous attack would be made by French forces in Syria against the Russian oil fields in Baku and that this two-pronged attack, 2,000 miles apart, would deprive Germany of its iron and oil without fighting the Nazis themselves. This plan has been described by historian Peter Calvocoressi as 'one of the wildest surmises of the war'. Vian in his war memoirs suggested that his Naval colleague, Admiral Sir Edward Evans, who like Cecil Parrott had a Norwegian wife and spoke Norwegian, was instrumental in persuading the British Government that, if we landed troops in Norway, after a token resistance there would be 'no serious opposition' from the Norwegians. Yet they had already protested when, as early as 6 January, we had informed them of our intention to mine The Leads and after that they had made their protest about the *Altmark* incident.

Vian makes it clear that troops were actually embarked on our ships, Admiral Evans had hoisted his flag in the cruiser *Aurora* and orders had been issued to sail to Norway with this expeditionary force (which, in effect, if it had got as far as Finland would have fought the Russians) when it was learnt on 12 March that the Finns had signed an armistice. In Vian's words: 'The whole basis of the plan had been knocked from under it. The troops were stood down [i.e. they disembarked] and orders rescinded.'

The day after the armistice, 13 March, the Labour MP Arthur Henderson asked Prime Minister Chamberlain in the House of Commons: 'Will the Prime Minister take this opportunity of neutralising German propaganda by making it quite clear that HM Government at no time threatened to violate the neutrality of Sweden and Norway?' Chamberlain gave the reply: 'There was never any threat to violate that neutrality' even though the expedition had been given orders to sail. Moreover, it is now known that only on the day before (12 March) he had instructed Major-General P. J. Mackesy who was in command of the British force, that it should land in Norway 'provided that it can do so *without serious fighting*' (my italics).

Six days later Chamberlain told the Commons that the Supreme War Council had agreed on 5 February to send 100,000 troops to Finland, that they had been ready in March, that 'no effective expedition could arrive in Finland except by passing through Norway and Sweden,' and that before they could be despatched or arrive in Finland it was 'necessary to obtain the assent of the Governments of those two countries.' He also said that Germany, on hearing rumours of the expedition, had threatened Norway and Sweden and that it had been proposed to the Finns that they should first make a public appeal to the Norwegians and Swedes, followed by a formal appeal by us, to allow passage of the expedition.

This, Chamberlain continued, had been done. The Swedes replied that they would allow small groups of volunteers (for Finland) but 'they could not grant a passage for any regular armed force because that would enlarge the area of the war and would turn Sweden into a battlefield.' He then stated unequivocally: 'But we did not on that account discontinue our preparations for the despatch of this force,' and further confirmed:

> We had repeated refusals from Norway and Sweden to permit passage of troops through their countries. Nevertheless, we went on with our preparations until they were complete and, even at the last moment, we could have sent the expedition if the conditions had changed.

The conditions did not change. The Finns first hesitated to give their assent and then, on 12 March, capitulated to the Russians.

If, as Vian recorded, troops were embarked and 'orders to sail had been given,' Chamberlain had been deceiving the House when he said 'there was never any threat to violate neutrality.' In matelot's lingo, it would have needed a lot of green in the eye to believe that, had the expedition sailed and reached Norway, it would then have obligingly returned if the Norwegians had persisted in not wanting it to pass through their country.

In the debate following Chamberlain's speech, the Independent Progressive MP, journalist, author and broadcaster, Vernon Bartlett, said that it was 'a very good thing' that the Finnish war ended when it did 'because we should inevitably have found ourselves at war with Russia, and whatever one's ideological views may be, we already have a big enough job on our hands to defeat Germany. Calvocoressi's verdict was: 'Great Britain and France had been saved by the Finnish collapse from making war on the USSR while they were still at war with Germany.' A Naval source gave the most forthright opinion on the proposed occupation of Narvik, Lulea (Sweden), Trondheim, Bergen and Stavanger: Captain Donald Macintyre DSO and two Bars, DSC, RN records: 'A more hare-brained scheme can seldom have been solemnly concerted by the leaders of a country at war.'

It is in this context that one finds extraordinary the omission of any mention of the proposed expedition to Finland via Norway and Sweden—indeed any mention at all of the Russo-Finnish war—in Captain Roskill's official *The War At Sea 1939–1945*. Since the troops, according to Vian, were embarked on Naval ships which would also have escorted them across the Norwegian Sea, it is odd that a Naval historian of Roskill's calibre in his punctiliously documented first volume failed to mention this episode. It was not until his later (1977) *Churchill and the Admirals* that there is mention of 'a plan (that) was prepared to land a force at Narvik to go to the aid of the Finns … '

Following the cancellation of the original expedition on 12 March because of the collapse of the Finns, Churchill had, by the end of the month, persuaded the Cabinet to ignore Foreign Office objections and to accept the Admiralty plan for mining The Leads. This is where Roskill, after the omission, picked up the story. The new plan was to be called Operation *Wilfred* but with it was to be another, a contingency plan, codenamed *R4*. This involved exactly the same arrangements as those for the 'Finnish' expedition, the same troops, ships and landing places in Norway, but this time it was only to be put into effect if the Germans reacted to our mine-laying by invading Norway.

The date ultimately fixed for Operation *Wilfred* and the conditional launching of *R4* was Monday 8 April (the day after our divisions on the Rosyth quayside). Confidential British and French notes outlining our intentions were delivered to the Swedish and Norwegian Foreign Ministries three days before. On 8 April Norway was informed that mines had in fact been laid. Cecil Parrott recalls that, when he went up in the lift of his *pension* that day, a normally friendly fellow guest nearly tore his eyes out. 'Look what you British have done!' she exclaimed. 'Now you have dragged us into the war' and Parrott's reaction was that he 'felt the Norwegian anger was fully justified'.

~~

As soon as divisions were finished on that Sunday, 7 April, on the quay alongside *Afridi*, Vian gave us a short spiel, the gist of which was that we would soon be 'enjoying' more action than we had seen so far. That was the limit of the information we were given. To add to the air of mystery, there was the rumour that troops had been seen embarking on the cruisers *Devonshire*, *Berwick*, *York* and *Glasgow* earlier that day. During the first dog watch we raised steam and that evening *Afridi*, her sister destroyers and the cruisers *Galatea* and *Arethusa* were steaming out of the Firth of Forth with our noses pointing nor'east.

We would have been even more mystified if we had stayed in Rosyth until the Monday and learned that the troops which had indeed embarked on the four cruisers were then ordered to disembark before the ships cleared port without them.

Unknown to us, probably while Vian was actually speaking, 35 RAF bombers were winging their way to the entrance of the Skagerrak where they would attack (unsuccessfully) a German battle-cruiser, two cruisers and destroyer escorts, all steaming north-west into the Norwegian Sea. It was not until the bombers returned to base nearly four hours later that Admiral Sir Charles Forbes, C-in-C Home Fleet, received this vital information and ordered every available unit to sea to intercept what he thought was an attempted breakout into the Atlantic.

So, though Churchill himself was at the Admiralty on the Saturday evening when heavy units of the German fleet were spotted, no countermeasures were taken specifically to bar an invasion of Norway. In fact, Forbes had been told that these reports were 'of doubtful value'. It was only later that it was admitted they had been correct and in fact were confirmed by the RAF bombers.

True, the battle-cruiser *Renown* sighted the *Scharnhorst* and inflicted damage on the *Gneisenau* before the German battle-cruisers were lost in intermittent driving snow and squalls of rain. But Admiral Raeder's purpose in sending these ships to the far north was a ruse which succeeded: it diverted the British fleet from his main operation, the invasion. On *Afridi*'s Lower Deck at this stage we had no idea that the Germans had already landed in Oslo, Kristiansand, Stavanger, Bergen,

Trondheim and Narvik. There was certainly confusion among those in command as to the enemy's intentions, from Churchill to the First Sea Lord, Admiral Sir Dudley Pound, to Forbes, and so on down the chain of command. Forbes was in the unenviable position, on board his flagship, the battleship *Rodney*, of having to decide (on inadequate information) which should be given priority: preventing *Scharnhorst, Gneisenau* and the heavy cruiser *Admiral Hipper* from getting into the Atlantic and playing havoc with shipping bringing vital cargoes to the UK, or preventing what he increasingly felt was the case, a possible invasion of Norway.[24]

By now Forbes knew *Renown* had engaged the German battle-cruisers and had severely damaged the *Gneisenau* and that the destroyer *Glowworm* on Monday the 8th had heroically rammed and ripped a gash in the side of the *Hipper* before sinking, for which Captain Gerard Roope was posthumously awarded the Navy's first VC of the war. It was an emotional moment when we heard about *Glowworm*'s fate over the BBC and thought of all the men who had gone down with her. Only thirty-eight were picked up and they became prisoners-of-war. In the early hours of Tuesday the 9th, Forbes had received enough information to make it probable that the invasion was underway. But Churchill and Pound, or the two in concert, and apparently without informing Forbes, had already given the order for the troops, earmarked for Norway, in Rosyth and on the Clyde to be disembarked so that the cruisers could put to sea to intercept the heavy German ships. This was the very diversion Raeder had intended we should take. Thus there were no forces available to oppose the German landings which were still, at this juncture, in their initial stages.

Forbes took the only decision possible: to send part of the fleet north to try to prevent *Scharnhorst* and *Gneisenau* (with which contact had been lost) returning to Germany while he himself and another force sailed south to intercept the invasion build-up. Early on Tuesday morning, 9 April, he proposed to attack Bergen but it was not until nearly midday that he received Admiralty confirmation to do so. Four cruisers of Vice-Admiral Sir Geoffrey Layton's 18th Cruiser Squadron were detached to do this, together with seven destroyers. *Afridi* was one of these, although by this time we were about eighty miles to the south of our objective and had to turn back and fight against a northerly gale in which we lost

---

[24] In the 'Conduct of the War' debate in the House of Commons on 7 May, with the advantage of hindsight Leopold Amery MP declared: 'The Navy went off in hot pursuit after that German decoy. Rarely in history can a feint have been more successful.'

another man overboard. It reduced our speed to a maximum 16 knots and it would be night-time before we reached Bergen.

Forbes had ordered Layton to keep his cruisers in the open and to send only the destroyers up Bjornefjord where it was believed the cruiser *Köln* lay. Later, our aircraft spotted two cruisers in the fjord and it was subsequently learned that, besides the *Köln*, there was quite a formidable force made up of the cruisers *Königsburg* [25] and *Bremse* as well as other units.

~~

Before I went below on the afternoon watch that Tuesday we all knew that we were to penetrate one of the fjords and make a torpedo attack on an unknown number of cruisers. The buzz had already started in the WT [26] office from one of the telegraphists or someone carrying signals to the bridge. Even in the open sea it would be a hazardous operation since we would be well within range of the cruisers' 5.9-inch guns before we could fire our tin-fish with any hope of success. From the comments I overheard, the consensus was that in the narrow confines of a fjord it would be suicidal.

Whenever I closed the hatch above my head before opening the boiler-room door and descending to the plates, I would suppress the fleeting thought that there were probably less painful deaths than being scalded by steam from a burst boiler as the result of an explosion by mine, bomb or torpedo. But, as I went on watch on this occasion, I was also conscious of the additional hazard of shells. *Glowworm* had been sunk by *Hipper*'s guns the day before.

One of my stroppier messmates gave vent to the alarm we all felt with a muttered outburst that went something like this: 'All right for them up top: the pigs get promotion and gongs for a death and glory lark like this. They'd probably give the skipper a DSO but what d'we get? A one-way ticket to fuckin' Paradise!'

In other wars men had been put in front of a firing squad for expressing such potentially demoralising sentiments. Joan and John Citizen are expected to admire the corporate valour behind an award to an

---

[25] The next day, 10 April, *Königsburg*, after being hit by Norwegian guns was dive-bombed by Fleet Air Arm Skuas, the first major warship in the war to be sunk in this way, as T. K. Derry pointed out in his official *The Campaign in Norway* (HMSO 1952).
[26] Wireless Telegraphy.

individual officer for a heroic deed and are not encouraged to ponder whether there might have been some under his command who were less than enthusiastic for self-sacrifice. When collective morale in wartime must be maintained, both among the fighting forces and the civilians at home, any expression of the view that 'faint-heartedness' can be more prevalent than just among 'craven exceptions' is regarded by the authorities as tantamount to giving comfort to the enemy. Yet we can be sure that identical opinions to that of Stoker X, tacit or expressed, were present aboard *Glowworm, Ardent* and *Acasta*. Their commanders, knowing the odds of surviving were nil, persisted in trying to inflict the maximum damage on the enemy prior to their own and their ships' companies' certain destruction.

Yet fear is not the handmaiden of clear thinking. Even in my beer-and-rum inspired observations to which the Lieutenant Commander in the Windsor Castle had listened so attentively, I had contended that there should not be such wide discrepancies in living conditions on small ships because every man on board, whether officer or rating, was equally exposed to danger. Disasters do not discriminate. When a commanding officer made a decision knowing that his ship was endangered thereby, he was obviously well aware that he himself and his officers were no more immune to that danger than ratings. Did Stoker X really believe that the thought of 'collecting a gong' entered the mind of a commanding officer when making an inevitably self-destructive decision? Even if, from Dartmouth onwards, a Naval officer throughout his career was steeped in the tradition of the service, with emphasis on the heroic from Grenville to Nelson, that did not produce a kamikaze mentality. Life must have been as dear to the COs of *Glowworm* and those other destroyers as to every individual on board.

One other flaw in my messmate's outburst was that it did not take into account the fact that Vian was himself obeying an order: that of the Commander of the Fleet who, in turn, was complying with Admiralty instructions. Moreover, it was an order that, as we now know, the man on the bridge, so remote from us working in the bowels of the ship, himself almost certainly felt was an unjustifiable risk. With typical understatement he would write in his memoirs that the proposed attack which he was to lead up the fjord would have been 'a considerable proposition'. It would have been in the dark; the position and strength of the shore batteries were unknown; he had no information about booms or other port defences to be negotiated, 'nor indeed how many warships we would have to tackle'. He concluded: 'There was not, therefore, the information necessary to make a plan, or time to give it to the destroyers in company, even had I been able to make one.'

From the *post factum* glimpse into his own thoughts on this occasion, it is difficult to believe that Vian, for all his conditioning in Naval tradition, did not have some personal qualms. It is, therefore, all the more remarkable that he subsequently gave the impression that he believed fear was never an element in the feelings of a ship's company. Nicholas Monsarrat quotes Vian's comment on his novel *The Cruel Sea*: 'There is a note, disagreeable to a Naval reader, of unwarranted fear. The crew of the *Compass Rose* were hunters, not the hunted, and to suggest the hounds were afraid of their fox creates an impression as demoralising as it is false.'

Unwarranted and false? No wonder Monsarrat dismisses Vian's reproof with a laconic, seemingly contemptuous 'Ha!'[27]

I am sure that every man aboard *Afridi* was relieved, even if he did not express it outright as many did, when the Admiralty cancelled the order to enter Bjornefjord. Whitehall had had second thoughts: it considered that Forbes was underestimating the enemy's strength by ordering only seven destroyers to attack what was certainly a superior force and which it was learned subsequently consisted of three cruisers, each with 5.9-inch and six 3.5-inch guns, although the shore batteries had not yet been taken by the Germans. Official Naval historian, Captain Roskill, however, had a different impression which was that the attack 'may well have achieved a valuable success' and that the decision to cancel it was 'ill-judged'.

Whatever relief we felt at the cancellation was premature in that by merely approaching Bergen we had stirred up a hornets' nest of enemy bombers which attacked our force repeatedly as we steamed to rejoin the main body. Both the cruisers *Glasgow* and *Southampton* were damaged by near-misses. Plunging and rearing in the heavy seas, there was no chance of accurate anti-aircraft fire and none of the bombers appeared to have been hit. The CO of our sister Tribal, *Gurkha*, was so irked by this that he turned her about into a following wind and sea so as to give his gunners a better chance of hitting their targets. He thereby isolated his ship from the rest of the force which continued steaming north and she

---

[27] In his *Action This Day* memoirs Vian gives an interesting insight into what he considered should be the order of a commanding officer's priorities if his ship were hit by bombs: ' … it amounted to losing one's reputation, in addition to one's ship and, possibly, life.'

was bombed and sinking when, at night, *Aurora*, located her. Survivors including the CO, were picked up.[28]

~~

As a mere second-class 'buff' stoker, it is extraordinary that I should have had any personal contact with the already renowned 'Vian of the *Cossack*', whose future illustrious career would eventually be crowned by him becoming Admiral of the Fleet Sir Philip Vian GCB, KBE, DSO, RN and merit being buried within a few steps of Horatio Nelson in the crypt of St Paul's Cathedral. The only occasion for a stoker to be spoken to by the CO—or indeed any rating apart from his cabin-hand (in Vian's case, Able Seaman Gammon), officers' stewards perhaps or others whose duties took them to the bridge—was if he were put in the Captain's Report and hauled in front of him on the quarterdeck for some serious misdemeanour. Lesser offences were dealt with by the first lieutenant.

No wonder, then, that I registered incomprehension when, during one quiet forenoon watch in the boiler-room, Cock Kent turned to me after answering an order through the voice pipe with an 'Aye, aye, sir!' given in a shade more deferential tone than usual, and announced with a bland grin: 'Nutty, the skipper want to see yer down aft.'

Since I merely returned a gormless gape, wondering whether this was another Cock Kent leg-pull, he assured me: 'I'm not flannellin'. The captain wants to see yer in 'is cabin.'

'Like this?' I queried, as I was, of course, in a boiler suit.

'Yus, just as yer are. Chop, chop!'

As I have already pointed out, the only time I had actually seen our captain was when he gave us that brief spiel on the Rosyth quayside. Our destinies were to a high degree in his hands and he was, indeed, as remote as the Almighty. I had picked up only one buzz about him soon after he became *Afridi*'s CO: that he differed in at least one respect from his predecessor who during air raids made the ship as difficult a target to hit as possible by sudden variations in speed and violent changes of direction. Not so Vian, or so it was contended, who took the minimum

---

[28] Vian quixotically blamed himself for this. Though in his memoirs he refers to Gurkha's CO as 'a noted gunnery officer (with) years of training', in his report as Captain (D) Fourth Destroyer Flotilla to Rear-Admiral (D) R. H. C. Halifax, he called him 'an inexperienced commanding officer (who) should not have been allowed to have become detached: the responsibility for failure to call him in is wholly mine.'

evasive action and was alleged to have declared that this was 'to give the gunners a chance' (like the *Gurkha*'s captain had done). Whether or not there was any truth in that initially, after further experience of the ship being the target of the bomb-aimers, he would certainly give orders for her to veer this way or that the moment he was informed a bomb had been sighted leaving a plane.

Puzzled and in some trepidation, I made my way aft. Vian was seated in his cabin. Around him, standing, were grouped three officers. I had never been in such intimate proximity to so much gold braid. Nor had I ever seen Vian bareheaded. This was more the face of an American tribal chief than of an Afridi, a beetle-browed Mohawk perhaps, with a steady gaze beneath a flat forehead, a prominent nose and chin, proud but not remote, keen but not (at this moment at any rate) severe. That was the impression of a more than somewhat awed young man on the lowest rung of the Naval hierarchy, additionally embarrassed by being in his working rig instead of his Number Ones.

The following circumlocutory exchange took place. Instead of Vian addressing me directly, an officer opened up with: 'We have been informed that you are a journalist. Is that right?' I admitted as much.

'What kind of journalist?' Vian asked and the lieutenant repeated:

'The captain would like to know what kind of journalist you were.'

'A reporter, sir.'

'He says he was a reporter, sir.'

'Ah yes, a reporter,' and after a moment's reflection, Vian suggested: 'Murders and things, I suppose?'

Since the officer didn't appear to be going to repeat this, I ventured a direct reply: 'No, sir. Only suicides so far.'

I wasn't being (I wouldn't have dared to be) facetious. The *Daily Mail* had a pride of crime reporters as well as a man permanently hovering in Scotland Yard's Press Bureau, a team which coped very adequately with murders. But I had once been sent by the news editor to a basement flat near Primrose Hill where a German student had put his head in the gas oven, leaving a note describing his mortification and depression at the Nazi persecution which had prevented him returning to his fatherland.

The self-deprecatory 'only suicides' cracked the ice and the entourage, on cue from Vian, permitted themselves a hint of a smile. Even the circumlocution was dropped. They could hardly have thought they had some high-powered Rothermere investigative reporter on board who might expose Naval shortcomings. Yet they must have been curious to learn that there was a Fleet Street journalist, of however limited experience, on the stokers' mess-deck. Perhaps this was a ripple from that ten-months' distant Commander Rump 'No. 1' episode.

Then came the inevitable question from Vian:

'What made you choose to become a stoker?'

'I wanted a change from pounding a typewriter, sir.'

'Ah ha … a beneficial change, do you think?'

A leading question: my personal degaussing gear warned me of a submerged mine. I replied as noncommittally but as honestly as I dared: 'Like the curate's egg, sir! Good in parts.' Not quite the enthusiastic answer I felt 'Vian of the *Cossack*' would probably have liked. He gave me a second's steady appraisal, then: 'I don't think there is anything else, is there?' the captain went through the courteous formality of asking his staff. There was a shaking of heads and I was dismissed.

~~

After the Bergen attack was called off we returned to Scapa to replenish our ammunition which had been heavily expended during the raids on the fleet. Lower Deck was cleared and this time it was Jimmy the One who briefly put the ship's company in the picture. The gist was that the Germans had already invaded Denmark and Norway, six Norwegian ports were already occupied and our government had decided to land troops in Central Norway, north and south of Trondheim, in the hope of recapturing that port.[29] We would ourselves be transporting sixty soldiers whom we were to make as comfortable as the cramped conditions permitted. Our exact place of landing would largely depend on intelligence reports of the speed of the enemy's advance.

The pongos clumped over the brow, most of them in leather jerkins and Balaclava helmets rolled up to make woollen caps, steadying shouldered kitbags with one hand and clutching Bren guns with the other. They were KOYLIs (King's Own Yorkshire Light Infantry) and Hallamshires, men from the territorial battalion of the York and Lancaster Regiment. The seamen played host, brewing up strong cuppas.

Since none of the guests were on our mess-deck, contact was fleeting and, as I had not heard about the previous embarkation and dis-

---

[29] 'The pincer movement as a strategic concept lasted one week, as a practical venture even less.' T. K. Derry ibid.

embarkation, I don't know whether these particular troops had been involved. But now at last they were about to be seaborne and to face unpredictable hazards.

Within a couple of hours of Jimmy-the-One's briefing, we were at sea and any worries Tommy had about the future were superseded by that malady which effectively concentrates the mind on self-pity: seasickness. Jack instructed Tommy in the art of slinging a hammock and getting in and out of it. Some squaddies, nevertheless, dived over the swaying hammocks trying to get into them or fell on the deck when trying to get out.

~~

On 12 April an irregular line of snow-clad hills took the place of the iron-grey arc which had been our horizon as we made the crossing from the Shetlands. This was Norway, a visible, invaded Norway, no longer a non-belligerent shrouded in mist, a visibility that was two-way and not always to our advantage. A distant plane hovered over the land, circled out to sea and disappeared. The white-mantled mountains loomed larger as we approached the island-studded coast.

We reconnoitred the port of Ålesund with the dual purpose of seeking intelligence on the whereabouts of the enemy and to check whether it was suitable for landing, not only our own troops, but those of the main force in the cruisers and troopships, of which we were the vanguard. We also had to make certain that the merchant ships in the vicinity were Norwegian, not German. Our six destroyers now split into two sections to continue the probe of the fjords.

Afridi threaded her way northwards through the channels between the islands and turned to starboard through the entrance to Moldefjord. We surveyed the town of Molde itself before pressing up the fjord, taking the most southerly prong of the trident that was Romsdal Fjord and inspected Åndalsnes at its entrance as a possible landing place for the main force. The Norwegians knew and we knew that our very presence would call down retributive havoc on their peaceful communities.

In these fjords we were dwarfed by the towering bastions of rock rising sometimes to 2,000 feet. The scouting plane had done its job: we were now attacked repeatedly by Junkers 88s and soon discovered our limitations. Not only was it often hazardous to manoeuvre in the restricted waters of the fjords, but the maximum elevation of 40° of our 4.7s seriously handicapped the chances of putting up a barrage, let alone hitting bombers that suddenly appeared in the ribbon of sky above the fjord and disappeared as quickly beyond the jagged rim of the mountain tops after dropping their bombs. It is a comment on the pre-war underestimation of the potential of the bomber made by the armourers of these recently built Tribal Class destroyers that they did not provide them with guns capable of firing at a steeper angle.[30]

We continued northwards, gave Trondheim Fjord a wide berth and by late the following afternoon, 14 April, entered Namsen Fjord, its only entrance being through channels between rocky islets.

In comparison with what we had so recently experienced, here it was a beautiful and strangely peaceful scene. *Afridi* kept an almost even keel as her bows parted the still waters of the thirteen-mile-long fjord. On some of the lower slopes the snows had melted, revealing a gentler, variegated landscape in contrast to the near-black crags and virgin snow-filled gullies above. On the little islets grew a profusion of slender, delicate silver birches and sallow shrubs near the water's edge where the boulders were covered with grey mosses. We steamed to the fjord's extremity where lay the town of Namsos.

The Germans had not reached it and it was decided to land a holding force from two of the cruisers consisting of 350 leathernecks[31] and armed seamen until the arrival of the main force. These men were transferred to three destroyers and landed at dusk. They were the first British troops to land in Norway.

When the main body arrived it was intended that Namsos should be the port from which the left hook to recapture Trondheim was to be delivered. This was codenamed, I would learn after the war, Operation *Maurice*, perhaps French-inspired with Chevalier in mind? Åndalsnes, over 150 miles south of Trondheim, was to be the port from which to launch the right hook.

Our own KOYLIs and Hallamshires were also disembarked, glad to feel terra firma beneath their hobnails. We all helped to carry their gear onto the quay. This was the first and only time during this campaign I would tread Norwegian soil. 'So long Tommy and the best of luck, mate!'

---

[30] When Admiral of the Fleet Lord Chatfield was C-in-C Mediterranean in 1931 he opined that 'attack on ships at sea by aircraft will be unremunerative in a few years.' Stephen Roskill in *Naval Policy Between The Wars* commented: 'Presumably this optimistic view was based on the anticipated but unproven effectiveness of the new multi-barrel close-range A-A weapons and the new long-range A-A fire control system.'
[31] Royal Marines, also known as 'bootnecks.'

was repeated, with variations, many times. We felt sorry for them; they had never been in action, were so lightly armed and had no armoured support. It seemed incredible that they had to do battle with the Wehrmacht which was already recognised as a formidable war machine due to Goebbels's propaganda and the swift invasion of Poland. As to defence against the Luftwaffe, there was not a single anti-aircraft gun to protect them. With us, they had shared the experience of air attacks and had at least seen us fire back, however ineffectively. Even this satisfaction would be denied them and they had probably already guessed there would be no air cover from the RAF, not unless an airfield could be found and held against the enemy who had already captured, and was using, Stavanger about 430 miles to the south.

At least we had given the lie to 50 per cent of the boast of the Nazi Foreign Minister Joachim von Ribbentrop ('Ribbondrops', as cartoonist Giles dubbed him): 'The German forces will see to it that no Englishman or Frenchman shows his nose in Norway or Denmark for the rest of the war.'

As *Afridi* pulled away from the jetty in the fast enveloping mantle of dusk, the troops were already marching up through the deep snow of the Namsos streets with multi-coloured wooden houses towards the snow-covered mountains behind.

~~

The powers-that-be decided that Namsos was no fit place for troops to disembark in large numbers in daylight. The cruisers and five grey-painted liners that had been converted into transports were diverted to a fjord 100 miles to the north and, on the evening of 15 April, we joined them as they approached it. Here, in Lillesjona Fjord, we fuelled from the Blue Ens'n oiler *War Pindari* and were attacked by bombers in the process. Being alongside the oiler, we could only fire from one side.

It was at Lillesjona that a colourful character was transferred to *Afridi* from *Somali* which had almost run out of ammunition and had to return to the UK.[32] He was in jodhpurs and cavalry boots, wore a Sam Browne belt and carried a walking stick, had a black patch over his left eye, displayed a red-topped Army officer's cap, had cultivated a moustache *à la* King Victor Emmanuel of Italy, and no hand was visible at the end of his left sleeve.

---

[32] 'The destroyer *Somali*, left at Namsos in support of the landing-parties, was heavily attacked by enemy aircraft and added her warnings to earlier ones of the danger of air attack.' (Major-General J. L. Moulton *The Norwegian Campaign of 1940.*).

This was none other than Major-General Sir Adrian Carton de Wiart VC, commander of the Expeditionary Force in Central Norway.[33] The buzz spread quickly that we had become the General's temporary headquarters until the force was established ashore. But I only got an occasional glimpse of him from afar when he was on the quarterdeck or when, invited by Captain Vian, he climbed the ladder to the bridge.

If I had known then what I now know from his autobiography, I would have paid more attention to that distant figure. For this was the Belgian-born soldier who, having already been wounded in the Boer War and lost an eye attacking Dervishes in British Somaliland, maintained that he had 'frankly enjoyed' the First World War in spite of being wounded in the hand in 1915 which led to its amputation at his own insistence. A machine-gun bullet through the back of his head in 1916 was followed by having his ear split by 'a bit of a shell' in 1917 and hit in the hip by another shell in 1918, thereby nearly losing a leg.

With him as his staff, the General, who was nudging sixty, brought aboard two younger men, also far removed from the common mould: the Arctic explorer Martin Lindsay (at this time an Army captain)[34] and someone who had been one of my favourite authors in my teens and had been described before the war as 'one of the best-known young men in England.' He was the Old Etonian, author-traveller and, at this time, Grenadier Guards Colonel Peter Fleming. I had spent many pleasurable hours of armchair rough-stuff trekking with him in *One's Company* and *News From Tartary*. I had been particularly interested in his first book, *Brazilian Adventure* published in 1933 to see whether it threw any light on the fate of the missing Colonel Fawcett and his son.

A few days earlier, in a break in his journey from London to Norway, Fleming had stayed in a Fleet Air Arm mess in Scotland. In a notebook[35] in which he had started to keep a diary, he wrote:

> The mess was composed of men who have been bombing Bergen in slow planes, leaving petrol and ammunition behind to

---

[33] Before boarding *Somali* he had flown from the Shetlands to Namsen Fjord in a Hudson flying boat which, in Peter Fleming's words, 'came under air attack while rendezvousing with a destroyer (presumably *Somali*) and his only staff officer was wounded; so for some days I found myself acting as his batman, driver, chief of staff and, mercifully, on rare occasions, cook.'

[34] Sir Martin Lindsay Bart (as he was known in 1962) became Conservative MP for Solihull. His books included: *The Epic of Captain Scott* and *Three Got Through: Memoirs of an Arctic Explorer.*

[35] See Sources and Acknowledgements p. 306.

make room for 500 lb. bombs. They have hard staring eyes and look fine. They are having another smack tomorrow just before we leave. They saw off one cruiser for certain. I feel very good and the war seems suddenly quite different.

The 'one cruiser seen off for certain' was the *Königsburg*.[36]

~~

The bombers attacked us again while we were still in Lillesjona alongside one of the transports taking troops on board. Bomb splinters punctured *Afridi*'s forepeak on the waterline but temporary plugging maintained our seaworthiness when we set out that evening for the 100-mile dash south to Namsos. Every inch of space on and below deck was taken up with some of the men from two of the three battalions of the Royal Lincolnshire and of the York and Lancaster Regiment, a total of 1,000 men whom the transports had brought over. They disembarked in the middle of the night of the 16th on the same quayside on which we had landed the KOYLIs and Hallamshires. The General and his staff remained on board.

The following evening we steamed to the mouth of Namsen Fjord and led in a Polish transport, the *Chobry*, which had also come from Lillesjona carrying the remaining battalion and some of the expedition's stores. The *Empress of Australia* had returned to the UK with a considerable quantity of stores still onboard, an unhappy omen of future bungling. Men and materials had to be landed so that *Chobry*, which would have been a sitting duck for the bombers in daylight, could get clear.[37] As it happened, it took two nights to land the stores.

In post-war British accounts there are conflicting dates as to how soon after the arrival of the British and French troops Namsos was bombed. Vian stated in his memoirs that German air reconnaissance had spotted the first troops—the Royal Marines and armed seamen—the morning after they landed at Namsos on the night of the 14th and 'attacks on the port soon began'. That tallies with Roskill in *The War At Sea* who wrote that 'the enemy's bombing had already produced difficult conditions at Namsos' before the cruisers and transport ships arrived at Lillesjona.

---

[36] See footnote p. 81.
[37] *Chobry*, which survived two near-misses approaching Namsos on 26 April, was finally bombed and sunk on May 14 on the way to Bodŏ.

Carton de Wiart, however, claimed that the British troops were most careful to obliterate all traces of their landing and that 'the Germans who flew over the next morning suspected nothing.' Likewise, Fleming affirmed that the landing went on for six nights without the Germans being any the wiser, despite their three-times-daily reconnaissance. Both Carton de Wiart and Fleming maintain that it was only after the battalions of Chasseurs alpins were put ashore on the 19th from four French transports and a cruiser that, because these troops made no effort to cover their traces and even opened fire with machine guns on the first planes that appeared on the 20th, the bombers then came over in force and, in the General's words, 'in a matter of hours Namsos was reduced to ashes.'

Captain Donald Macintyre in his book, *Narvik,* claimed that because the four French troopships and escorting cruisers steamed up Namsen Fjord in daylight on the 19th (that is two days after we led in the *Chobry* in the early hours while it was still dark) there was no hope of concealing their presence and they were bombed in the fjord while approaching Namsos. In that case there was no reason why any effort at concealment should have been made by the French troops ashore when the bombing began on the 20th. Roskill confirms that four French troopships, escorted by the French cruiser *Emile Bertin* and destroyers, reached Namsen Fjord on the 19th and were led in by our *Cairo*. The convoy was attacked in the fjord and the *Emile Bertin* was hit [38] but the troopships discharged the French troops and went home again before daylight (about 02.30) on the 20th before the bombers attacked 'in strength.'

By this time *Afridi* had departed, after putting the General and his two-man staff ashore, and set course for Scapa to repair, refuel and ammunition ship. We were destined to make only two more voyages to Norway.

~~~

Our next crossing was to Åndalsnes, the southern hinge of the jaw that was intended to close on German-occupied Trondheim. Since our speed was restricted as always to that of the slowest ship in the convoy, our progress was slow. It was approximately 650 miles between Scapa and Central Norway and for about three-quarters of the outward-bound voyage, we could be reasonably sure of unmolested passage; the nearer we got to the Norwegian coast, the more likely Luftwaffe attacks became,

---

[38] Three bombs hit the *Bertin* but none exploded.

usually heralded by spotter planes shadowing us well out of range of our guns. If the coastline was still low on the horizon when we went below for the forenoon or afternoon watch, we would only know if we had entered a fjord by the different sounds bombs made exploding under the water. In the open sea it was a single muffled crump of greater or lesser intensity according to its proximity, but inside a fjord, there would be an echo of some seconds duration as the explosion reverberated off the submerged rock walls.

When I occasionally kept watch in the engine-room, even these sounds, which gave some indication of where we were, were almost drowned by the throb of the turbines which reduced conversing to only essential shouted instructions; otherwise, exchanges had to be made with the mouth within an inch or two of a hopefully receptive ear.

My job in the engine-room was to log changes in speed as the turbines' revolutions were clocked up on an indicator and orders on the telegraph connected to its twin on the bridge. Once during a watch I would take the temperature reading of the turbines, of water intakes and outlets, and check the amount of lubricating oil in the sumps.

Engine-room watch-keeping was one of the less fresh parts of the curate's egg I had in mind when questioned by Vian. Whereas the temperature in the boiler-room could be icy—operating above the Arctic Circle, off Bodö for example, we were wearing our duffle coats—the temperature in the engine-room could be anything from 90° to over 112°F (32°–48c°). In the tropics it could be up to 130°F (56°C). It was a moist heat that sapped the energy during a four-hour watch. The hottest job of all during that time was wiping down the blue-steel turbine casing. We were not allowed to drink cold water, a sure recipe for stomach cramps but, like boxers between rounds, we would take a mouthful of what was always tepid water, rinse the mouth, gargle and spit it out into the bilges.

During the middle watch there was at least the compensation of 'pusser's kye' made from slabs of unsweetened chocolate. Chunks of this were placed in a kettleful of water and boiled up by hanging this receptacle, not the domestic, tea-brewing variety but open and lidless like a painter's kettle, on a steam gland in one of the boiler-rooms. When the valve was turned on, a jet of steam sent the brew racing and bubbling inside the kettle. When ready, the SPO in the boiler-room would ring us through in the engine-room and I would climb the ladder, pass through the blackout canvas over the hatch, make my way along the upper deck and down into whichever of the three boiler-rooms the kye had been brewed. From then on it was a severe test of my ambidexterity. With one hand I would hold the brimming kettle; with the other I had to clutch the rail of the near-vertical ladders, lift and lock again behind me the air-lock doors and hatches and climb up and down the ladders of the other two boiler-rooms. On the upper deck more often than not it would be pitch black as the ship raced through the night, swaying and dipping, spray or waves sweeping inboard. With my free hand I would hold onto one of the sliding hangers attached to the lifeline and steer an erratic course for the next boiler-room or back to the engine-room for my fellow watch-keepers to have the remainder of the kettle's contents. It was only by a miracle (or my legerdemain) that any kye was left.

My last port of call was the gear room which was accessible from the engine-room only. Here, a leading stoker would keep watch. It was cooler but never cold, a clean and comparatively quiet number since it was one-man watch-keeping and the only place where I saw the watch-keeper invariably with a paperback. On the other hand, its very isolation must have put an extra strain on the nerves of gear room watch-keepers when the ship was in action.

My fellow watch-keepers in the engine-room were an engine-room artificer (ERA) and a leading stoker, one on the port, the other on the starboard throttle, and perhaps a chief ERA. There would be another stoker looking after the vaps (the evaporating plant which converted sea-water into fresh water for the boilers). On entering or leaving harbour and when the ship was at action stations, white-overalled Commander (E) Halliwell would be standing beside us. This was his 'bridge'.

ERA Scott represented for me the embodiment of reliability. He was probably in his early thirties, pale from hundreds of hours in this atmosphere; tense, only relaxing his grip on the throttle to wipe sweat from forehead, face and neck and ever alert to give rapid swings to the throttle at an instant's command of a change of speed. Even if he had wanted to be sociable to anyone as lowly in the engine-room hierarchy as a buff stoker, the noise would have been a barrier to fraternising.

~~

Depending upon who was watch-keeping, there could be a more sociable atmosphere in the boiler-room, at least when we were not in action and especially during the latter part of the first watch and during the middle watch when a few hours of darkness gave *Afridi* a respite from the bombers. There were five stoker petty officers and I kept an occasional watch with four of them.

'Lofty' Christopher Coombes was a perpetually good-humoured man, usually with a smile playing around his mouth. Even when he was leaping about the boiler-room on his long legs, his dank, tow-coloured hair flopping over his ears and eyes gave him a wild and most un-pusser appearance. The day would come when we would think he had a charmed life.

Don Budgeon was the opposite of Coombes, a little intimidating on early acquaintance, with a jutting jaw giving him a misleadingly pugnacious aspect. In reality, he was also a kindly and considerate man and, typically, he would meet his fate doing a good turn for his oppo. The other two were Geordie Allen, long-nosed, quiet and canny, and Sam Hardy, gnomish, with hard-bitten features, his angst less under the control the others managed to keep and our mutually well-intentioned efforts to converse foundered on a dearth of common interests.

Most of my boiler-room watch-keeping was with the fifth, SPO 'Cock' Kent. This was my good fortune since he had an inexhaustible supply of lore about the peacetime Navy, and was articulate and fluent. It was difficult to gauge his age for he combined pepper-and-salt hair with epidermal softness, lack of wrinkles and a slight flush over the cheekbones; one could be wrong by a decade either way. That he had been caught up in the Invergordon mutiny of September 1931 provided only a slender clue since, in his detailed description of its causes, I don't recall whether he was in the 1919 or 1925 rates of pay bracket. The cause of the mutiny was, in Stephen Roskill's words, ' … beyond doubt … the severity of the pay cuts as first announced and the inept manner in which the Admiralty presented them to the fleet.' The mutiny lasted four days and involved nine ships.

Cock may have been born within sound of Bow Bells and though his 'local' when he was up-homers was the Askew Arms in Acton, his rhyming slang was certainly no affectation and was as spontaneous as his dropping of aspirates and substituting *k* for final *g* in his spoken English. His wit was tart and sly, delivered deadpan to keep me puzzling whether innuendo lurked behind the words.

But he was serious enough when talking about pay and conditions in the service. When he got to know me after dozens of hours of watch-keeping together, he would urge me to expose what he regarded as the inadequacies and injustices in the 'Peas and Gravy' when I got back to Civvy Street.

~~

It could have been during the middle watch on one of the nights of our slow progress towards Åndalsnes that Cock asked: 'Nutty, did I ever tell you the one about Shiner Wright and the loaf of bread?' When I shook my head he then recounted a story which went something like this. Propped up by the oil-fuel pump to steady himself against the ship's slow roll, puffing at his briar, and glancing every now and again at the pressure gauge, he began:

> Shiner was a killick stoker on the *Verulam*, one of the old V and Ws.[39] 'E was a decent bloke but always gettin' in the rattle, nothin' serious but 'e'd been warned next time 'e was up before Jimmy the One 'e'd almost certainly lose 'is 'ook.[40] Well, on the occasion I'm talkin' about, *Verulam* was oilin'. The fuellin' trunk was snakin' in board from the tanker alongside, across the upper, through the port flat and the 'atch leadin' down to the stokers' mess into No. 1 oil-fuel tank below. Got it?

I mentally traced the path of the thick, flexible pipe and nodded.

> The 'atch cover of the tank was 'orf and the open tank was directly beneath the ladder leadin' up from the mess-deck to the port flat. Chiefy [41] 'ad cleared the stokers out of the mess and posted Shiner at the top of the ladder with strict instructions not to let nobody down the ladder in case they dropped somethink into the tank. So, there was Shiner, standin' firm as a barrack stanchion and not lettin' nobody down the mess.

Cock sucked hard on his pipe which threatened to go out before he had hardly started his yarn. After he had got it going again he went on:

> Just then, along comes the bosun's mate pipin': 'All messmen to the galley' to collect their staff-of-life. Shiner was the stokers' messman and 'e knew the bread locker was as bare as Old Ma 'Ubbard's cupboard. If 'e didn't go and collect the bread 'is

---

[39] V & W class destroyers, survivals from the First World War.
[40] Demoted from Leading Stoker to Stoker.
[41] Chief Stoker.

messmates wouldn't 'alf create! So 'e was in a bit of a two-an'-eight, 'orns of a dilemma. Any'ow, 'e 'esitates awhile, then says to 'imself 'Fuck this for a lark, I'm not goin' to let m' messmates down.' So 'e slips orf to the galley and comes back clutchin' about a dozen loaves, one on top of the other. When 'e reaches the 'atch of the stokers' mess, 'e sneaks a quick dekko to make sure nobody's seen 'im—Chiefy in particular. Then 'e gingerly descends the ladder.

Well, I reckon Shiner's lucky star was 'avin an eclipse that day. 'Orf topples a bleedin' loaf from the top of the pile plumb into the gapin' mouth of the tank. Shiner 'eard it splash into the black muck below . 'Stone a fuckin' crow,' 'e mutters, stows the rest of the loaves into the food locker, nips up the ladder, smart-like, and takes up 'is position as if 'ed never left the spot, like the boy wot stood on the burnin' deck. By rights, o'course, 'e should've reported 'is droppin the perishin' loaf. But not Shiner. It would've meant the tank 'avin to be drained and 'im and 'is messmates sloppin' around in the oil-fuel lookin' for the bleedin' loaf. Worse, as far as Shiner 'imself was concerned: 'e would be put in the rattle and certainly lose 'is 'ook. So, 'e don't say nothink to Chiefy nor to nobody else and when the fuellin' was finished, the 'atch cover was secured and not another soul was any the wiser.

Cock's pipe had really gone out by this time. Taking his pouch, he filled it deliberately and lit up again. He peered into the furnace to make sure the cones were not carbonising and, satisfied, resumed his place against the fuel pump. I gathered there must be a sequel to Shiner's mishap.

It was about a week later. Shiner 'ad almost forgotten about the loaf. Any'ow, 'e wasn't botherin' *'is* loaf about it no more. *Verulam* was afloat doin' exercises with 'alf the fleet. All the old custard tanks was there: *Rodney, Renown,* the *'ood* and the rest, weighed down with gold braid, includin' the blessed Admiral of the Fleet. All of a bleedin' sudden, *Verulam* starts belchin' black smoke. A few wisps at first, then buckets of it pour from 'er funnels as if she was layin' a perishin' smoke screen. The skipper nearly takes orf. 'E swings the engine-room telegraph 'imself to: 'STOP MAKING SMOKE' and when this don't 'ave no effect 'e orders Jimmy the One to bellow down the voice pipe to enquire, polite like, what the bleedin' 'ell they think they're doin' down there? The skipper was in for a proper bollickin' from the Admiral and 'e knows it. 'E didn't 'ave to wait long either. The Aldis on '*ood* started blinkin' and Bunts[42] took down the message, as far as he could make it out through the smoke.

Cock now assumed the haughty tones he thought appropriate to an admiral:

> Would *Verulam*, repeat *Verulam*—not Vesuvius—'KINDLY STOP ERUPTING.' There was more of it. Somethin' about givin' away the position of the 'ole bloomin' fleet. The skipper was nearly 'avin' twins. 'E calls up the Senior Engineer on the blower and tears 'im orf a strip. The Senior tears a strip orf the Chief boiler buster.[43] Chiefy in turn balls out the SPOs in each of the boiler-rooms. It was gettin' just like one big 'appy family. The temperature of the oil-fuel was tested. The fan pressure was checked. The stokers chipped the cone of every sprayer clean as a baby's bum. They went through every routine in the Stokers' Manual. But *Verulam* still went on layin' down more and better smoke per square foot than Battersea Power Station in a November pea-souper.

Cock paused to allow the mental image of this enormity to sink in, took a couple of sucks at his pipe and proceeded to the dénouement:

> And then ... and then it began to get thinner. Quite fast and stopped. Stopped as mysterious as it 'ad begun. Everyone was bewitched, buggered and bewildered. Wot could 'ave come over *Verulam*, playin' a dirty trick like that when she was in 'igh class company? Lettin' the poor old skipper down a treat. Nobody 'ad a clue. For 'oo could 'ave guessed a perishin' loaf 'ad got stuck in the oil-fuel system and gummed up the works until it got burned to a cinder and finally disintegrated? Not a bleedin' soul. Except Shiner. And 'e was keepin' 'is trap shut. Too bleedin' right 'e was!

---

[42] Bunting tosser—a signals rating.
[43] Chief Stoker.

~~

The reason for the slowness of the convoy to Åndalsnes was that it included a fully-loaded tanker only capable of doing five knots. The first part of the voyage was as usual uneventful, the sporadic appearance of RAF or Fleet Air Arm escorts being as effective a deterrent to the enemy as it was a morale booster for us. But the nearer we got to Norway the less protection from RAF fighters could be expected, since the distance was too great for them to operate there and return home. When Gladiators were brought to Norway aboard an aircraft carrier so that they could use a frozen lake as an airstrip, they were knocked out by the Luftwaffe almost as soon as they arrived.

The Luftwaffe attacks were again heralded by a single scouting aircraft well out of range. It disappeared and an hour or so later the Junkers were on the scene. The escorting cruisers with their 6-inch and the destroyers with their 4.7s tried to keep the predators from attacking the convoy with fuel and other vital supplies for the troops. Bofors, pom-poms and point fives would be brought to bear when the barrage was penetrated. Red tracers arced into a sky in which hung dirty puffs from myriad bursts of high explosive. Yet our antagonists seemed impervious to all this HE bursting high above the convoy. If one bomber left the fray trailing black smoke, it would disappear over the steep hills and the gunners would be deprived of the satisfaction of seeing it plunge into the sea.

Great gouts of water would spurt up as bombs missed their targets. Harassed by the gunfire in the open sea, the bomb-aiming was usually erratic. Even in the long fjord leading to Åndalsnes, despite the limited elevation of our guns, the Junkers scored no direct hits although near-misses caused minor damage. Some of the ships seemed to bear a charmed life. When we were within 400 yards of a tanker, a Junkers dived and released its bomb which I saw plummeting directly for the vessel. It dropped within what must have been a few yards to starboard— and failed to burst. Had it exploded, the ship, loaded with petrol, would have been a floating torch within minutes.

For me such topsides viewing was exceptional. If we were down below when action stations sounded, we remained in the boiler-room or engine-room until the 'all-clear' was piped. On one memorable occasion this meant thirteen consecutive hours down below, sustained by cheese sandwiches and kye. But this routine was deemed unsatisfactory and was changed. Later on, during a period of continuous action, we alternated our normal watch below with being closed-up at our action stations. Mine was the for'ard guns' supply party.

As expected, the peaceful little towns with their wooden houses, steeply canted roofs and white churches with pepper-pot towers which we had reconnoitred before landing our troops, had paid the price. At Molde, bombed two days after we had surveyed it, I saw for the first time what would become all too familiar back home, in France, and even in Burma: a bomb crater. Perhaps because it was the first one I had seen, it seemed huge. Writing home, I used that anachronistic epithet: 'big enough to take a coach and horses'. Åndalsnes was a still-smoking ruin when we reached it. The convoy's 'vital' supplies, brought over intact despite the Luftwaffe's efforts, were too late. It had been decided that our foothold in Åndalsnes was untenable. There was no offloading. *Afridi* turned about, negotiated the forty miles through the fjord with fewer attacks than when we entered it, and made for the open sea.

~~

Back in Scapa, we were given another 'progress report' by Jimmy the One. Progress, of course, was an ironic misnomer. The sight of the smouldering ruins of Åndalsnes so soon after reconnoitring the unscathed town sixteen days before had been depressing. The port had been bombed incessantly since 25 April. Up to that point, few of us would have realised just how in vain the effort had been to supply our forces or the significance of that failure in the context of the Central Norway campaign as a whole. Now its magnitude was revealed concisely by Lieut-Cdr Meyrick, and with no attempt to conceal how desperate the situation was.

The expeditionary force we had helped to land, he explained, had been too small and under-equipped to stem the Germans who were now reinforced by armoured units from the south of Norway. Furthermore, the complete absence of supporting aircraft for our troops, owing to the impossibility of finding a landing strip, had sealed the fate of the campaign. In fact, as already mentioned, the Germans had captured six ports, including the capital, although their 8-inch cruiser *Blücher* was sunk by the Norwegians in Oslo Fjord with the loss of many assault troops and the capture of the general and the admiral in command of the operation. The invaders were thus landed and installed and airfields secured without a shot or shell being fired at them by Anglo-French naval or military forces, and often despite heroic resistance by the Norwegians, epitomised by the twenty-day withstanding of the siege of Hegra Fort.

In the circumstance, the First Lieutenant continued, the British and French troops had fought courageously in the face of impossible odds. The two-pronged attempt to re-take Trondheim had been abandoned and the Admiralty had, that day, decided that the troops in Namsos and Åndalsnes must be re-embarked before they were completely cut off and enveloped. After much procrastination the final decision by the British War Cabinet to abandon Operation *Hammer*, a Naval frontal assault on Trondheim, was made on 20 April. General Carton de Wiart recommended consideration of the withdrawal of the Anglo-French expeditionary force on 23 April, and the actual order to evacuate Åndalsnes and Namsos was made on 27 April. The extent of Chamberlain's duplicity in deceiving both the Norwegians and the French about these decisions is spelled out in François Kersaudy's *Norway 1940*.

The Åndalsnes evacuation was to take place during the nights of 30 April to 1 and 2 May. *Afridi* was to assist in the withdrawal from Namsos. We would sail immediately, in command of a screen of five destroyers. Another four had already gone ahead, escorting the cruisers, *Devonshire* and *York* and the French *Montcalm*, and three French transports; the whole were under the command of Vice-Admiral John Cunningham.

There was about to begin what Captain Roskill would describe as 'one more venture, perhaps the most desperate since it was increasingly probable, as each day passed, that the enemy would realise what we were doing', that is, extricating the 5,400 troops from Namsos:

Meyrick had covered the essentials. In the circumstances, that was enough. It was just as well for our morale that we were ignorant of how ill-conceived had been the venture from the beginning. Nor did we know some of the farcical details that came later, and the confusion that reigned in Whitehall right up to this moment of evacuation. No less an authority than Admiral Forbes himself would observe: 'The scale of air attack that would be developed against our Naval forces off the Norwegian coast was grievously underestimated when the operations were undertaken.'

As to details, the Chasseurs alpins, ski troops trained for mountain warfare ideal for this kind of terrain, found on landing that they could not use their skis because essential parts were missing, as were their mules, their sole means of transport. Apparently the ships that had been carrying these items were bulky and of too deep draught to be brought up the fjords and positioned alongside the inadequate wharves. The only British troops trained as skiers were a battalion of the Scots Guards and they were disbanded when the plan for invading Norway and Sweden to help the Finns fell through. Similarly, the two anti-aircraft guns landed for the temporary British base at Ålesund were declared 'utterly useless' by its CO and the ammunition 'a potential menace'.

Even Carton de Wiart, doughty old warrior though he was, had decided that it was quite impossible to advance on Trondheim because of inferior equipment and lack of air support.[44] He would sum up the situation in a memorable phrase: 'I could see very little point in remaining in that part of Norway like rabbits in the snow.' There followed a profusion, or rather a confusion, of orders and counter-orders from Whitehall.

Nor was the decision to pull out of Central Norway passed onto the Norwegians, not even to King Haakon (whose army was still fighting and an embryo guerrilla resistance forming) until after he had been evacuated from Molde by a cruiser and landed in Tromsö in the far north. The Norwegian C-in-C, General Otto Ruge, had gone over the brow of the Tribal destroyer *Tartar* to join his staff on board but when told they would not be put ashore in the north of their country, they disembarked and stayed behind in the flames of Molde to attempt to carry on the fight.

~~

The Norwegian coast was shrouded in an impenetrable mist through which the bigger ships at least would be unable to navigate. Mountbatten was to record how he got Cunningham's approval to take his own *Kelly* and other destroyers in 'a mad rush along the seventy miles or so of Norwegian coast to Namsos' in an endeavour to evacuate the first night's contingent under cover of this fog. However, it took them all night from 1–2 May to probe Namsen Fjord, navigating by using their ASDIC pings against its steep sides. Luckily, the fog suddenly lifted at 05.00 when Mountbatten found *Kelly* was only 100 yards from running head-on into half-submerged rocks. 'All that day we played hide-and-seek with the German bombers, in and out of scattered fog banks,' he would recall.

Our sister Tribal, *Maori*, was not so lucky: the bombers spotted her mast sticking out of the mist and she sustained damage and twenty-three

---

[44] Captain M. D. Rahilly RN (rtd) recalls: 'My most lasting impression (as a lieutenant on board the Tribal destroyer *Nubian*) is of General Carton de Wiart shinning up a jumping ladder over our ship's side, despite having only one arm and one eye and saying to our Captain: "Well, this has been a total cock up!"' More prosaically, *Nubian*'s CO would recall that when Wiart came aboard he declared that, unless the Germans could be drastically restricted in their air activities within a very short time, 'the expedition was doomed'.

casualties; five of them died from their wounds. But no one on board either saw or heard the bomber.

Like the rest of us, Mountbatten had to wait until dusk before the Namsos evacuation could commence. It had already been decided that, because of the bombing, any attempt at a daylight withdrawal was out of the question. Yet, on account of the German pressure on our troops, it would have to be attempted in one, instead of two, nights, a feat Carton de Wiart thought impossible. He would write: 'But the Navy did it and earned my undying gratitude.' It was the next evening, 2 May, that we steamed up Namsen Fjord, leading in the transports, followed by the cruiser *York* and another Tribal, the *Nubian*. In the last few days the fjord had been the scene of furious encounters between the bombers and the ships of the 15th and 16th Anti-Submarine Striking Forces detailed to protect the landings from U-boats. Generally, the only anti-aircraft armament of these slow-moving ASDIC trawlers were 12-pounders, Lewis guns and Oerlikons. Four had been sunk, the *Aston Villa*, *Gaul* and *St Goran* in the previous two days, the bows of one of them suspended grotesquely from a crag. Altogether, eleven of these ASDIC trawlers were sunk out of a total of twenty-nine sent to Norway.

The sloop *Bittern* also had to be sunk by a sister ship after an ordeal which had lasted from soon after entering Namsen Fjord on the morning of 30 April until late afternoon. It was an ordeal graphically described by Gunner John Connor, a Manxman, as seen from his hilltop anti-aircraft gun-site above Namsos:

> Almost immediately the Stukas came screaming down at *Bittern* but as her guns and ours opened up, the first bombs fell well wide of the ship. As the main target for the Stukas, there was rarely a moment when she had not been forced to twist, turn and weave back and forth across the fjord in her desperate fight for survival. The Stukas' tactic was to attack in threes, two diving on her from in front and one from astern. She survived numerous near-misses. Together with our Bofors guns we put up an impressive barrage of flak. But further waves appeared and one Stuka coming in from astern scored on her quarterdeck. We saw the flashes and then heard two huge explosions, the second as an ammo locker blew up. We could see that much of the stern had been blown off and as we continued to fire at the Stukas, fire broke out and the rear of the ship was engulfed in thick, black smoke. During the

whole of this action *Bittern*'s forward guns kept firing but soon we could see she would have to be abandoned.[45]

Norwegian rowing boats set out from the shore to pick up survivors; others were rescued by the destroyer *Janus*. Bombardier Harry Killingbeck remembered 'several sailors began to swim towards our and two other gun positions. A few made it, others were machine-gunned in the water.' *Janus* sank the wreck of the *Bittern* with a tin-fish. Twenty *Bittern* men died that day. An American Fox and British Movietonenews cameraman Bonney M. Powell, who had filmed the ruins of Namsos and sent the reels down to the quay where they were taken on board *Bittern*, watched from a hill as they were sent to the bottom. Her CO, Lieut-Cdr R. H. Mills, claimed *Bittern* shot down two bombers that day. A few days later her survivors were transferred to the Town Class cruiser *Carlisle*, which had already suffered casualties on 28 April when attacked by five dive-bombers. Splinters from near-misses or machine-gun attacks fatally wounded an officer and caused other casualties to guns' crews and in the following days there would be three more burials at sea.

~~

Before the war Norway had been at peace for 126 years. The people of Namsos had led a moderately prosperous life, sustained by the fish from the fjord and earning their living from half a dozen saw mills, a canning factory, a woollen clothing workshop and a dairy products' plant which supplied the surrounding area. News that their country was at war reached them during the morning of Tuesday 9 April when it was broadcast by Radio Norway. It was naturally the main topic of conversation but there was no outward sign of panic, rather, as one of its senior citizens recalled to me sixty years later:

> … a tense and disturbed anticipation of what was going to happen in our country. Later that day when it became obvious Oslo had been taken over by the Germans, we listened to other local radio stations, the news bulletins always preceded by King Haakon VII's march *Alt for Norge* (All for Norway) which stayed in our minds for the rest of the war.

---

[45] *Stukas Galore* by J. E. Connor in the regimental museum of the 15th (Isle of Man) Light Anti-Aircraft Regiment RA in Douglas.

My informant was Jens-Anton Andersen, a local historian and archivist whose father, Henrik Andersen, aged forty-six in 1940, held the important position of harbour master in this community of 3,600. He had telephone contact with all the pilots along this coast of Central Norway.

Leading figures in Namsos met during the morning and elected a committee which immediately started working on an evacuation plan. The emphasis was on mothers, children under fifteen, the old and the sick who were chosen from the electoral registers of the town's twenty-three wards.

In Namdal the district through which the Namsen River flows into the fjord, the first mobilisation posters went up but created considerable confusion when hundreds of young men discovered that the extra boats and trains to which it referred were not running. Around Namsos itself there were large groups who had no idea where to report, whether to travel to the next town, Steinkjer, or stay in the Namsos area. Jens-Anton (fifteen at the time) distinctly remembered 'the sight of an elderly bank manager outside the Namsos Savings Bank in his old-fashioned retired major's uniform from the 1920s. To us teenagers it all seemed strange and rather comical.'

His father had been in contact with the pilots at Flatanger on the Namdal coast who reported that on the morning of the 8th they had seen flashes and heard gunfire out at sea. This must have been the engagement in which the *Hipper* sank the *Glowworm*.[46] This and reports from Radio Vigra, the station at Ålesund south of Kristiansund, that the Germans were advancing from their invasion points and had captured Vaernes airport near Trondheim the next day, was bringing the war closer to Namsos where tension was mounting. The more or less uncontrolled evacuation continued while crowds of young men with rucksacks and cases wandered around not knowing what to do.

The Heinkel and JU 87 (Stuka) bombers flew over in small groups carrying out reconnaissance to establish whether there was any troop activity. 'Once they discovered there was no anti-aircraft fire,' said Jens-Anton Andersen, 'the pilots flew close over the rooftops, so low that we could clearly see the pilots and gunners. Some of them indulged in displays of their flying prowess by flying between the radio masts, either trying to intimidate or overawe us. They always came at a fixed time, two or three times a day, and because there was no shooting or bombing, we could safely stand in the streets and squares and watch them fly over, the

---

[46] See Preface and p.80.

black crosses and swastika on the tail perfectly visible.'

While the Norwegian Government and King Haakon refused to surrender, the Germans installed Vidkun Quisling as their puppet prime minister. In his archives, Jens-Anton has a copy of a leaflet dropped over the Namdal area by the Germans:

NORWEGIANS!
The Norwegian and German troops are together protecting your homeland. Do not allow yourself to be panicked by criminal English agents who want to turn your country into a battlefield.

Lay down your arms! Go back to work!

The High Command informs you that all those supporting the former government's mobilisation order or spreading false rumours will be court-martialled. Any civilian encountered with a weapon in his hands will be shot. Any person causing damage to equipment used in transport or by the intelligence service will be shot. Any person who engages in any means of war against the law courts will be shot.

Norwegians! If you really love your Fatherland, go back to work!

Jens-Anton's sarcastic reaction was typical of the majority of Norwegians: 'It was the first greeting we in Namdal received from those who said they came as our friends.'

On 12 April Harbour Master Henrik Andersen received a call that two British warships had been spotted to the south the previous evening and were steaming north-east, possibly making for Namsen Fjord. Indeed, two evenings later (14 April) the first Allied landing on Norwegian soil was made when the advance party of 350 seamen and Royal Marines from the Town-class cruisers *Glasgow* and *Sheffield* and *Afridi*'s KOYLI 'passengers' disembarked on Namsos quay.

That morning Col Peter Fleming and Capt Martin Lindsay took off from Scapa Flow with instructions from London to find out whether Namsos had been occupied. As their Sunderland flying boat approached the Namdal coast, they received further instructions from Captain Pegram in Glasgow to go direct to Namsos and to be sure 'to observe complete secrecy'. They then circled the town (a manoeuvre which failed to yield the required information) and landed at Bangsund in an inlet of the fjord. A fisherman in a rowing boat assured the officers that there were no Germans in the vicinity and Lindsay was rowed ashore to request the telephone exchange to stop all outgoing calls. He proceeded to Namsos by car. Meanwhile, Fleming had flown there in the Sunderland and addressed a crowd of curious but anxious people who were not quite sure that he was not a German officer in disguise. After the war he would say that it was Henrik Andersen, while 'still under a cloud as a putative impostor, who persuaded the four pilots whom the Navy needed, to go out and guide the destroyers in.'

~~

For the people of Namsos, the sudden arrival of Allied troops in their midst brought the war to their very doorstep. For the young men the sight of their own age group from another country in uniform emphasised their own predicament. Impressed on Jens-Anton's memory was 'the aimless wandering around of young Norwegian men who should have been mobilised'. It was a fertile atmosphere for rumours, mainly without foundation, about enemy infiltration into the Norwegian officer corps, about the number of German troops and where they were operating. It took considerable time for the Norwegian forces in the Grong area to check and scotch a story going the rounds that German paratroops had dropped only about fifteen miles to the north-east of Namsos. And there was speculation as to the Allies' intentions and strategy.

At the same time practical steps were being taken: an air raid warning system was devised whereby a lookout on Bjorumsklompen, the steep hill that rises behind the town, had a direct line to the police station which had the number of the Namsos church bell-ringer. It was claimed that he took no more than forty seconds after the message came through to the police station for the chimes to ring out. The first air raid warning was at 5 a.m. on 15 April. That was also the day press self-censorship started in the town's three newspapers.

As a teenager Jens-Anton was one of those who were evacuated into the countryside after the British had landed and there were fears the Germans would start bombing. In fact, there were not many civilians left in the town. When, nearly six decades later, I met seventy-four year-old Jens Anton, he produced a copy of the order given by Hitler on the eve of the Führer's fifty-first birthday and signed by General (later Field

Marshal) Wilhelm Keitel, Chief of Staff of the Armed Forces. Top Secret and restricted to twelve copies, it stated:

> The Führer and supreme Commander of the Wehrmacht has ordered the Luftwaffe to destroy, *without consideration for the civilian population,* those towns on the coast other than those we have occupied but which are occupied by the English or which they intend to take. This order from the Führer is especially directed to destroying the roads and rail tracks nearest to Namsos and Åndalsnes.

Oberkommando der Wehrmacht   Berlin, den 19. 4. 1940
W F A N r. 8 2 7 / 4 0 g. K d o s. A b t. L

        12. Ausfertigungen
        10. Ausfertigung

GEHEIME KOMMANDOSACHE

Der Führer und Oberste Befehlshaber der Wehrmacht hat der Luftwaffe befohlen, Orte außerhalb der von uns besetzten Küstenplätze, die von den Engländern besetzt sind oder durch englische Verlautbarungen als besetzt gemeldet werden, ohne Rücksicht auf die Zivilbevölkerung zu zerstören.

Zunächst ist dies vom Führer für Namsos und Andalsnes angeordnet. Hier sollen auch die Bahnen und Straßen möglichst nahe diesen Punkten unterbrochen werden.

Der Chef des Oberkommandos der Wehrmacht

(gez.) K e i t e l

V e r t e i l e r

Hitler's Top Secret order to the Luftwaffe, signed by Chief of Staff of the Armed Forces, General Keitel, to destroy Namsos and Åndalsnes 'without consideration for the civilian population'.

In contrast, our Government's instructions 'to govern the conduct of all forms of bombardment,' at this stage of the war, included a section which read: 'It is clearly illegal to bombard a population area in the hope of hitting a legitimate target.'

In his proclamation of 13 April, King Haakon had already stated: that 'the powerful opponent has not hesitated to bomb the civilian population in towns and country districts.'

Jens-Anton was categoric about the precise date, 20 April, and time the first bombs fell on Namsos. He was quite positive that Vian had been misled into thinking that the first troops which landed had been spotted the next morning (15 April) and that the town had then been bombed. Spotter planes certainly came over two or three times a day at regular times but he agreed with Peter Fleming that the landing went on for five nights undetected. From the fisherman's farm in Namsen Fjord where he was an evacuee, young Jens-Anton watched the Luftwaffe's attack on 19 April on the large convoy, including the four French troopships.

It is generally agreed that the French troops who disembarked on the night of the 19th were the first to fire on the German planes. One French officer would describe in his memoirs [47] how the bell of Namsos church rang out an aircraft alert at about 9 a.m. on that beautiful spring morning, as it had done several times already, the first at 4 a.m. when it was daylight. It seems he was not unduly bothered because each time it had merely been German planes passing over the town from different directions. So, this time he was walking nonchalantly in the street and when he saw a big plane flying over, he thought it innocuous despite the

black crosses on its wings. But 'suddenly a huge pointed object dropped from the plane and started falling, comparatively slowly it seemed. When it reached the ground, the earth shook. That was the first bomb. Machine-guns spat fire from some of the Chasseurs concealed in a copse at the foot of the cliff behind the town but the bomber went on its own sweet way.'

The first two Allied soldiers to land in Norway following the German invasion of 9 April 1940 were Colonel Peter Fleming *(left)* and Arctic explorer Captain Martin Lindsay. They were flown in to Namsen Fjord to see whether Namsos was still free and suitable for an Allied landing.

Peter Fleming, who of course knew nothing about Hitler's order, was not at all impressed with 'the passionate French firing their machine guns' after all the trouble he,

---

[47] Olivier Nesque *L'Expédition de Namsos.*

Martin Lindsay and Henrik Andersen had taken each morning to conceal the presence of the British troops by removing all tell-tale signs from the quay of the previous night's disembarkation. He would write thirty years later that it was 'mainly thanks to Andersen that for five nights we won the game of hide-and-seek.'

In his notebook at the time, Peter Fleming wrote:

> Carton de Wiart lounged about in his red hat and refused the disguise of a Naval balaclava. No heroics but a genuine unconcern. The Germans were machine-gunning and killed one Frenchman. The station was going up in successive bouts of black smoke, with timber flying above. The bombs floated down over our heads. Quite a few duds … They went for our trawlers in the fjord and eventually sank one. In a quieter moment I went down and got a signal off for the General through a Naval officer in the cellar, where a man was lying under the table and is now almost certainly dead. They blew the town hall to hell with incendiaries. The church was gutted, the hours showing like a skeleton on the clock-face as though it was eternal … Casualties vague and no one seems interested: no tears, no anger, no searching. Quay still OK though charred.

The anti-submarine trawler which Fleming noted had been sunk was HMT *Rutlandshire*. After she had fought off repeated attacks, a bomb exploded under her stern lifting her out of the water and she ran aground on a shelf of rock within about a hundred yards of the little island of Hoddøya in Namsen Fjord. The crew either swam ashore or reached it by Carley float, scaled mountains to reach a farmhouse and were eventually given shelter by the inhabitants of the nearby island of Ötteroya. Through the initiative of Ordinary Seaman James Norman Memory, RNVR who borrowed a pocket mirror from his hosts, his heliographed signal to one of our ships resulted in *Nubian* picking up all twenty-seven of the crew who otherwise would almost certainly have become prisoners-of-war once Namsos was occupied by the Germans. The *Rutlandshire*'s CO, Skipper Lieut John Wilson RNR, was awarded the DSC, Memory the DSM. Sixty-one years later, Wilson's son and grandson visited Ötteroya and thanked the islanders for succouring the crew.[48]

---

[48] The full story can be viewed on the website: *www. royal-naval-reserve.co.uk*.

It was precisely on Hitler's birthday, shortly after 09.00 on 20 April that the first flight of bombers came over the town, flying high. When not meeting any anti-aircraft fire, the following waves doubled back around the 1,400 foot mountain behind the town and dived to about 600 feet to release their bombs at 09.15. The first one hit a sawmill near the harbour. As the Führer had ordered, the railway station and rolling stock were blasted but, on the first day, the harbour quays were not badly damaged. Conforming to the order not to spare the civilians, incendiaries rained down on the mainly timber homes and shops.

The bombers returned to the aerodrome at Vaernes near Trondheim around 11 a.m. There was a two-hour lull before they returned in even greater strength to complete their work of destruction. Between 2 and 3 p.m. the whole centre of the town was ablaze. The Lutheran church was gutted and only the stone fabric still stood (as I would witness twelve days later). By 5 p.m. a couple of houses in the old town were all that had survived. The school in which the British soldiers had stored their equipment and stores was a shambles. The planes even flew at low-level and machine-gunned the streets and the wooded hills outside the town where Norwegian civilians and some troops were sheltering. It is estimated the Luftwaffe made over sixty sorties.

Capitaine Raymond du Pavillon of the 5th Demi-Brigade of the Chasseurs alpins in a graphic contemporary account of the bombardment wrote:

> The Germans had complete mastery of the air and it is clear they decided to obliterate the whole town. They fly so low that we can see the bombs being released from the aircraft; we count them—four or five explosive bombs, ten to twenty incendiaries but, because they are released at such a low level, there is no time for them to whine before they explode. We can make out the shapes of the pilots and machine-gunners and clearly see the aerials hanging from the fuselages and the black swastikas. Not all the bombs explode on impact but some time after they have fallen.
>
> Everywhere is burning now and the fire spreads outwards from house to house. The sky is black with smoke and a great black cloud hangs over what yesterday was an attractive town. The hospital has been hit but continues to function as a military hospital. The town is a pile of ashes, only brick chimneys marking where houses once stood.

This scene would become only too familiar. When du Pavillon wrote those words, the only city that had suffered bombing by the Germans was Warsaw and the only open, undefended town comparable to Namsos which had been deliberately razed was the Basque town of Guernica bombed by the Nazi Condor Legion almost exactly three years before in the Spanish Civil War.

Miraculously, and in spite of many evacuees coming back during the lull to shop for provisions, only three civilians were killed. Other fatalities were a Norwegian and a French soldier [49] and, according to Andersen's recollection, eight British, either Naval ratings or Royal Marines. Many civilians and some service personnel, on first hearing the bombers returning, managed to dive to safety into the concrete cellars of the dairy produce factory.

When our sister Tribal, *Nubian*, returned that night her CO, Captain William Ravenhill, RN, would recall: 'When the town came into view the sight was remarkable. The whole place was a mass of flames from end to end and the glare on the snows of the surrounding mountains produced an unforgettable spectacle.' Although there were further raids the next day, as well as on the 28th and 30th, the town could hardly have been 'in flames … every building was burning' on 2 May as Mountbatten's biographers contend. Certainly daylight on the 21st revealed nearly all the buildings in the harbour in ruins, including the wooden wharves. Splinters from bombs ripped into the interior of the Andersen's flat. Sixty years later Jens-Anton showed me these jagged shards, one of the books they had damaged and the nose of one of the dud bombs Peter Fleming had mentioned in his notes. Carton de Wiart was already contemplating recommending total withdrawal.

~~

Now, on the night of 2 May, the only sounds coming from the harbour ruins we could hear aboard *Afridi* were the shuffling of soldier's boots on the stone quay and their subdued voices as they queued up to board two of the transports, *El-Djezaïr* and *El-Kantara,* which had managed to berth, one alongside the other. In the dim light I could just see soldiers in berets, smell wafts of Gauloises or Tsiganes in the crisp air and hear

---

[49] The French memorial in Namsos cemetery has the names of seven soldiers but some may have been killed in fighting outside the town.

muttered snatches like: 'Merde alors! J'en ai marre d'acculer ici' and another voice affirming: 'Il me fait chier aussi.' Such grumbling probably reflected the frustration of all the troops, French and British alike. It was cut short by an NCO's curt order: 'Ta gueule, toi!' as if les Boches were already closing in through the ruins and would hear their voices. They had, after all, waited for us the night before when we had been unable to get up the fjord because of the fog. They had then had to go back into the snow-wrapped hills before daybreak and hang around all day before returning for this, the second night's attempt to get them away. As one French officer would recollect after the war: 'Many men did not take this change of plan as philosophically as they should have done.'

There were three French transports in all, the two at the quayside and anchored offshore *El-Mansour* and our cruiser, *York*. Mountbatten's *Kelly* had been the first to take on board a number of French troops that must have exceeded her own complement. Since then there had been a shuttle service of destroyers and surviving anti-submarine trawlers ferrying troops out to the transports. For their exploits in the last few days and the next few hours, the crew of one of the trawlers, *Arab*, would earn their CO, Lieut Richard Been Stannard RNR, the Victoria Cross. He, his crew and that of the trawler *Gaul* had taken an anti-aircraft gun ashore a few days before and fired on the bombers. Now, just before reaching, at daybreak, the open sea, *Arab* would shoot down a Heinkel III. But *Gaul* herself had already been sunk.

According to Olivier Nesque's account, General Audet remained on the quayside until the last of the Chasseurs alpins had been embarked before himself going aboard *El-Djezaïr* where Rear-Admiral Cadart, responsible for the troopships, wanted to get away immediately but Audet insisted on remaining until the last of the British troops had been lifted. *Afridi* ferried a battalion of the Royal Lincolnshires to *El-Mansour*, the first of the French troopships to leave Namsos, before we returned to the damaged but still functioning quay.

~~

I had been able to witness the activity on the quayside before going below at midnight for the middle watch. The roster had just been changed by 'Big Bill' Bailey, the chief stoker, who had replaced, during the Hartlepool refit, the elderly chief with the whining ''ands off cocks, on socks!' routine. Now, all the stokers were watch-keeping in places different from those to which they had become accustomed in the last months and with different SPOs. Whatever the reason for this reshuffle, the result was to be of vital consequence for some of us, fatal for others. So, instead of going down No. 1 boiler-room with Cock Kent, I joined SPO Sam Hardy in No. 3, the furthest aft of the three boiler-rooms. Although we were hove-to alongside the jetty, naturally, we had steam up ready to slip on the instant. Hour after hour went by, however, with little to do except pace up and down the plates like a caged animal since Sam was his usual taciturn self. I missed Cock's yarn-spinning.

It was after 03.00 that, without warning, our pom-poms started firing. My first thought was that perhaps the French NCO who had told his men to keep their voices down had not been unduly cautious after all, that the Germans had indeed entered the ruins of the town and a rearguard action had started to which we were giving support. Down below we were as uninformed as to what was going on up top as passengers during a train hold-up.

Sam leapt to the voice-pipe and rang up to find out what was going on. He turned to me, evidently relieved: 'We've taken the last of the squaddies aboard and we're blowing up their transport on the jetty.'[50] Almost immediately after the firing stopped we got under way.

As I discovered later, we had indeed taken 'the last of the squaddies'. All the soldiers in Central Norway, both French and British, had been embarked. Those in Åndalsnes and Molde would by now be in home waters, perhaps already safe and dry. Not a ship or man was lost in this phase of the evacuation. *Afridi* had waited for the rearguard at Namsos. They were thirty-five men, mainly in the Territorial Battalion of the York and Lancaster Regiment, and their commanding officer, Lt-Col C. G. Robbins. They had blown up the last bridge behind them about the time I had gone on watch below and it had taken them about two and a half hours to cover the ten miles or so into Namsos because of the treacherous snowbound road. Earlier, General Carton de Wiart had apparently hoped to take passage with us. He expressed his disappointment when he heard his baggage had been taken aboard *York* and thought he had better not be separated from it. Peter Fleming joined him in the cruiser.

At approximately 03.50, after giving a final inspection to the oil-fuel cones, chipping away the last suspicion of clinker and rubbing the plates

---

[50] In the Namsos archives contemporary photographs and film show the amount of British military equipment, including about ten Bofors guns, abandoned intact, and documents left behind in the retreat from Steinkjer which were used by the Germans for propaganda.

down with a piece of cotton waste soaked in the malodorous sperm oil, I nipped up the ladder, along the upper, through the blackout canvas, down into the stokers' mess-deck, gave my relief a shake and returned to No. 3. Another five minutes and he turned up; the middle watch was at an end, and so was the forlorn expedition to Central Norway. For this operation *Afridi* had been the first ship to enter Namsen Fjord (though *Kelly* was the first alongside Namsos quay) and we were now the last ship to leave.

At 04.00 on this 3 May 1940 it was already light as, before turning-in, I gave a last look across the dark green water of Namsen Fjord.

~~

The local commander of the Norwegian troops, Colonel Ole Getz, got wind, only the day before, via one of his officers liaising with the Allies at Namsos, that the British and French were going to embark on ships. But he was in the dark as to their destination. He is supposed to have thought that they were for an assault on the Agdenes Fortress at the entrance to Trondheim Fjord. Only when the troops were embarking did he receive a brief message from Carton de Wiart that 'with the most profound regret we are obliged to evacuate this sector.' Enclosed was a letter in similar vein from the French C-in-C, General Sylvestre Gérard Audet. Even then it was not clear that we were pulling out of the country altogether. Getz had no alternative but to surrender to the Germans.

Before the final Allied evacuation from Norway in June, Narvik was captured in order to destroy its iron-ore and copper-exporting installations. This was successful except for the sinking by *Scharnhorst*'s guns of the aircraft carrier *Glorious* in spite of the heroic attempts to defend her by her sole destroyer screen, the *Ardent* and *Acasta*, with the loss of most of the companies of all three ships. Thus ended the last chapter in the Norwegian campaign. Captain Donald Macintyre in his book, *Narvik,* summed up: 'A defeat it had been, most certainly. Being on perhaps too small a scale to merit description as a disaster, it was not transformed in the eyes of the British public into a heroic episode as was the catastrophe of Dunkirk.'

We were leaving behind the friendly people of Namsos who had paid a very heavy price for being caught up in a conflict which would become world-wide. They had shared the tribulations of the British and French forces who had made a belated, inadequate and inevitably vain attempt to stem the invaders of their country. Now, they had to endure, though none of us knew then for how long, another five years of alien occupation.

Henrik Andersen, at a desk facing a hole blown through the wall of his harbour-master's office in ruined and desolate Namsos, would years afterwards, admit to how lonely he felt after the last Allied troops left. He would not be lonely for long: the Germans arrived the day after we left and installed his double, a *hafen-kapitän*, ostensibly to deal with the German commercial and military aspects of the job but also no doubt to keep an eye on Henrik. Though their orders were to try to fraternise and win over the people they were 'liberating', most Norwegians remained aloof and did no more than they were obliged to do just to exist alongside the *herrenvolk*. Henrik's son, Jens-Anton, was making his own teenage contributions to non-co-operation: removing the fuses from unexploded fire bombs and dismantling the engines of Citroens abandoned by the French so that neither could be used by the invaders. Later, he would be one of the many people who gave food on the quiet to the maltreated Red Army prisoners-of-war who were forced to work constructing roads and railways, fortifications and other buildings. Twice a day, morning and evening, a column of these PoWs would pass close to the Andersens' rebuilt house and Jens-Anton and his friends would slip them fish, potatoes and other vegetables, bread, cod-liver oil and so on, although these were in short supply under civilian rationing. The German guards punished the prisoners severely if they discovered any of this *verboten* food.

When he was seventeen, Jens-Anton got a job with a Norwegian steamship company which the Germans used for sending provisions for their troops to about twenty places along the coast. This provided him with opportunities to 'divert' such goodies as canned herring into the hands of his grateful fellow citizens.

In the immediate environs of Namsos there was no armed resistance. Nevertheless, alongside the general passive resistance and help for the Russian PoWs, telephone wires were cut, signposts turned in the wrong direction and clandestine newspapers were produced. There were two secret radio stations operating in the vicinity, continual contact was kept up with the Shetlands and assistance given to agents to land in Norway and for Norwegians to escape to Britain, an activity which earned the soubriquet 'The Shetlands Bus Service'.

As these activities grew, so did the German efforts to detect and suppress them with increasing ruthlessness. In October 1944 the Gestapo arrested Henrik Andersen, accusing him of not having been sufficiently cooperative. Actually, he had been working with the Resistance since mid-1940 and was in contact with Britain through the 'Bus Service'.

Either deliberately or under torture he had been given away and was first taken by the Gestapo to their headquarters and torture chamber in the Misjons Hotellet in Trondheim. This has been renamed the Hotel Augustin in Prinsens gate where there is a plaque on the wall honouring Bjorn Eriksen, a twenty-seven-year-old member of the Resistance who jumped from the roof rather than betray his comrades. Henrik Andersen was tortured, too, by sadistic Quisling collaborators called the Rinan Group[51] and once confided in his son that he had contemplated suicide for the same reason as Bjorn. But his fellow prisoners who bore Henrik a sturdy respect and affectionate solicitude kept a discreet vigil on their harbour-master to make sure nothing of the sort happened.

Henrik was condemned to death by the Gestapo. Ironically, he was only saved from execution by the intervention of his German co-harbour-master who, like most of his compatriots, slipped back to Germany as swiftly as possible when the war ended. We will never know what motivated his untypically humane intervention. Henrik's sentence was commuted and he was was kept in a succession of concentration camps in Norway. But in January 1944 he was taken by train with another batch of prisoners from Trondheim to Oslo for shipment to a camp in Germany. The Norwegian Resistance managed to sink the ship before the prisoners were embarked and, instead, Henrik spent the last months before VE Day in the Grini concentration camp near Oslo. He returned to a 'home' which in December 1944 had been taken over by the Gestapo. They had thrown out his wife and Jens-Anton and before scuttling back to Germany, ransacked the house.

Henrik was awarded the MBE for his wartime services and was conspicuous in his dress uniform returning the salutes of the ships' companies during post-war courtesy visits to Namsos by the Royal Navy. But he paid dearly for his courage and loyalty to the Allies. To the end of his days—he died in 1970 aged seventy-six—he suffered from the effects of his torture, every month having to go into hospital for a blood transfusion.

~~

We will leave *Afridi* steaming homewards through Namsen Fjord with her extra complement of thirty-six soldiers. Years will pass before the

---

[51] Rinan and six of his gang were shot after the war.

almost forgotten swoosh of a falling bomb from an unseen and unheard aircraft—a repeat of *Maori*'s experience—and a fountain of water only feet away from another Tribal's bow would bring back vivid memories of the events during the rest of that 3 May 1940, rounding off the story which Commander Rump, RN had all unwittingly begun. [52]

---

[52] See Chapter 17, Tribals Again, p. 271.

SECOND TURN–*Terra Firma et Trepida*

Hull, in 1941 the UK's third busiest seaport after London and Liverpool, was probably the most persistently bombed provincial city in Britain. The biggest blitzes were on the nights of 7 and 8 May 1941. Pictures show fire raging in the British Cake and Oil Mills and tin-helmetted men of the NFS (National Fire Service) in the ruins of another part of the city. *(Photographs courtesy of the Imperial War Museum)*

Chapter 7

Humber Watershed

The British were not merely making the best of things when, after the fall of France, they professed themselves well satisfied to stand alone. Had they been closely analysed at the time, the nation's reactions might well have proved an alloy in which much was base: conceit, stupidity, xenophobia, fecklessness and wishful thinking—these, among other flaws, might have been found in the gleaming brass of its self-confidence.

Invasion 1940: Peter Fleming

The city that suffered most [in the provincial blitzes] *was Kingston-upon-Hull. It was an easy target night after night. Hull had no peace.*

Home Secretary Herbert Morrison

Exactly a week after *Afridi* steamed out of Namsen Fjord on 3 May 1940, *blitzkrieg* entered the English vocabulary.

The German attack started on 10 May against the Netherlands, Belgium, Luxembourg and France simultaneously. By the 24th the Allied armies were facing certain defeat and it was only General von Runstedt's order for a three-day halt which permitted the miraculous British evacuation from Dunkirk. This began (after those from Boulogne and to a lesser extent from Calais) on the 27th and would continue, under relentless bombing, until 4 June. Nearly 340,000 men (a third of them non-British) managed to reach our shores from Dunkirk, a small French town between Ostend and Calais, in an armada of vessels of every kind which sailed to the rescue from all around Britain. It was accomplished through the superlative efforts of the Navy, both by its top commanders and, especially, by the strenuous and indefatigable work of the destroyers which, apart from taking aboard thousands of troops from the beaches, mole and harbour, and fighting off the Luftwaffe, engaged in gun duels with German artillery ashore. Apart from over 200 other types of vessel, six destroyers were sunk, including *Grenade* with which *Afridi* had been involved in rescuing men from another bombed destroyer on 3 May.

I had returned to Pompey barracks after the Namsos evacuation. In the last days of May the order came over the Tanoy many times a day for men to fall-in on the parade ground according to their messes. There, regulating petty officers called out the names of individual ratings who were needed to man the hundreds of craft of all descriptions which formed the rescue armada. Every time the stokers' mess was called I fell-in with the others but my name was not on any of the lists. It was not until 12 June, nine days after Operation *Dynamo*, the Dunkirk evacuation, had officially ended that I was given a draft chit to HMS *Beaver II*.

Beaver II, I discovered, was not a destroyer nor was it seaworthy. It was a stone frigate, the RN base in the Yorkshire city of Kingston-upon-Hull. Specifically, I was to join the Humber Boiler-cleaning Party which conveyed very little to me at the time. Hull was an unknown quantity but Humber rang a bell: *Afridi* and the other eight ships of the 7th Destroyer Flotilla and two cruisers had been part of the Humber Force based on this so-called river which is the tributary of six others but has no source. Even more mysterious was the instruction on the chit to report (to my surprise) to a hotel. I arrived at Hull's Paragon Station with my kitbag and hammock. Thankfully, I didn't have to walk far: I found the hotel in nearby Anlaby Road. I reported to a middle-aged petty officer with spectacles sitting in the foyer. He had a generally laid-back air and was evidently enjoying a quiet number away from the usual Naval discipline and wartime dangers. He explained that I would only be in the hotel for the night and then be billeted elsewhere. I was to stand by for a coach to arrive at 08.00 the following morning, he said, to take me to the docks together with the rest of the Humber Boiler-cleaning Party. Meantime the rest of the day was my own.

It was by now late afternoon with the mid-June sun still shining as I strolled up Anlaby Road and discovered West Park. I went in and as I strolled past a bench I was hailed. 'Hullo sailor!' said a woman whom I reckoned was around thirty and had a child in a pram. It was a nice surprise; Hull was evidently a friendly place. I had never been greeted by a complete stranger of the opposite sex apart from the usual accosting 'Hullo dearie. Feeling naughty tonight?' I used to get in the Bayswater Road on the way to Hyde Park to exercise my dog. Professional ladies wouldn't sun themselves on a bench with a pram, would they? Was she just a comely, friendly Yorkshire mum taking the initiative because she wanted company and a natter? We chatted as she wheeled the pram through the park. When she got to her home, I was invited in for a cuppa. She was alone, she said, with a twinkle that had only one interpretation. She wouldn't be a jiffy while she put the nipper to bed. This done, any vestige of a doubt as to what to expect was of brief duration. This woman of initiative slid onto my lap and started embracing me with a passionate and infectious gusto.

Enjoyment of my unforeseen adventure was tempered by inhibitions. I was shocked that this was happening with her baby upstairs and even more when she told me her husband was at sea on a minesweeper. So I was more than half relieved when she apologised for not being able to take me for an 'all night in' because of the child. But that little hitch to consummation could be easily overcome, she assured me, with the help of an accommodating neighbour who would baby-sit in her own home the following night.

The assignation never materialised. By one of those coincidences, which in stories seem contrived, I did have a meeting of sorts with her a year later. In the crowded carriage of a Paragon-to-Doncaster train, the first leg of the journey to King's Cross, I squeezed into the only available seat and only then glanced at my fellow passengers. Right opposite was the West Park mum. Beside her was a matelot with an HM Minesweeper cap tally. We recognised each other instantly and with an almost imperceptible headshake she silently pleaded that I should make no sign of knowing her, which for the sake of all three of us I would never have dreamed of doing. I don't think she exchanged a word with her husband, as I presume he was, until we all got off at Doncaster and, wherever they went, I made sure I didn't follow.

~~

The living quarters of the boiler-cleaning party was the Etheldreda Mission, a terracotta brick building with an outside iron fire escape, lying back from George Street close to the bridge crossing the sluggish River

Hull. It had been a convent and had its own adjoining graveyard. The Church Army had taken it over and ran it as a hostel. In place of the erstwhile nuns there were now elderly men with apparently little or no other means of subsistence who hung about the ground floor in cloth caps smoking briars or drinking cuppas.

Also billeted at the hostel were young seamen who were staffing the *Beaver II* base which was in another part of the city. But the majority of Etheldreda's Naval personnel were the permanent boiler-cleaning stokers. There were about half a dozen of my own age in the party, some of them survivors from ships that had gone down. Eric Bettes, for instance, had been on the *Grenade* at Dunkirk. But most of the party were three-badge men who had done their twenty-one years' service and had been called up from the RN Reserve for the duration. There were no officers, no chiefs, no petty officers. So, no bullshit either: we maintained our own 'discipline'. Those who preferred to do so even 'went ashore' in civvies.

In charge of the hostel was a grey-uniformed, cherubic-faced Church Army Captain named Sangster, in his early forties with a permanent air of bewilderment. That was not surprising since his world, looking after his comparatively docile ancients, had now been invaded by a host of men whose every sentence was punctuated with what he would certainly consider obscenities and who made this former convent ring with ribaldry.

Etheldreda's upper floors consisted of corridors of wooden-partitioned cubicles, each just big enough for a single, grey-blanketed bed, a collapsible card table and a chair. As there was a two-foot gap between the top of the partition and the ceiling and another large gap under the door, there were no restrictions on the passage of cold air in the winter nor, all the year around, on the chatter, shouts, singing, whistling, farts and snores of the occupants. On each door was a brass plate with the name of its one-time inmate: Sister Mary, Sister Martha and so on. The irony was much appreciated by the three-badge men who would never tire of fantasising with variations on the same theme: 'Fancy a hairy-arsed stoker bashing his bald-headed bishop on a bed which Sister Agatha used to sleep in!'

Apart from the purple language, there was another reason why Captain Sangster kept, to the best of his ability, aloof from his Naval paying-guests: the food dished out to us was qualitatively and quantitatively worse than anything Oliver Twist could have complained about. Since the captain symbolised the Church Army, which was being paid by the Navy for our maintenance, he was the butt of our resentment.

The most vocal members of our boiler cleaners were Jim Wybird and Harry Sturla, an inseparable couple, three-badge men, both going thin on the top. Jim being the slightly older of the two, Harry treated him with the respect due to an Old Testament prophet. It was Jim this and Jim that and 'Don't you think so, Jim?' They were East End Londoners of a type now almost extinct, their humour synchronising with the Old Time music hall patter of their youth. Jim was fleshy from nose to paunch, ponderous, a pipe smoker. Harry was sharper featured, quicker in his movements, smoked fags and every now and then would make some dramatic exclamation in Yiddish which he had probably picked up from his Stepney neighbours.

'The Church Army's bleedin' miracle, I calls it.'

'Wot's that, Jim?'

'Makin' rosie lee without tea, milk or sugar.'

'Yus, quite right, Jim. Fuckin' maiden's water, that's wot it is, Jim.'

That was their verdict on the liquid that came out of the urn which was trundled into the room where we ate our breakfast and the last meal of the day at six o'clock, whatever we liked to call it: tea or supper. Etheldreda's staple diet, which the Church Army apparently considered adequate after eight hours of cleaning boilers, was one Cornish pasty per man. With cotton-wool bread and a scrape of marge, that was supposed to suffice for the next fourteen hours. Jim, Harry and the rest of their Chatty-Chatham-based [53] mates knew enough West Country lingo to give a Cornish pasty its native monicker: tiddy oggy. So it was that whenever Etheldreda Mission hove in sight from the coach which brought us back from the docks, without fail it would be greeted with yells of 'Tiddy Oggy 'Ostel ahoy!' with the frequent variation: 'Starvation 'Ostel ahoy!' After a day's grafting in the boilers, Harry would exclaim: 'M'belly button's flappin' against m'bleedin' backbone, Jim.' To which his fellow sufferer would rejoin: 'Yus, 'Arry, I could eat a scabby 'orse, m'self.'

For breakfast we might get a plate of watery tinned tomatoes, 'train-smash' in Navalese, and if we were lucky, a near-invisible sliver of bacon, washed down with the inevitable dish-water chai. 'Wot'd you do, 'Arry, if yer old woman dished up sumfin like that?' Jim would ask, looking down his large proboscis at a meagre portion of baked beans.

---

[53] Chatham RN barracks, long since closed down.

'Cowboys gorge, ain't it, Jim? I'd shove it hard, right acrorst the table at 'er and she'd 'ave to field it.'

We did get, however, a comparatively substantial lunch in the dock canteen, its quality and quantity varying with the dock. In the largest, King George Dock, there was a big canteen where we invariably had a fresh meat course, presumably because rations corresponded to its numerous clientele of dockyard workers. In the Albert Dock, however, there was only a small hut where a man-and-wife team ran a café. Here the lunch was predictable, what Jim and Harry called nuts-and-bolts, steak and kidney pud, probably out of tins. Hungry as I always was, I had no complaints.

Complaints about Starvation Hostel were certainly made by Jim and Harry to our stoker petty officers who presumably passed them on through higher channels. But the SPOs had their own billets in private houses and they seldom even descended from the coach which took us to and from work. Once or twice during the time I was at the Etheldreda Mission an officer did come to inspect our evening meal after a particularly trenchant complaint but there was no lasting change for the better. The men's resentment was fuelled by the knowledge that the food in the barracks and at sea was excellent compared with that available for the tightly rationed civilians. Furthermore, since Etheldreda was not a Naval establishment, the Naval personnel also had to forfeit their daily tot.

~~

That the cleaning of a destroyer's boilers was no sinecure and meriting more than a nightly tiddy oggy for tea was evidenced by the very existence of a permanent shore-based boiler-cleaning party. Its *raison d'être* was to give the sea-going stokers a chance to get boiler-cleaning leave, to go home after weeks at sea. It also relieved them of a chore they loathed doing. To get an idea of why this was so calls for a short description.

In theory a destroyer's boilers should have been cleaned after approximately every 900 hours of steaming. But with the ever-growing pressures of the war at sea, this was now the exception and destroyers were docking after 1,000 hours or more of steaming. Scale and even rust formed inside the three steel drums of each boiler as well as inside the hundreds of tubes connecting the lower drums to the big one above them. Most destroyers had three boilers. As in any chimney, soot from the oil-fired furnace was deposited on the inside of the funnels or smoke-stacks, while clinker formed between the tubes since these were in direct contact with the furnace. All this could affect the raising and maintaining of steam to the turbines and, in consequence, the ship's manoeuvrability. So boiler-cleaning was vital to the ship's efficiency.

When a destroyer went into dry dock for this essential refurbishment of its intestines, the opportunity was often taken for a general refit. Dockyard mateys, as Jack called them, would swarm over the vessel. Down below, there would be mainly boilermakers and fitters and, working anywhere on board, carpenters, electricians, welders and painters. From looking shipshape and Bristol fashion (the ship's normal appearance in harbour) she now exceeded her Jimmy the One's worst nightmare.

When we went on board our job would be divided into two sections: internal and external. Internal meant cleaning the inside of the steam drums and water tubes; the external: cleaning inside the funnel and removing the clinker from between the outside of the tubes. In the top drum two men could sit upright in comparative comfort while they paid out down the inside of each of the hundreds of tubes a dynamo-powered 'snake'. This was a small round steel brush that revolved inside a flexible steel casing. Each time the fast-rotating brush was pulled up and out of a tube, it brought with it a little cloud of powdered rust and pulverised lime scale. Of the whole boiler-cleaning process, this was the plum job. Jim and Harry, no doubt maintaining stoutly that this was 'skilled' compared with the other functions that we performed, were always given the top drum by our SPOs. I, or other members of the party, only got a chance of working in the top drum when Jim and Harry went on leave.

It was a job that required the maintenance of a slow but steady rhythm, gently, without forcing, pushing the snake down each tube and as gently pulling it up and withdrawing it. ('Much easier if it 'ad 'air around it,' Harry would muse nostalgically.) If the revolving brush were to break off or get stuck in a tube, there would be hell to pay.

As in cleaning the oil-fuel tanks, lighting for these operations was by a single bulb at the end of a flex or wandering lead, with the juice coming from a dockside dynamo.

The other internal (we called it infernal) job necessitated us crawling through the apertures of the lower drums which were just wide enough to wriggle the shoulders through. Once inside, it was only possible to lie on our bellies or backs or, at best, to kneel crouched double. Although of course the boilers had been emptied, a certain amount of sediment, a rusty sludge of the consistency and colour of cocoa, usually remained and had to be mopped up with cotton waste. Then, the steel walls of the drum had to be wire-scrubbed, including between the orifices or bells of the tubes, before we crawled out of the drum. Next, with a brush and fanny-full of plumbago—the same black lead with which old-fashioned fire grates used to be coated and polished—we would climb in again and 'paint' the whole of the inside with it.

When this was dry, probably the following day, we would crawl back into the drum to polish off the plumbago. Since part of this process had to be done on one's back, especially the belling—touching each tube's orifice with the revolving steel brush to make them twinkle like stars—the plumbago fell in showers on one's upturned, rag-wrapped face.

The so-called external phase began with climbing up the vertical ladder inside the funnel which might be divided in two by a steel partition if it was the outlet from two boilers. Starting at the top, we would wire-scrub the entire surface of the interior, loosening the oil-fuel soot and gradually working our way down to the bottom. This in itself was a grimy operation but some ship's engineer officers insisted that the inside of the funnel should then be coated with linseed oil. Clothes were particularly resistant to being dhobeyed after such treatment.

Next came the 'sawing' of the clinker from between the tubes, from both inside the furnace and the wings of the boiler-room.

What I found to be the most unhealthy part of a generally insalubrious process was yet to come. Air hoses were rigged to a compressor and we then had to high-pressure blow between the tubes to remove any remaining soot or clinker. Everyone, except the man doing the blowing, cleared out of the boiler-room into the fresh air. Within seconds of the compressed air being switched on, heavy clouds of soot billowed around the boiler-room, obscuring even the dim lights of the lanterns at the end of the wandering leads.

No masks or protection of any sort were provided by the Navy for any of this work. No matter what we wrapped around our faces, eyes smarted and streamed, noses ran and the powdered lime scale, plumbago and oil-fuel soot penetrated boiler suits and clothing to the skin.

During the winter months especially, since there was no heating except perhaps the dockyard mateys' brazier on the upper deck, I wore the inner-lined black leather German seaman's trousers I had acquired to keep myself warm under different circumstances. They were held up with cord in lieu of braces. Under the boiler suit I wore an odd assortment of old civvy shirts and pullovers. Handkerchiefs and rags covered my nose

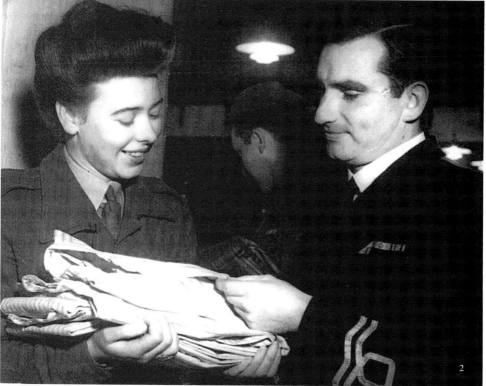

(Top) August 1939, No. 1 (second from left) with three of the First 500, self-conscious in a strange uniform and *(Above)* May 1946, an ATS in the clothing depot at London's Olympia Exhibition Hall shows No. 1 a selection of demob shirts.

Admiral of the Fleet Sir Philip Vian GCB, KBE, DSO and two bars, RN (1894–1968) and (*above*) as Captain (D) on the bridge. This picture was probably taken following the *Altmark* episode when Vian had temporarily transferred to *Cossack* during *Afridi*'s refit in the Co Durham port of West Hartlepool. After the Namsos evacuation he would again command *Cossack*.

(*Opposite page left*) In the engine room of HMS *Tartar*, a Tribal class destroyer, an ERA (engine-room artificer) controls the throttle on one of the two turbines and behind him a stoker logs the changes in revolutions. Note the fanny hanging up behind him. The temperature could be over 42° in northern latitudes. (*Opposite right*) A stoker in the maze of asbestos-lagged pipes in a destroyer's boiler-room. The only exit and access is by a near vertical ladder. It leads via the platform on which this stoker is standing and an air-lock door to a very confined hatch space; another short ladder gives access to a hatch-cover which opens on to the upper deck and must only be lifted when the water-tight door behind the man exiting is shut. Otherwise, the strong draught from the huge fans would draw the furnace flames into the boiler-room.

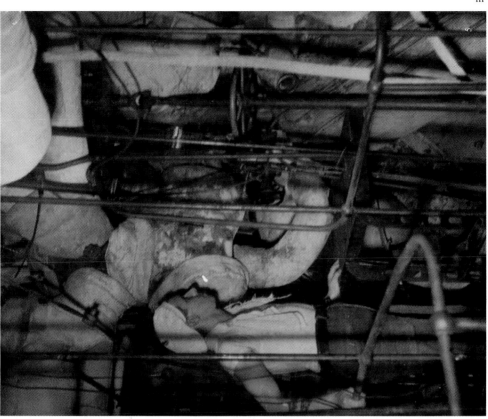

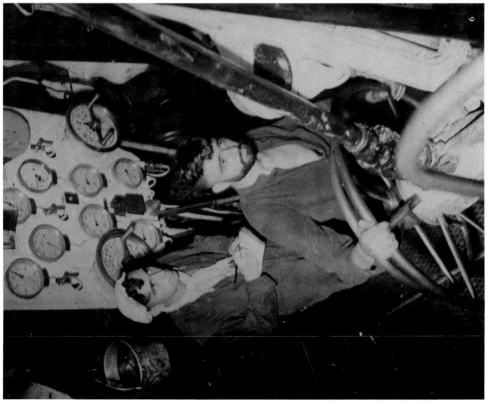

(Left) German troops, unopposed, landing at Trondheim from the battle cruiser *Admiral Hipper* on 9 April 1940.

(Below) A picture taken from the *Admiral Hipper* of oil-clogged men from the destroyer *Glowworm* clinging to a Carley float before 31 of them managed to get on board the heavy cruiser. A rope was thrown to *Glowworm*'s CO, Lieut-Cdr Roope RN but he was too weak to hang on to it. He was awarded a posthumous VC for ramming the German ship.

(Top) Chasseurs alpins officers aboard one of the French transports. *(Above)* Major-General Sir Adrian Carton de Wiart VC, Commander-in Chief British Expeditionary Force in Central Norway, and his French opposite number, General Sylvestre Gérard Audet. *(Namsos Museum)*

Photograph courtesy of the Imperial War Museum

(Above) The sloop HMS *Bittern* bombed and ablaze in Namsen Fjord. *(Below)* British troops unloading at Namsos from the converted Polish liner MV *Chobry* on 17 April 1940. *(Namsos Museum)*

(Top insets) Low-flying Heinkels over Namsos. *(Main pictures)* Namsos before and during the blitz of 20 April 1940.

(Top) Desolation after the blitz. Apart from some French soldiers in the hills above the town firing machine-guns at the raiders, there was no anti-aircraft defence. Namsos was the Second World War's first 'Guernica', the undefended town blitzed by the Germans in the Spanish Civil War. *(Bottom)* German officers survey the destruction left by the Luftwaffe.

Photograph courtesy of the Imperial War Museum

(*Above*) British troops embarking on the French troopship *El-Djezair* during the night of 2–3 May 1940. (*Below*) In the winter of 1940–41, from the Bastion of German-occupied Namsos, the local commander, Colonel (later General) Fischer, reviews a parade of the Wehrmacht invaders with other officers.

Three maltreated Russian POWs at Namsos photographed after liberation in 1945. With other foreign labour and some Norwegians, they were forced by the Germans to work on fortifications like the bunker *(top)* in the Utvorda coastal fort dominating the approaches to Namsen Fjord. When the anchor *(inset)* from an old sailing ship which the Germans had brought from Holland was going to be used in the making of ferroconcrete for a new quay at Namsos, Harbour Master Henrik Andersen approached the leader of a Russian POW gang who spoke German and persuaded him to get them to dig a deep hole. Clandestinely, the anchor was dropped into it and covered up. After the war it was dug up and is one of the memorials for Soviet prisoners.

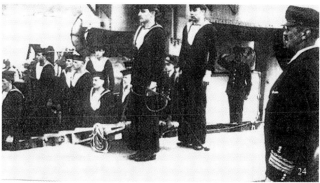

(Top left) Jens-Anton Andersen, fifteen at the time of the blitz, seen here in 2002 with a book from his home damaged by the bomb splinter he holds in his right hand. At his feet lies the nose of an unexploded bomb. *(Top right)* His father, Harbour Master Henrik Andersen MBE, free after detention in concentration camps, salutes HMS *Hotspur* as she pays a peacetime courtesy visit to Namsos. *(Above left)* The inseparable Royal Naval Reserve pensioners, Stokers Jim Wybird and Harry Sturla, taking a lunch-time rest in Hull's King George V Dock. They usually had what was considered the 'plum job' in the boiler-cleaning routine: inside the top steam drum *(right)* of a destroyer's boiler, carefully playing a dynamo-powered revolving steel brush at the end of a flexible 'snake' down the insides of hundreds of tubes. Should the brush get stuck or break off inside a tube, the stoker, whoever he was, would be in real trouble. Each time the brush was withdrawn it brought up a little cloud of powdered rust. 'Masks' were old rags.

(Top left) No. 1 (in German black leather trousers) with two other Humber boiler-cleaners on board the destroyer HMS *Express*. With the whole of her fo'c's'le blown off by a mine, *Express* was in dry dock for months and was the Humber boiler-cleaners' stand-by job. *(Right)* Some of 'Starvation Hostel's' stoker (and young seamen) inmates. The three standing on the right in the back row are from left to right: 'Rotherham Robby', 'Ye Olde English Gentleman' and 'Scouse'. Above: D-Day: '05.55: Deep roar of aircraft going south … continues intermittently for 25 minutes … We were told at the briefing that there are 10,000 aircraft in this show.' In the background of this Official Naval Photographer's picture of gliders being towed by Allied planes are the battleships *Warspite* (left) and *Ramilles*. Nearer the camera, a destroyer races westwards.

(Top) A silenced German gun in a log emplacement positioned for raking the beach. (Centre) Royal Marines dismantling *teller* mines attached to stakes which were submerged at high tide and a close-up of an explosive device wired to a stake. *Main picture*: Royal Marines neutralising beach obstacles on the afternoon of D-Day.

(*Left*) Royal Marine Corporal Tandy demonstrates how he guided his Landing Craft (Assault) loaded with troops to a D-Day beach after its steering gear was smashed. He was often submerged up to his armpits in the choppy seas. Tandy was awarded the Distinguished Service Medal.

(*Below*) Jimmy Southcott, a First World War veteran and naval correspondent for the London evening newspaper, *Star*, interviewing RN Commandos on the beach at La Rivière.

34

35

Pictures left behind when German troops evacuated a dug-out at Fécamp in Hitler's 'West Wall': three Field Police and three snaps of young women—German or French? One of the two on Fécamp beach hides her face from the camera. It could be the same three *feldgendarmerie* in the background.

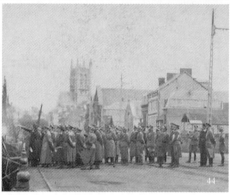

Nazi propaganda pictures: *(From top)* Wreckage of RAF planes; a German soldier inspects a woman's cart; a high-ranking delegation on Fécamp's quayside (the figure in front appears to be giving the Nazi salute); sketches of the Wehrmacht in action; the wave-lapped cadaver of a pilot (most likely British); the Nazi *Hakenkreuz* flies from a naval vessel.

(Previous page:, top) Landing craft approaching Walcheren in Operation *Infatuate*, 1 November 1944 to clear the Germans from the mouth of the River Scheldt. Official Naval historian Captain Stephen Roskill, RN maintained that for the 'Green Berets', the Royal Marine Commandos, this was 'the most formidable of any assault from the sea during the war.'

(Previous page, centre) Rockets from rogue LC(R)s (rocket landing craft) exploding among our own vessels and the camera catches the fate of one of them seconds after impact. *(Previous page, bottom)* A medic is in the foreground of this craft, still well off shore. The Admiralty censor has blotted out an object on the left. *(This page,: top)* Shells bursting on the Walcheren town of Westkapelle, the commandos' objective. *(Centre)* The top of a windmill is just visible through the smoke shortly before the run-in at 09.45.

(Pictures on this and previous page were taken by Official Naval Photographer, Lieut M. H. A McNeil, RNVR.)

56

57

(Top) Two of HM Submarine *Shakespeare's* crew have climbed overboard and are plugging a hole blown by gunfire from a Japanese armed merchantman which prevents her from diving. Another shell wounded Petty Officer Telegraphist Harmer's feet and after 20 minutes he was washed into the sea.

After the ordeal, including repeated attacks by bombers, surviving crew members *(left)* watch the approach of a fol boat with medical supplies and food from their sister submarine, HMS *Stygian*.

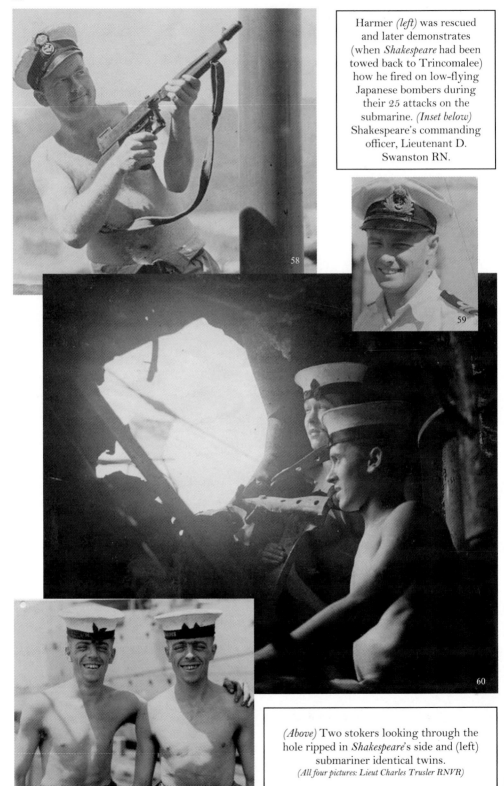

Harmer *(left)* was rescued and later demonstrates (when *Shakespeare* had been towed back to Trincomalee) how he fired on low-flying Japanese bombers during their 25 attacks on the submarine. *(Inset below)* Shakespeare's commanding officer, Lieutenant D. Swanston RN.

(Above) Two stokers looking through the hole ripped in *Shakespeare*'s side and (left) submariner identical twins.
(All four pictures: Lieut Charles Trusler RNVR)

(Top) Japanese swim or tread water amid the wreckage of their ship sunk by British East Indies Fleet destroyers. Several chose drowning to capture and one man hammered the side of a destroyer with a shell. Those who were rescued are dhobeying on the destroyer's upper deck *(above)*. Another managed to hang himself with his own loincloth.

(Pictures: Lieutenant Charles Trusler, RNVR)

(Top) Four of the seven South-East Asian women survivors from the Japanese submarine-chaser *Teshio Maru* sunk by the guns of the destroyer HMS *Volage*. They were probably intended to be 'comforts' for the Japanese troops on the Andaman Islands. *(Above)* HMS *Newcastle*'s 6-inch guns fire a salvo prior to the assault on Cheduba, an island on the Arakan coast of Burma (today's Myanmar).

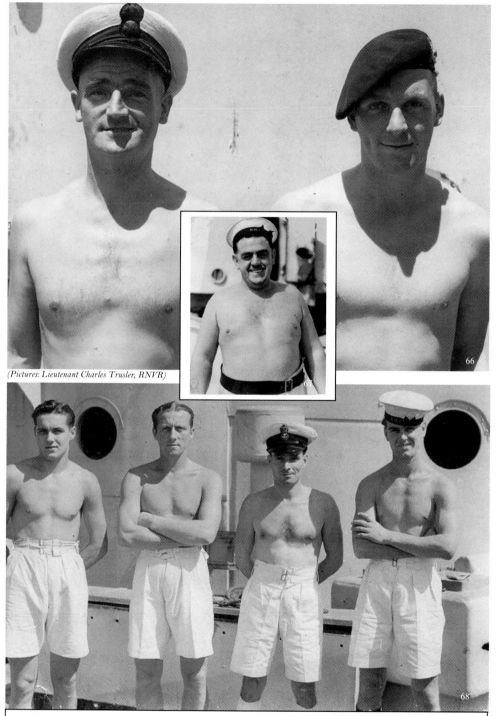

(Pictures: Lieutenant Charles Trusler, RNVR)

Contrary to custom not to put men of the same family on the same ship (to avoid a double bereavement) there were on the cruiser HMS *Newcastle*. *(Top)* Chief Supply Assistant W. J. and his son, Royal Marine Kenneth Squire from Lancaster and *(above)* two sets of brothers, Ordinary Seamen Anthony J. and John R. Barnes from Middlesborough and Stoker Petty Officer A. F. and Stoker J. Woodman from Swansea. *(Inset)* Able Seaman 'Tubby' Goss from Plymouth had served eight years on *Newcastle*.

(Pictures: Lieutenant Charles Trusle,r RNVR)

(Top) Royal Marines training for jungle warfare in Ceylon (Sri Lanka) and *(above)* on 26 January 1945, approaching the island of Cheduba in *Newcastle*'s whalers.

(Top) Wading ashore on Cheduba and, later,
(below) Chedubans help the Marines land stores.
(Pictures: Lieutenant Charles Trusler, RNVR)

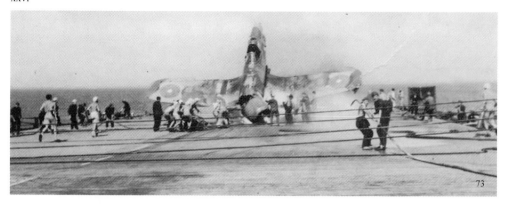

(Top) A Corsair fighter crash-lands on the flight deck of the carrier *Khedive*. *(Below)* As seen from *Venus*, three sister destroyers, *Volage*, *Verulam* and *Virago* in Operation *Sunfish*, a search-and-destroy sweep of north-west Sumatran inshore waters. *(Pictures: Lieutenant Charles Trusler, RNVR)*

Picture: National Film Archive

Pictures: Lieutenant Charles Trasler

75

76

(Top) The brothers McLaglen. Left: tough guy Victor in Hollywood and Lieutenant Leopold RNVR in Colombo. Who had the bigger line-shoot? *(Below)* Japanese soldiers pose for a snap beside their vehicle in the grounds of a commandeered Rangoon bungalow.

77

78

79

(Top) Artist Francis Chapelet's impression of the bombing of the rescue efforts after the French destroyer *Bison* had been hit by a dive-bomber on 3 May 1940 during the evacuation of Allied troops from Central Norway. *(Insert)* Captain Roger Bouan who was killed instantly when the bomb hit the bridge. *(Musée Naval de St-Martin-de-Ré)*. With the USA still neutral, the American media gave revealing views of the war which would have been considered bad for morale in the UK. This artist's impression *(right)* in *Life* magazine of 27 May 1940 was captioned: 'German dive bomber dives with one 1,100-lb. bomb on the British destroyer *Afridi* of the crack Tribal class and proceeds to sink it. Flying usually in a formation of nine, the dive bombers attack in threes. It cannot often sink warships.' This statement was too premature, unfortunately, and a contradiction of the headline to the article it illustrated: DIVE BOMBER PLUMMETS ON TARGETS. Also shown was a Luftwaffe pilot in the cockpit of a Stuka, over the caption: 'He may faint in zooming.'
(Rex Features & Life Magazine)

80

(Above) Afridi men after being landed in a troopship at the Clydeside port of Greenock entrain for Portsmouth where they were give 'survivors' leave.

(Left) the thirty-year old, Hamburg-born, Paul-Werner Hozzel with the rank equivalent to Flight Lieutenant, commanded the Luftwaffe group of four Junkers 87 dive-bombers which dropped the two bombs on *Afridi* and sent her to the bottom forty-five minutes later. He is wearing the Iron Cross (2nd Class) awarded for operations during the Nazi invasion of Poland which sparked the Second World War.

83

84

85

86

87

When *Grenade* came alongside the bombed *Bison*, Ordinary Seaman William Ridgewell *(top left)* saw through a porthole 'the terror on the faces' of men trapped on a messdeck; Ordinary Telegraphist Jack Levy *(top right)* was one of thirteen telegraphist ratings killed when *Afridi's* W/T office got a direct hit and Warrant Telegraphist R. Mellor, RN was the only one of *Afridi's* officers who died. *(Above right)* Bombardier Harry Killingbeck said that 'a few of *Bittern's* men made it. Others were machine-gunned in the water.' *(Above left) Afridi* signalman Harold Kirk, as he was in 1940, said: 'The flames caught me and I was badly burned' and *(left)* Harold in 2000 visiting an island in Namsen Fjord with Radio Telegraphist Jean Raoul *(centre)* who, on board the French destroyer *Tartu*, heard the last messages from the stricken destroyers *Bison* and *Afridi*. John Gritten *(right)*.

Ambassador Richard Dales unveiling the British memorial in Namsos on 17 May 2000 while *(below)* the Defence Attaché, Commander David Stanesby RN, stands at the salute. Veteran Olav Olsen, who during the German occupation escaped to England to fight-on in the Royal Norwegian Navy, is about to toll the ship's bell salvaged from the bombed anti-submarine trawler HMT *Aston Villa.* George Pears *(sitting right, holding Union flag)* was with the Hallamshire Battalion of the York and Lancaster Regiment in the Namsos evacuation.

88

89

On 17 May 2000 French and British veterans of the Norwegian campaign and their families watch from the Namsos Bastion a colourful Norwegian Constitution Day procession of children and young people *(below)*. It was from the same Bastion that local German commander Colonel Fischer reviewed the Wehrmacht parade in November 1940.

90

91

and mouth during the dirtiest parts of the job, the whole topped by a battered matelot's cap with no tally ribbon.

The boiler-cleaning on one destroyer could take up to a fortnight and when finished it was inspected by her senior engineer or engineer commander together with *Beaver II*'s Chief Engine-room Artificer Lapthorne with torches, gloved hands and white overalls as if the ship's viscera were susceptible to human contagion. There were wry grins and some uplifted digits behind the backs of this immaculate inspection team by some of us who had wrought this miracle of sanitisation.

After inhaling these clouds of soot and, to a lesser extent, the plumbago, our chests wheezed for days. These effects were unhealthy enough for those of us who were young and strong but the older men (with the exception of Jim and Harry) were not spared the worst phases of this work. Some of them already had chest complaints and one man had only one lung. Yet these were the conditions in which they worked year in and year out, some for the duration. The lives of these men, especially those who already seemed prematurely aged, may have been shortened. This seemed unnecessary, even allowing for the extra effort and hardship that could be expected in wartime, and I persuaded an MP to ask in Parliament why such men were sent to permanent boiler-cleaning parties and why all of us were not provided with masks. The First Lord A. V. Alexander gave a totally irrelevant answer to the effect that there was no greater incidence of chest complaints in the engine-room than in any other branch of the Navy. Unfortunately, the MP did not see that this was a complete evasion of his question, which referred specifically to stokers doing this job every working day and not to engine-room personnel in general, and did not pursue the matter with a supplementary question.

~~

The job did have its perks. The stokers on these ships showed their appreciation for our relieving them of this work and for providing the opportunity for a few more days leave by piling on us tins of food before they left—all of it strictly rationed outside—as well as tins of pusser's tobacco[54] and duty-free cigarettes.

Another of our inveterate three-badge comedians was a Scouser. He had liquid blue eyes and would comb into a fetching curl the tuft that

---

[54] Issued monthly to the Lower Deck at duty-free prices. The cigarette tobacco would be rolled by hand with or without a machine and the resulting fag was known as a tickler.

stuck out like a promontory on his forehead between gulfs left by a receding hairline. He also had a beautiful set of teeth which I suspect were removable. His combination of disingenuous innocence and devilment most women he encountered found irresistible. Far from being shocked, most were highly amused by his risqué witticisms, especially by the absurdity of his opening gambit: 'Ever done it standing up under the bed, darlin'?'

One day I was walking with Scouse through St George's Dock, with sacks on our backs. These were full of 'rabbits', tins of all kinds of food unobtainable by civilians, which could either be taken home on the next leave or would be an open sesame to the favours which certain ladies of Hull were adept in providing. This bounty had befallen us thanks to the thoughtfulness of the stokers on a destroyer which was paying-off before being recommissioned and our friends were only too pleased to show their appreciation of our relieving them of the boiler-cleaning chore. So the remaining stores in the stokers' mess quickly found their way into the sooty old sacks in which we carried our dirty working gear. Scouse and I shuffled through the dockyard loaded with our share of the loot, including tins of pusser's tobacco—all of it contraband. If caught, we would certainly be for the high-jump.

Suddenly, to our dismay we spotted two HM Customs officers sitting on the bogey of a crane right beside the way we had to go. They were intent on examining some document one of them was holding. To turn back would have been to court suspicion. 'Leave this to me,' counselled Scouse. 'Don't say a word.' When we got abreast of the Customs men, Skouse without looking at them and bending even more under the weight of the sack, let loose a stream of profanities audible enough for the officers to have heard had they been inquisitive about the contents of the sacks. 'Fancy askin' us to carry a load of boiler-cleanin' gear as 'eavy as a set of main engines all this road when they could've brought the bus alongside and loaded it straight on. That's stoker POs for yer—as useless as spare pricks at a Christenin'.'

We passed unchallenged. Scouse's imprecations against our SPOs stopped abruptly and a lid came down over one of those blue eyes as they turned to me. 'A near shave,' he conceded.

In fact, several times our bus would be stopped by the dockyard police and they would come aboard and open one of our bags in a perfunctory inspection, but they never copped us. There were, however, some tense moments as we went slowly through the gates knowing that we had contraband concealed on board. Relief was expressed when we were on the city side of the gates, Etheldreda-bound. Then from men with a long poaching tradition there would be merry cries of: 'Rabbits! Tuck their ears in!'

~~

I never thought of counting the number of ships whose boilers we cleaned in Hull and across the Humber in Immingham Docks. They included destroyers launched in the mid and late thirties: I, J and K classes with names like *Intrepid*, *Impulsive*, *Javelin* and *Kandahar* and even an ancient Norwegian destroyer that had managed to escape. There were also some of the V and Ws, First World War veterans like *Verulam* and *Whitshed*, which were still doing sterling work, mainly escorting convoys.

Churchill (Prime Minister since the Norwegian débâcle), after requests to President Roosevelt as early as May 1940 for 'the loan of forty or fifty of your older destroyers to bridge the gap' before our own destroyers came off the slipways, eventually managed in September to clinch a deal whereby fifty of these American contemporaries of our old V and Ws were bartered for the lease of British bases, mainly in the Caribbean. This was fifteen months before the Americans entered the war. The first five of these four-funnel ancients arrived here in September but it was not until well into 1941 that they became fully operational. Several of them came to Hull for boiler-cleaning and we were able to see such innovations as coffee machines which the Americans had installed for the benefit of the British crews who had crossed the Atlantic to take these superannuated relics out of their inter-war mothballs and bring them back to the UK.

On several of these lend-lease and other destroyers I met again characters who have already appeared in this narrative: Nobby Clarke, Class 10's chief gunner's mate instructor at Devonport; Stoker Petty Officer Cock Kent, my watch-keeping yarn-spinner; another *Afridi* SPO, Sam Hardy, with whom I had shared my last watch; and Stoker Achilles Daunt, the young voluntary exile from Ireland who had got engaged to someone whose father owned a laundry. He was hoping to buy himself out of the Andrew as soon as the war was over and go into a conjugal dhobeying partnership. All these 'old ships' greeted me warmly but were surprised to find me still in a boiler suit instead of with gold braid on my sleeve.

I fell foul of one innovation on these Yankee destroyers: a bar of lye, a soap apparently used by their matelots which I was assured would work miracles on our begrimed boiler-cleaning gear. What nobody had told me was that the 'miracle' contained caustic and in diligently rubbing my boiler suit I removed enough skin to have my hands and arms up to the elbows in bandages for over a week.

There were no baths or showers in Tiddy Oggy Hostel. Basins only were available, both for our ablutions after returning from our soot and plumbago clothes-penetrating exertions, as well as for dhobeying our boiler-suits and underwear.

We had one 'fall-back' ship. Whenever there was a lull, that is, when the sea war was so intense that the demands on our destroyers obliged them to steam well beyond the limit at which they should have had boiler-cleaning, we would go aboard what remained of HMS *Express*. She had been converted into a mine-laying destroyer in August 1939, had taken part in the Dunkirk evacuation and after the fall of France was part of the destroyer flotilla that laid mines off our east coast as part of preparations to frustrate a Nazi invasion. She also laid mines in enemy waters.

At the end of August 1940 our reconnaissance aircraft spotted a large force of German craft off the Dutch coast, steering westwards. This was interpreted as being part of Hitler's invasion preparations and *Express* with her sister destroyers were ordered to intercept. But the destroyers themselves ran into a minefield the Germans had laid to protect their invasion fleet. *Esk* and *Ivanhoe* were sunk. *Express* had the whole of her fo'c'sle right up to the bridge blown off by a mine and her commander was among those who died of their wounds. Nevertheless, by some dexterous feat of seamanship, the survivors managed to bring her back to port. It was said that the Hull dockyard workers refused to work aboard her until a Naval party had cleaned up the vestiges of human remains with which it was festooned.

It had taken a long time to rebuild the fore part of the ship and our party had cleaned her boilers at a leisurely pace. We would return repeatedly to loaf around her dismal and, in winter, draughty interior until the next destroyer came in for our therapy. At least our loafing aboard *Express* kept us out of sight. By December 1941, however, she was in the Indian Ocean picking up survivors from the bombed and sinking *Prince of Wales*.

But *Beaver II* suddenly came up with another idea for under-employed boiler-cleaners.

~~

After Dunkirk the evacuation of British, French, Polish, Czech, Canadian and Belgian troops continued, not only from other Channel ports but from the west coast of France between Brest and St Jean de Luz near the Spanish frontier. Destroyers were the principal handmaidens in these operations which went on until 26 June. Including those from Dunkirk, over half a million men were brought back to the UK to fight another day. When France capitulated on 22 June 1940, Britain alone was at war with Nazi Germany and with Fascist Italy. Mussolini had declared war only on 10 June when the success of Hitler's blitzkrieg was assured. Throughout that summer—indeed right up until the invasion of the Soviet Union the following 22 June—we felt our own invasion was not only possible but very likely. In fact, as we subsequently learned, Hitler had given orders in July 1940 for preparations for the invasion, Operation *Sealion*, to be completed by the following month. Nor did we know at the time that *Sealion* was postponed in September after the failure of Goering's Luftwaffe to eliminate the RAF's capability to oppose an invasion or that *Sealion* was finally abandoned in February 1942. This was because Hitler's invasion of the Soviet Union had not proved the walkover he had expected and he needed the troops earmarked for *Sealion* for the Russian front.

So, over here after the fall of France there were frantic preparations for resistance to sea and aerial invasion. The Home Guard was formed and fortifications were established on the beaches and coast and wherever there were potential objectives which air-dropped troops might attempt to capture, as well as at points of strategic resistance to an invading army. Signposts were removed and church bells forbidden to be rung except to warn of an invasion.

Among the rumours that percolated through to us in Hull from the south was a rumour (which was incorrect as it turned out) that German troops had attempted to land somewhere on the south coast but the sea had been set alight with flaming petrol. Charred Wehrmacht corpses were even supposed to have been washed ashore.

It was in this atmosphere that the Royal Navy's redoubtable Humber Boiler-Cleaning Party set out on an approximately seven-mile route march, with packs and rifles, from Starvation Hostel to the village of Cottingham. In the time-honoured not-to-reason-why military tradition, the purpose of this exercise was not explained. It could have been that *Beaver II* feared that a lull in boiler-cleaning might lead to demoralisation in the ranks, or perhaps it was thought the morale of the worthy citizens of Hull needed a boost in these alarming times.

To a twenty-one-year-old many of my fellow boiler-cleaners were antediluvian, even compared with those hale and hearty middle-agers, Jim and Harry. These were men who belonged to a less happy breed, most of the time morose, plaintive and manifestly unhappy at having had to return to the not-so-Merry Andrew after slinging their hook with twenty-one years' service behind them. They were returning, moreover, not to some quiet number like watch-keeping in a barracks boiler-room but to this inescapably dirty and health-hazardous job. These were the equivalents of Falstaff's 'ancients' pressed into military service before the battle of Shrewsbury, the 'scarecrows' he said he flatly refused to march with through Coventry, as ours were to march through Hull.

The men who fell-in for the route march included 'Seedy Boy' (or should it be Sidi Boy?), a nickname given him by Harry and Jim presumably because of his Levantine complexion and grizzled fleece. Seedy/Sidi Boy who resented the epithet with its racist overtones lived in a state of almost perpetual indignation. On this day his eyes darted from side to side as he poured scorn in a torrent of phallic vituperation on whoever had thought up 'this fuckin' lark.'

But where Seedy Boy snarled loud and clear, alongside him was a gnome with eyes almost hidden by tufted eyebrows who muttered no less pungent imprecations but, for the most part, under his breath: 'Soddin', jumped-up, poxy whoresons, I shit 'em … ' formed part of the just audible cascade of invective.

In contrast to these two was Ye Olde English Gentleman, so dubbed partly because he patronised a Hull pub of that name, partly because he considered himself a cut above his fellows and always maintained an upright bearing. As if to accentuate the difference in his tastes from those he would term 'the hoi polloi', Ye Olde English Gentleman would only smoke a particular brand of cigarettes which came in a sea-green packet imprinted with three castle turrets. For my benefit he would resort, when he could catch my eye at work, to a little charade. In the black beret he sported on the job to cover his balding pate he would stand in his dirty overalls in a wing of the boiler-room, taking a breather from sawing the soot and clinker from between the tubes, his sooty, rotund face wreathed in an affected smile of bliss. With his left hand on the handle of a saw, its other end resting on the plates as if it were the elegant cane of a Van Dyck cavalier, Ye Olde English Gentleman would place a cigarette between his lips with an exaggerated sweep of the hand, inhale with closed eyes, expel a ring of smoke and, holding the fag delicately in mid-air, proclaim in enraptured tones the name of the brand: 'W. D. & H. O. Wills' Three Castles Hand-made!' pre-dating television commercials by decades.

Ye Olde English Gentleman had a slight palsy which was even more noticeable as he waited for the route march to start. A pack on his back, webbing equipment, gaiters and clutching a First World War Lee Enfield (but with no ammo), he relished no more than the others of his age group the prospect of a seven-mile march.

Not only our stoker petty officers—one rather frail and probably consumptive, the other ostensibly able-bodied but no chicken—but even the elegant Chief Engine-room Artificer Lapthorne turned out for this morale-boosting occasion.

Apart from the few grumblers, the march at least began through the city centre in buoyant, almost hilarious mood, in large part due to the flow of badinage from characters like Jim, Harry and Scouse. They regarded the whole exercise not with bitterness but with light-hearted, pragmatic scepticism as to its purpose and value. 'With such a fine body of men, why should England tremble?' was Scouse's comment as he surveyed the shuffling column of mainly superannuated stokers who had never shouldered a rifle since their initial squad drill when joining the Peas and Gravy well over a quarter of a century before. Reflecting the historic rivalry between the Upper Deck and the Engine-room branches, Jim expressed the opinion (inevitably endorsed by Harry): 'Job for fuckin' dab-toes,[55] not 'airy-arsed stokers.'

'Quite right, Jim. Leave it to fuckin' sand-scratchers to parade with muck-sticks,[56] not the likes of us. 'Oo thought this one up, d'yer think?'

'Don't ask me, 'Arry. Some cunt.'

'Nah, Jim, a cunt's useful.'

'A useless piece of ullage, anyways. Not an injuneer, yer can bet yer life on that. Some young sprog just left Dartmouth with a brand new ring on 'is sleeve, it wouldn't suprise me, 'Arry. If only Adolf could see this Kate Carney outfit!'

''E'd throw in the towel right away, Jim. Specially when he found out we'd got sweet fuck-all to put up the spouts of our muck-sticks. Not a round between the bleedin' lot of us.'

---

[55] Dab-toes and sand-scratchers were the stokers' somewhat patronising nicknames for seamen.
[56] Rifles.

Perhaps it was the column's leavening of young blood, perhaps just the novelty of seeing a body of armed Navy men marching through their city which prompted greetings from the pavement such as: 'Well done, Jack!' with sometimes the addition of good-humoured, sarcastic but entirely unmalicious remarks like: 'Now we've got the Navy, we don't need to worry!'

Encouragement like this usually came from women and, when it did, Harry and Jim would immediately start singing a duet beginning: 'It's the Navee wot gets the gravee …' Our column sent two women into a paroxysm of giggling which inspired one-track-minded Harry to hazard a guess as to its cause: 'Reckon they've got an 'air acrorst it, Jim,' to which his chum rejoined: 'More than likely, 'Arry.'

Some semblance of order, even of keeping in step, was maintained as we marched through the city, though at a pace hardly brisker than that of a funeral cortege. However, the further we progressed along Cottingham Road (and pedestrians and any other observers became scarcer) whatever efforts had been made by our weaker brethren to keep up were demonstrably relaxed. Gaps began to appear in the column and it was not long before even Scouse's ironical 'fine body of men' looked like Bonaparte's retreat from Moscow.

Well before our destination, stragglers like Seedy Boy and the gnome had fallen by the wayside. There they sat as we passed them, some with their boots off, without even the strength to cuss any more. They were eventually picked up by our docks coach which, in fact, after sandwiches and liquid refreshments in Cottingham, returned us all to Starvation Hostel. To march the seven miles to Cottingham had been ambitious; even to contemplate marching back would have meant for the majority an outright mutiny or giving up the ghost on the spot.

~~

Although he was not one of the sorry band of chronic moaners, Rotherham Robby was among the early stragglers on the route march. Robby was roly-poly with a sunny temperament. Alas, it failed to irradiate as far as his feet, and his fallen arches forced him to be one of the first to fall out, sit on a grass verge and remove his boots to let sun and air soothe them. 'Don't forget yer daisy roots this time!' shouted Harry with a knowing grin. For it was not the first time he and the rest of us had seen Robby bootless out of doors.

One morning, we clambered as usual aboard the dockyard coach outside Starvation Hostel and took our seats, already in our boiler suits and assorted gear ready for work. 'Where's Robby?' growled the gravel-voiced SPO with the ginger hair. He had made a head count and found one of us missing. 'Dunno, didn't see him at breakfast,' someone volunteered. 'Went up-homers, didn't he?' suggested another. There were corroborative nods. 'Up-homers' was a version of the euphemism 'getting your feet under the table' or in plain language finding a 'regular' woman friend who would substitute for the missus back home in London, Liverpool, Rotherham or wherever.

There followed a discussion as to what Robby might say and do when he went up-homers. Harry, who no doubt had his own local sheet-anchorage, suggested: 'Up them stairs, Ada! Open them pearly gates!' Another suggested the variant: 'Are you ready, luv, for a stroke of the "O be joyful?"'

We waited. We waited ten minutes, perhaps fifteen. Ginger kept ostentatiously consulting his watch with evident growing impatience. Gruff and with a slight stammer adding to a superficial uncouthness, to his credit he had never yet followed his staccato bark with a bite. But what would he do now? Unless one was sick, not turning-to for duty was a serious offence. He would surely put a younger rating in the rattle. But Robby was a three-badge man and he had never given trouble before. It would be almost embarrassing for Ginger to report a man of his own age, length of service and, like himself, a called-up reservist. 'I'll give 'im another five minutes,' Ginger snapped. We waited until four minutes went by. Ginger was just looking at his watch prior to giving the driver the nautical: 'Let's slip!' when an extraordinary figure padded from around the corner and ran, panting and bare-footed, towards us. It was Robby, his near-bald head capless and dressed only in a vest and bell-bottoms. 'Sorry!' he blurted out between gasps. 'Give me 'alf a shake to get into boiler rig!' and he disappeared into the hostel. There was some bizarre conjecturing within the coach as to what had happened to him, the more experienced of the up-homers getting pretty close to the truth.

If Robby's perennially cheery face was capable of registering shame, it now came as close to it as ever it would as he climbed aboard, still tucking a sweat rag around his neck.

> Said 'er 'ubby wouldn't be 'ome for another ten days, didn't she?
> I 'eard him coom through t'door and shout 'Maggie!' as I dived

into coobud. She managed to keep 'im talkin' so 'e didn't coom into t'bedroom but there were no chance of gettin' rid on 'im. So, before I sooffocated like, I tiptoed out o' coobud, raised t'window, all stealthy like, climbed through, dropped on me paws and scarpered. Clean forgot m'boots in t'panic. 'Ope Maggie finds 'em before 'e do. Any road, it's never up-homers there no more.

~~

The Luftwaffe had been raiding Hull or its environs with increasing persistence from soon after I joined the boiler-cleaners. At first in small numbers and usually with the oil tanks at Killingholme as the target, then areas of the city itself were bombed. But the BBC never named Hull as such. It was always: 'There was a raid last night on a North-east town.'

Against the supposed advantage of not telling the enemy which city they had been raiding, as if they didn't know, was the effect on morale of the people of Hull who became increasingly irritated at this persistent concealment of their ordeal from the rest of the country. It was not until after the war that the Home Secretary, Herbert Morrison, pointed out that 'night after night Hull had no peace.' Figures issued later, presumably after access to German military records revealed the precise number of bombers involved, show that in one March 1941 raid, seventy-eight came over Hull, killing seventeen, and by the 16th of that month over 2,200 people were seeking to be re-housed. On the 18th there was a seven-hour raid by 378 bombers and people did not shuffle out of their shelters into bed until four o'clock in the morning. When the air raid warning sounded everyone was supposed to go to the nearest public shelter. This applied not only to people in the street or the pubs but to the majority of those who were at home in their terraced houses with no garden in which a private Anderson shelter could be installed.

As late as May 1942, when raids had virtually stopped elsewhere following the Nazi attack on the Soviet Union the previous June, Hull experienced another heavy onslaught and even in July 1943 people were still getting killed in their homes before they could get to a shelter. After all the seventy raids on this anonymous 'North-east coast town,' it was estimated only 65,000 out of the city's 93,000 houses were unscathed and by the middle of May 1941 it was estimated that about a third of the population were leaving the city, although it is not clear whether this was nightly or for a longer period.

By far the heaviest raids (though I have no figure for the number of bombers) were on the successive nights of 7 and 8 May 1941, the dates to which Hull citizens were generally referring when they spoke of *the* blitz. I had been in many raids at sea and almost exactly a year previously I was within yards of three exploding bombs. Yet it is the night of 7 May which is indelibly etched as my date with fear. At sea one was always in the company of others when it is much easier to control reactions to danger or at least to maintain a calm exterior. But on 7 May I was on my own and feeling very isolated.

When the sirens started I was somewhere near the Wilberforce Monument. The anti-aircraft guns opened-up almost immediately and, conscious that what goes up must come down, including jagged pieces of shrapnel, I took shelter in the Queen's Gardens dugouts that had been hastily prepared (like those in Kensington Gardens) in 1938 at the time of the Munich crisis. Not very close to any main thoroughfare, these dugouts were hardly ever used and certainly not another soul was in the section I was in that night.

If nearly 400 planes had come over on 18 March there must have been many more on 7 May. Alone in that dugout I felt that the whole of Goering's Luftwaffe was overhead in a perpetual stream aiming their bombs at me personally. As their engines droned with that distinctive pulsating throb which millions had learned to dread—in Warsaw, Rotterdam, London, Coventry and other British towns and cities—as the tearing swoosh of falling bombs was all too audible above the racket of the barrage, and the ground shuddered from their explosions, I was a very frightened person and behaved like one. If I could have scrabbled even deeper into the dugout, I would have done so. I have often wondered since: if that was the effect a few hours of bombing had on me, why in the First World War, after months and years of shelling, did not many more men suffer from shell-shock than, apparently, actually did?

In support of my theory, the following night the blitz was at least as heavy yet my nerves were well under control because I was in a crowded shelter. Danger shared was danger sustainable. Long before the all-clear, I was out of the shelter helping to tear away at smouldering debris with other impromptu would-be rescuers, which went some way to shoring up my slipping *amour propre*. The only personal damage on this second night was a ruined tiddley suit.

In daylight after these two raids I saw destruction I would not see for another three years, in some of the towns in Normandy. There were whole streets of still smouldering ruins, craters, some nearly twenty yards wide like the one beside what had once been the Ritz on Holderness Road, one of the cinemas I used to frequent with my girl friends. The Rank flour mills, just the other side of the River Hull from the Etheldreda Mission, went on smouldering for months, polluting the air with a distinctive bitter-sour stench. The Reckitts factory, now a burned-out husk was just down the road from the hostel. (I recalled my mother using 'Reckitts Blue' for the laundering.) It is recorded in the history of Pocklington School, twenty-five miles away, that doors and windows shook when landmines floated down by parachute, exploded and devastated whole streets in Hull.

One man who had been on his own, at least in the latter hours of the blitz but whose self-confidence was not in the least affected, was Scouse. He had returned to Starvation Hostel with a skinful of beer under his belt, gone up to his cabin, taken off his shoes, lain on the bed without bothering (perhaps lacking the power) to undress further, and Morpheus had carried him away to a land where the throb of raiding planes sounded like plucked harp strings and bomb blasts, the clash of cymbals. Even when a near-miss blew the window frame onto his bed, Scouse did not wake. The following morning he was surprised to find his feet sticking up through where a pane of glass had been. He was without a scratch.

Although bombs had fallen in the docks, the dry docks where our destroyers used to berth for their refits were untouched. But there was a job of a different kind waiting for some of us boiler-cleaners. With the Army bomb-disposal squads stretched beyond their limits, the Humber Boiler-cleaning Party, after its renowned display of moral fibre on the route march, was called upon to fill the breach. There was a bomb crater in King George's Dock about the width of three double-beds. In the muddy yellow pool at the bottom was, invisible, an unexploded bomb. Volunteers of the 'you, you and you' variety were called for by our SPOs. Married men were exempt. Except for Scouse, who to his credit genuinely volunteered, that left us, the few young bachelors. Somebody, presumably the squaddies, had shored up the sides of the hole with timber. For days we dug and hauled up in buckets mud from that hole, trusting that the conditions which had caused the bomb not to explode on impact—perhaps the softness of the ground—would remain the same. Eventually, when the Army hauled it out and we saw it dangling from a crane, it looked monstrous.

~~

One or other of the young members of our party, disenchanted with boiler-cleaning and perhaps with having to work among so many elderly men, would put in a request for a draft to a sea-going ship. For some there were more complex and impelling motives. Such was the case of 'The Ram', as I will dub him to preserve his anonymity. His sexual appetite was boundless and totally undiscriminating either regards age or gender, with the inevitable result that he was several times off duty, hospitalised. However, he met his fate: a young Hull maiden who resisted his advances for months but eventually became pregnant. The Ram slapped in a request for a draft and duly found himself aboard a cruiser in the Med. But his conscience, remorse and the discovery of true love did eventually impel him to the altar or register office and, after the war, to conjugal domicile back in Hull.

Another of my young workmates, who had an on-off relationship with a blonde, blamed her (without proof) and actually assaulted her when he, too, suffered 'a dose'. He then decided he had had enough of the fleshpots of Hull and requested a draft. That left still fewer young green bottles hanging on the wall. But when my turn came it was for a very different reason.

The Nazi invasion of the Soviet Union in June 1941 had initially looked as if it was going to be another blitzkrieg or, as Harry put it more than once: 'They're going through Russia like a knife through butter, aren't they Jim?' By August, Kiev had fallen. In September the siege of Leningrad began, and would not be lifted for twenty-eight months and nearly a million Russian deaths later. Sebastopol was invested in October and captured in June 1942 and, in December, the Nazis were within twenty miles of Moscow. But in that month the Red Army started its counter-offensive. The five-month titanic struggle for Stalingrad ended in February 1943 with the surrender of Hitler's Sixth Army, its Field Marshal von Paulus and twenty-four generals, followed in the summer by the biggest tank battle in history, at Kursk, with the loss to the Wehrmacht of half a million men.

All this was stirring news for a country which had been fighting Hitler on its own. The US did not enter the fray until the treacherous Japanese attack on Pearl Harbor decimated its fleet on 3 December 1941 and Hitler and Mussolini declared war on her five days later. For three years, here in Britain, at first tentative and then increasingly vociferous calls were made to open a second front in Western Europe to relieve the pressure on an embattled Soviet Union and help its counter-offensive (inexorable but conducted at huge cost to its troops) and to expedite the defeat of Hitler. In one of his famous aphorisms Churchill spoke of the Red Army tearing the guts out of the Nazi armies. 'Open the Second Front' demonstrations in Trafalgar Square attracted up to 60,000 and shoals of letters and telegrams were sent to MPs and to the government with the same demand.

I was caught up in the emotional atmosphere of the time and perhaps it was, in retrospect, in a moment of impetuous naïvety that I got a blank telegram form from the post office, wrote a message to Churchill calling for the opening of the Second Front, signed it myself and went around several of Hull's pubs inviting people to put their signatures to it at a penny a time to cover the cost. It was sent from Hull GPO with its fifty signatures to No. 10. I will never know at what stage it was intercepted but it was surely no coincidence that my draft chit to Pompey Barracks arrived a few weeks later.

Chapter 8

Change of Course

The shortest distance between two points is a straight line.

Euclid

anae, according to Greek mythology, was a beautiful princess who was imprisoned by her father in a brazen tower because he had been told by an oracle that his daughter's son would kill him. Jupiter, the most powerful of the gods, managed nevertheless to seduce her by disguising himself as a golden shower. Baby Perseus was the result. Dad cast mother and son adrift on the sea but the wind drove the boat to an island where, in the nick of time, they were saved by fishermen. Perseus, needless to say, would eventually kill his grandfather unintentionally.

It would seem inappropriate that one of His Majesty's ships should be named after someone who was forced into a small boat which was nearly wrecked. That, however, was the name of the cruiser to which the Portsmouth drafting office sent me. HMS *Danae* was laid up in Swan Hunter's dry dock in Hebburn-on-Tyne undergoing a refit at the end of a commission. The most fertile of fantasists could never recognise in this disreputable looking old lady any resemblance to her namesake, the lovely mythical princess, although, in a way, this *Danae* too was being ravaged. There was nothing gilded, however, about the shower of dockyard mateys who had descended on her and, in the course of replacing the lady's organs and giving her a facelift, dropped fag ends, empty packets and other litter among the chaos of cables that lay on her filthy decks like snakes stunned by the cacophony of hammering, drilling and the hissing of electric welding.

Whatever she had been, *Danae* in 1943 was an old class of cruiser. At the outbreak of war she had been part of the 9th Cruiser Squadron on the South Atlantic station based on Freetown, Sierra Leone. A year after I left her she would be turned over to the Polish navy and renamed, much more appropriately, after that seafaring prince of story tellers, Josef *Conrad* Korzeniowski.

Since there was nowhere on board that was habitable, we were given shore leave every day and I went 'up-homers' to hospitable cousins who lived in a Durham village. After weeks, *Danae*'s refit was nearing completion and we could live on board. She was recommissioned, that is she had a completely new ship's complement, and order was gradually restored. Instead of boiler-room watch-keeping I was assigned to assisting the engineer's writer, a leading stoker. Since we were all new to the ship and, as far as the chief stoker was concerned, unknown quantities, I have no idea why I was given this particular job. But within a few weeks it would start a chain of circumstances that would mean a radical alteration of course to my career in the Navy.

Ironically, in spite of my having told Captain Vian that I had wanted 'a change from pounding a typewriter', here I was back at a desk job in the tiny engineer's office. But I would still be doing at least one part of my former *Afridi* routine: when *Danae* entered or left harbour my place would be in the engine-room logging orders from the bridge and the turbines' revolutions.

And so it was that after *Danae* had been towed and nudged by tugs into the Tyne and was about to start her first engine trials after the refit, I was standing beside the engineer commander and senior engineer behind the engine-room artificers on the throttles. Almost immediately following the first order for Slow Ahead and the turbines began to turn, their hum was shattered by a raucous clatter and grinding from the port turbine. The engineer commander instantly gave the order to Stop Engines and the Chief ERA swung the throttles to shut off the steam to the turbines. *Danae* was towed back to her berth and a buzz word started circulating around the ship: SABOTAGE.

Newcastle CID were called in and, after a while, on our desk in the engineer's office chopped-up pieces of metal, each about 15 mm. thick with jagged edges, were laid out carefully by a grim-faced Commander (E).

Either someone had left by mistake or, as was suspected, had deliberately placed a monkey wrench under the port turbine casing. The blades of the turbine had chewed it up but had themselves been stripped.

This was not an auspicious beginning to a new commission. It had already been evident that *Danae* was not going to be a 'happy ship,' the description of a ship's company which had a good relationship between officers and Lower Deck and a CO who inspired respect. The seamen were complaining about the commander, but not being my department, I never learned what were the specific routines he initiated which made him so unpopular. Since our CO was a four-ring captain, it was the commander who had the responsibilities of a destroyer's First Lieutenant or 'Jimmy the One.' In our engine-room department there was one leading stoker who developed an obsessive animosity for his fellow Scot, the senior engineer, an RNVR two-and-a-half-ringer.[57] I have never known a man turn so livid with rage and hatred as did our Jock after some encounter with the senior. He probably considered himself at least as knowledgeable about marine engines as this 'jumped-up, civvy whoorson' and resented being given orders he considered unjustified or technically inept. I watched him in our mess nursing his wrath, growing more morose as day succeeded day, even vowing he would 'kill the bastard' if he could get away with it.

Apart from these personalised antipathies there was a general resentment to the idea of 'going East'. We had been given no official indication as to our destination but, whether it originated with the dockyard mateys or something they had been installing which pointed to a spell in a hot climate, the galley buzz had been from the beginning that *Danae* would soon be ploughing furrows in the Indian Ocean or, worse still, in the Persian Gulf. 'The hottest spot on Earth', my messmates described it, 'and this old tank is not equipped for the tropics.'

By this time, April 1943, there was a totally different spirit in the land compared to the backs-to-the-wall feeling of 1940–41. Only two months before, at Stalingrad, the Nazis had suffered their first major defeat. The previous October, our Eighth Army had decisively defeated Field-Marshal Rommel at the battle of El-Alamein in North Africa and the Allies had landed in Morocco and Algeria in vessels that had sailed directly from the US and UK. It was these first whiffs of ultimate victory against the Germans which no doubt played a part in the resentment

---

[57] Lieutenant Commander.

aboard *Danae* at the thought of being sent to the Far East, to the 'forgotten war' against the Japanese or, perhaps even more galling, to somewhere like the Persian Gulf where there was no visible enemy at all.

Had someone put the wrench in the turbine out of spite against an officer or to delay *Danae*'s departure for somewhere east of Suez? Or had it been unmalicious but absent-minded carelessness? I never discovered. But one man did suffer as a consequence and, from my observation of him, he was most unlikely to have been guilty of either sabotage or an unintentional lapse. He was a chief engine-room artificer who had impressed me during *Danae*'s refit as being the most hardworking and conscientious of any member of the engine-room department. Most of his colleagues got through their work without a stain on their boiler suits but he went into the machinery's most inaccessible parts to check that the dockyard mateys had done their work properly and was usually begrimed with oil or grease. It was his bad luck that he happened to be the last person to inspect the port turbine before the casing had been lowered. He was theoretically responsible for the wrench, although someone could have deliberately slipped it there at the last moment when his back was turned. When we had already left the Tyne weeks later, he told me he had been given a draft to a small ship. This virtual demotion without actually being reduced in rank must have worried him considerably. His immediate concern was that he suffered from chronic seasickness and had the Naval equivalent of a doctor's certificate to say that he should not serve on any vessel smaller than a cruiser. His draft was to a minesweeper lying across the bay from where we were at anchor.

~~

On the presumption that I was going to be aboard *Danae* for a long time, I had enrolled for a Pitman's shorthand correspondence course. I had been learning it at evening classes prior to my call-up. I had to be prepared to resume my work as a reporter whenever the war was going to end and had to keep my hand in as far as shipboard routine allowed.

It was after the turbine had been repaired and the engine trials completed successfully that we had at last steamed to Scapa Flow for working-up trials. One day, the Commissioned Schoolmaster (with warrant officer rank) poked his head into the Engineer's Office when I was on my own. Since there was nothing else to do, I was occupied with my correspondence course.

'Shorthand? What use are you going to make of that?' queried the schoolie and I explained my reason for doing the course.

'How long have you been a stoker?' was his next question and I explained that it was nearly four years.

'Four years on the Lower Deck and you're a journalist? Incredible! Why aren't you in the Press Division?'

'Never heard of it, sir! What is it?'

He advised me to slap in a request to see the commander immediately so as to start the process of transferring to the Press Division, Admiralty. Nobody on board *Danae* had heard of the Press Division. The Jaunty, to whom I had to give my request to see the commander, assumed it was the branch that operated the postal service between ships and shore; the commander had never heard of it but permitted me to put in a further request to see the captain. Nor had the captain heard of it but gave his consent for a signal to be sent to the Admiralty on my behalf.

In due course and while we were still at Scapa a signal came back: Stoker Gritten was to report to Commander Dillon-Robinson at the Admiralty for an interview.

I made the 500-mile journey by ferry and train from Scapa to Whitehall. I passed through the Admiralty entrance behind the statue of Captain James Cook, reported at the security desk and just had time to glance at the glass case containing the first letter Nelson wrote after losing his right arm at Tenerife before being directed to the room of the Press Division's chief. If I had any qualms about meeting this personage at the lofty end of the Naval hierarchy compared with my lowly rank (I was actually Stoker First Class by now with a good-conduct badge) I need not have worried. Cdr Dillon-Robinson, RN was the epitome of geniality. Well-built and florid, his natural amiability would have put the most timid of awestruck ratings at ease. He had checked on me at the *Daily Mail* (he put it more tactfully than that) and if only he had known of my existence a couple of weeks earlier, he could have taken me on board immediately. As it was, he had just filled a vacancy for an ONR (Official Naval Reporter).

But first, said the commander, he must put me in the picture as to the functions and aims of the Press Division and an ONR's duties. He had not gone far when echoes reached me of another interview, way back in the summer of 1939, with Cdr Rump. There were striking similarities. The Army, Cdr Dillon-Robinson explained, and the RAF in particular, had been getting good publicity because they had built up effective public relations outfits while the Silent Service, four years into the war, was still shy of PR. (I didn't tell him that nobody aboard my ship from the captain down had even heard of the Press Division.) This had to be changed. Apart from immediate exigencies, we had to think about service estimates after the war. Definite shades of Rump, I was thinking. Then again, our American allies were becoming increasingly involved over here and they mustn't entirely steal the show, must they? It was his responsibility to build up a department of professional journalists who had served on the Lower Deck and some of them had been executive officers and even commanded ships. There was a team of sub-editors in the Admiralty Press Room, the others were Official Naval Reporters attached to bases from which HM ships were operating both in home waters and abroad. They wrote stories about the exploits of these ships or anything that they could dig out about individual members of a ship's company so that it could be filtered back to their hometown local papers. The ONR's stories were subbed and censored in the Admiralty and issued to the media via the Ministry of Information. There were also Official Naval Photographers (ONPs) who usually worked in liaison with the ONRs.

What Dillon-Robinson called the 'immediate exigencies' was the need to boost the morale of the fighting men, of their families and the civilian population at large. This was later reiterated in my letter of credence signed by Admiral Arthur Power when I joined the British East Indies Fleet staff in 1945. He requested that every assistance be given to me in the performance of my duties:

> ... which are to obtain material, particularly of human interest, about ships and personnel which can be used by the Department of the Chief of Naval Information. [By then the Press Division had changed its title.] In addition it is his duty to obtain material which can be used under Admiralty guidance to attack enemy morale.

Having put a damper on my hopes by saying that a vacancy had just been filled, the commander now made amends: 'I'll tell you what I'll do. You return to your ship and I'll see to it that you are drafted straight away to your base. Then, at the first opportunity you will be made an ONR with the rank of sub-lieutenant RNVR.' In other words, I had to return to *Danae* and before she left Scapa I would get a draft back to Pompey where I would wait until another signal notified me of my meteoric promotion and new duties.

My immediate feeling was one of elation. I had not formed any particular friendships aboard *Danae* whose ship's company had not had time to shake down. Furthermore, she was evidently sailing into a backwater, away from the main enemy, Hitler, and now there would be a better opportunity to be involved in the subject of that telegram I had naively sent from Hull.

On the other hand I would miss the camaraderie of the Lower Deck, the intimate living, working and going ashore together, companionship that was unlikely to be repeated.

~~

I returned to Scapa and waited for my promised draft to Portsmouth. That was in July. Week after week went by. At last our working-up trials were completed and one day in August, *Danae* steamed into the Atlantic set on a southerly course. I was still on board.

By the time we reached Gibralter, there surely would be a signal for me to return to Pompey. But though we were beneath The Rock long enough for me to get sorely roasted by the unfamiliar Mediterranean sun, I was still on board, and continued to be when the chunk of Africa a Frenchman had felicitously named Cap Bon slipped astern on our starboard quarter. A long string of Italian submarines was being escorted into captivity somewhere between their bases in Pantellaria and Lampadusa following the capitulation of Italy on 7 September. There was still no signal when we reached Malta, the 'George Cross Island' and 'Hands to bathe over the side' was piped in the insanitary Valetta harbour; nor when the gully-gully men came alongside at Port Said; nor when we passed more Italian warships anchored in captivity in the Great Bitter Lake. Neither was there any signal when we reached Suez with its wreak of crude oil; nor at Aden where the heat was so intense, awnings were rigged over the quarterdeck and it was stifling on the mess-decks. And so we steamed ever south, parallel with the low, olive shoreline of the Somali and Kenya coasts until we reached Mombasa in the second week of October.

We had crossed the Equator but long before that the warnings that *Danae* would prove a most uncomfortable ship in the tropics had been confirmed. The heat did not improve tempers and affected some in strange ways. Jock became even more morose and his imprecations against the senior engineer more sinister. There was another stoker who, sitting at the mess table, would jump to his feet unpredictably and yell 'Heil Hitler!' at the top of his voice before sitting down again and quietly resuming whatever he had been doing.

There was also a near mutiny, or at least talk of refusing to turn-to, when, instead of our normal Jamaica rum, the tot had tasted so queer the grog-drinkers spluttered at the first sip and most refused to drink it. This surely was an unprecedented situation. The stock of Jamaica had run out and when it could not be replenished, South African rum had been substituted. So great was the fuss that the supply officer had to respond and when Jamaican rum was still not obtainable (probably sunk by a U-boat in the Battle of the Atlantic), a compromise was found: Australian rum. It was still not as good as Jamaican but the hullabaloo subsided.

~~

The day after we anchored at Kilindini off Mombasa, the long-awaited signal arrived: I had been promoted to Temporary Acting Sub-Lieutenant (Special) RNVR and should 'return immediately by the most direct route' to report, via HMS *Victory*, to the Press Division, Admiralty.

Following a single run ashore with two of my messmates, the next day all my repressed regrets about leaving the Lower Deck, which I had inwardly nursed between Whitehall and Mombasa, welled up as the skiff pulled me shorewards away from *Danae* for the last time. Under the influence, not only of my own tot, but of sippers from well-wishers, I felt very emotional.

My orders were to report to HMS *Tana II*. Though not afloat, this could hardly be described as a 'stone frigate'. A few miles outside the port of Mombasa, in a clearing between jungle resonant with chattering monkeys and the silver sands of a deserted beach,[58] was a tented encampment for Naval ratings. Bungalows were painted brilliant white for officers and at the entrance, the White Ens'n flew from a jackstaff on the quarterdeck with its base surrounded by a flowerbed with HMS *TANA II* artistically laid out in pebbles from the seashore, also painted white. This bizarre ship was commanded, so I was told, by a peacetime editor of the *Mombasa Times*.

---

[58] Today there is a waterfront of hotels and the 'Paradise' at Kikambala was demolished by terrorists in November 2002.

If I had imagined that 'return by the most direct route' had meant the briefest of fleeting acquaintances with this jungle 'ship', I was in for protracted disillusionment. The Regulating Office, I would discover, was staffed by lotus-eaters.

I settled in to my boy-scout-type bell tent which I shared with other ratings and enjoyed the amenities. These included heads, unique for one of HM ships, which consisted of a row of lavatory seats with hinged covers over a ditch, at one end of which burned a perpetual wood fire fed by local Africans employed by *Tana II*. Sitting on these guaranteed smoked hams and genitalia.

During one off-duty spell in my tent I was startled by a shout. One of the Africans who had been cutting the grass around the tents had sliced in two a snake which had reared up in the path of a forward sweep of his sickle. Another day I was detailed off to be part of an escort of two prisoners, Naval ratings who had been caught in the heinous crime of gambling. We took them from their ship to a Naval prison camp and, once through the gates, we watched for a few minutes the treatment meted out to these unfortunates. In the midday sun, only 4° from the Equator, they were immediately ordered by a gunnery petty officer to lift their heavy kit-bags (which stood at least hip-high from the ground) above their heads and start doubling over the parade ground. 'Abaat-turn!' he bawled after they had gone a few yards. No sooner had they done a 180° turn than: 'Abaat-turn!' he yelled at them again. Then, almost on the instant: 'Abaat turn!' so that they were almost spinning like tops on their own axis before he shunted them off in another direction, still at the double and bearing their kit-bags aloft.

I felt exhausted myself just watching this sadism. But before we were treated to any more, two other seamen who had finished doing ninety-day jankers were handed over to us to escort back to their ships. One of them told me that the worst part of the punishment was not being allowed to smoke, that some vomited when they had their first drag after such long deprivation, that he himself had managed to make fags of a sort by wrapping lavatory paper around tea leaves or even the fluff from the lining of his uniform.

One of the more bizarre duties in this strange 'ship' was the posting of one solitary sentry to patrol, not the clearing where the tents were nor the adjacent seashore, but a certain path leading through the jungle on the perimeter of the camp. When my turn came to keep the morning watch (4–8 a.m.) I had plenty of time to ruminate on just what practical function

I was supposed to be performing. Who was I guarding the camp against with my old ammo-less Lee Enfield? The Germans were 3,000 miles away in North Africa (actually within a couple of months of surrendering to the Allies), the Japanese were 4,000 miles to the east and, for all their fiendish Oriental cunning, were hardly likely to be creeping through this particular jungle to disturb the CO's artistically planted white pebbles. Even if I were supposed to be guarding the camp against potentially delinquent Kenyans, not even a 14-carat cretin could believe they could not get past a single sentry who had been given strict instructions to keep to this one path and not stray off it.

It was in such a sceptical attitude to guarding this outpost of empire that I was gradually lulled by the velvet darkness, the hum of flying insects and chatter of night birds into a pleasantly relaxed mood. The pre-dawn light found me concentrating all my attention on a fight to the death between two ants, each at least 2 cm long. They must have been well-matched because the contest was interminable. At least I didn't see the end of it because suddenly there was a dull thud close enough to make the ground tremble slightly under my feet. From crouching, watching the contending ants (my rifle propped up against a tree), I jack-knifed erect. Some leaping beast landing on its paws? Or the heavy footfall of the Master at Arms catching me out in gross dereliction of duty? It was neither animal nor mineral but vegetable: less than a yard away a coconut had dropped from a great height. What I picked up was the weight of a cannon ball. It would have been an ignominious end to my distinguished Naval career to be slain by a coconut.

After three weeks of this relaxed but senseless routine I put in a request to find out what had happened to the 'return by the most direct route' signal. More days passed before I was sent by the Regulating Office to an airline office in Mombasa to get a plane ticket to the UK. Here, the first enquiry was whether I had been inoculated for typhus and yellow fever. Since this had been overlooked by the lotus-eaters no ticket could be issued in case I contracted one of these diseases when the plane touched down in West Africa, the wartime 'direct' flight from East Africa to Blighty.

Since I was disturbing their quiet number, *Tana II*'s regulating POs were now so anxious to get rid of me they scrubbed around the inoculation and the next day, 26 November, that is, twenty-five days after leaving the *Danae* and over three months after returning to Scapa from the Admiralty, I was sent to a troopship waiting in Kilindini harbour. This turned out to be the Slow Boat to Suez, like a peacetime cruise, a voyage in which at night I swung in a hammock slung on the upper deck beneath a canopy of stars, lulled by the gently modulating swish of phosphorescent waters against the ship's side.

Most of my fellow passengers were the RAF Base Accounts Unit normally stationed in Cairo which had been moved to Kenya when Rommel looked like breaking through to Egypt and, now that the Germans were in an Allied pincer movement, the unit was returning to Cairo. Both these hundred or so airmen and a few score East African Rifles had boats and local (no doubted sweated and certainly sweating) labour laid on already at Suez to transport them and their gear ashore to complete their journey by road. No arrangements had been made for the handful of Naval personnel left on board. No boats came to fetch us and no one apparently knew of our existence. We hung forlornly over the rails for hours until the couple of Naval officers in our party managed eventually to get some craft to come alongside and we manhandled our baggage over the steep side and down into the boats. There was another delay on the quay until a coach was laid on which took us north along the Suez Canal to another tented encampment, HMS *Saunders*. Like the humped, four-legged variety, this was a ship of the desert, not far from the Great Bitter Lake.

~~

The boredom of living under canvas in the midst of a featureless landscape was only relieved by the excellent meals cooked by Italian prisoners-of-war though I felt uncomfortable at being served at table by them. After all, Italy had not only surrendered but had tried to make amends for the bombastic ambitions of Il Duce by declaring war on Germany the previous month. These were not professional waiters but matelots like ourselves. Though I had no doubt they were only too glad to be out of the war, it seemed unjust that they should be put to the indignity of serving meals to their victorious erstwhile enemies.

Apart from a ride in a Sherman tank by courtesy of the rearguard of the Eighth Army, the only other relief from ennui was a 'run ashore' in Ismailiya. This was my first experience of large-scale poverty and disease. Appalling were the numbers of the sightless and the maimed and children with flies feasting on suppurating eyes. Sitting at a table in a café, I felt a tug at my jumper, looked around and saw no one. A more insistent tug followed and again I looked around, and down this time. It was not much more than half a man with a tray of mother-of-pearl ornaments for sale strapped to a torso that ended just below the hips where his legs had been amputated and supported on a platform with rollers.

It was here in Ismailaya that I witnessed one of the oldest tricks in that unwritten book: 'How To Separate Jack From His Pay'. A young Egyptian went up to a matelot in the street, just in front of me: 'You want to buy stolen diamond, Jack? Very cheap. Send home to girl—she love you. Very genuine. Look!' and I watched as, darting glances over his shoulder in a pretence of making sure no coppers were in the offing, he made a short scratch on the nearest shop window. Jack fell for it, parted with several English pounds and pocketed—for the moment well satisfied with his 'bargain'—a worthless piece of glass.

~~

Frustrated at this new hitch in the 'immediate return' to the UK, I waited only a week before putting in another request, this time to *Saunders'* Regulating Office. Several days passed before, presumably, another signal came from the Admiralty confirming that I should be hastened on my way. I was given a train warrant and travelled solo to Alexandria to join the Town Class cruiser HMS *London* for homeward passage.

I was by no means the only passenger. Down aft there were not only some Jenny Wrens but a miscellany of females who were all out of bounds to other ranks: civilian secretaries, interpreters and typists. They had been part of Churchill's entourage at the four-day meeting in Teheran with Roosevelt and Stalin, where the post-war division of Germany and the frontiers of Poland had been decided. Winston himself had been flown home but his Chief of Staff, General Hastings ('Pug') Ismay was on board and gave a briefing to a large and attentive audience in *London*'s hangar. I was surprised at the provocative questions put to him by the men. Was this a presage, if we had had the foresight to divine it, of the 'surprising' defeat of Churchill nineteen months later in the 1945 General Election?

Geraldo's dance band minus Geraldo himself (he had flown home, too) were returning after entertaining the troops and were accommodated in the chiefs' and POs' mess, suffering from our rough passage through the Med and the Bay of Biscay. I chummed up with several of the players and helped them ashore and through Customs with their gear when we arrived in Greenock on Christmas Eve. We shared a carriage on the train and, well on our way to London, the drummer began taking watches bought in *Cairo* from all of his pockets. As he laid them on the seat he announced the price he had paid for each one and estimated the profit he hoped to make when he flogged them in London. Waiting without comment until he had finished was the trumpeter who then reached for his case in the rack, took out the shining instrument and displayed from one end to the other almost twice the number of watches. So that was what I had carried for them through Customs. But I was not offered any share of the loot.

It had taken four months to get from Scapa Flow to Portsmouth, putting the Navy's concept of a direct route at odds with Euclid's. But any residual frustration at the delay was offset by being home for Christmas and by the news on Boxing Day that *Rawalpindi* [59] had at last been avenged: *Scharnhorst* had been sunk off the North Cape by the 14-inch guns of the battleship *Duke of York*, by gunfire from cruisers, and our destroyers had given the *coup de grâce* with eleven tin-fish.

---

[59] See Chapter 3.

Commander John Dillon-Robinson, RN, chief of the Press Division, Admiralty, 'the epitomy of geniality'. In the Admiralty picture, with glasses and telephone, he is sitting between a Wren and another officer.

THIRD TURN–*Wavy Navy*

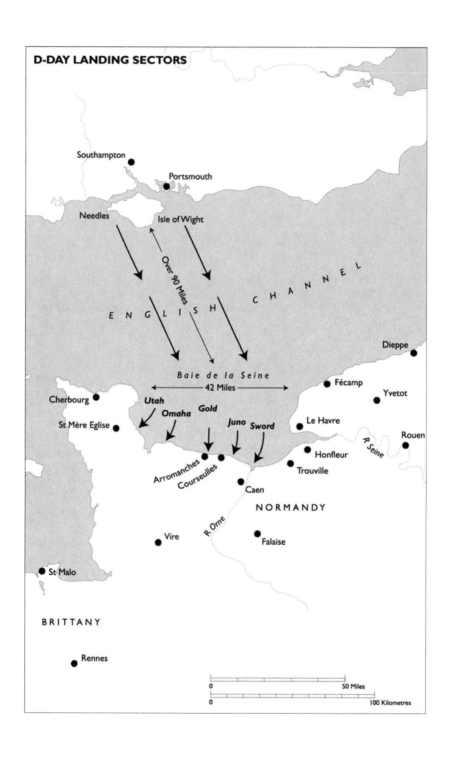

D-DAY LANDING SECTORS

Southampton

Portsmouth

Needles

Isle of Wight

Over 90 Miles

E N G L I S H   C H A N N E L

Dieppe

Baie de la Seine

42 Miles

Fécamp

Yvetot

Cherbourg

Utah

Omaha   *Gold*

Juno *Sword*

Le Havre

Rouen

St Mère Eglise

R Seine

Arromanches

Courseulles

Honfleur

Trouville

Caen

N O R M A N D Y

R Orme

Vire

Falaise

St Malo

B R I T T A N Y

Rennes

0   50 Miles

0   100 Kilometres

Chapter 9

'Greatest 'op in history, sir!'

You are soon to be engaged in a great undertaking: the invasion of Europe.

General Dwight D. Eisenhower

From the bridge of Scylla it was a heartening sight to see the vast concourse of landing-ships and craft set out in accordance with the plan which we had worked on for so long.

Action This Day: Rear Admiral Sir Philip Vian

... the incredible sight of slowly circulating, firing, burning sinking, jammed, capsized, shifting or anchored ships.

Flesh Wounds: David Holbrook

Nothing could dampen the exhilaration of those who had survived [the landing at La Rivière], *sitting as wondering sightseers on ground that over four long years had attained for them the alien and mysterious status of the dark side of the moon.*

Overlord: Max Hastings [60]

Seconds after the Wren had dropped the signals on our desks, Jock looked across at me and said evenly: 'This is it. The balloon's going up.'

---

[60] Reproduced from *Overlord* by Max Hastings (Copyright © Max Hastings 1984) by permission of PFD on behalf of Sir Max Hastings.

Official Naval Photographer Lieut (S) 'Jock' Russell, RNVR [61] had just returned with me to our cosy little office in the house commandeered by the Navy on Parkeston Quay, Harwich, after doing our morning duty visiting one of HM ships. It may have been *Widgeon, Guillemot, Mallard* or another corvette or one of the MTBs (Motor Torpedo Boats). According to wardroom convention (which I was learning fast), once 'the sun was over the yardarm' it was the normal time in harbour for officers from chummy ships to drop in for elevenses. Jock and I combined business with bonhomie by getting our stories for the Press Division over a gin and orange. Stories and Jock's pictures would go by courier to the Admiralty where (just as Cdr Dillon-Robinson had explained) they were subbed, censored and distributed through the MoI (or Ministry of Disinformation as it was inevitably dubbed). A couple of days later they often appeared in the London evening papers. One that never got past the censors was about our visit to the first of the heavily-armed 'sea forts' which had been towed to its anchorage eight miles off Harwich in February 1942. These sea-forts were intended to harass bombers on their way to London and deter mine-laying E-boats.

For us two these were halcyon days in the spring of 1944 (with romantic overtones). We were well aware they would be of short duration. All the signs—for example, the ever-growing influx of Americans in uniform and the ban on wives visiting British servicemen in coastal areas—indicated that the Allied attempt to land somewhere in Western Europe could not now be long delayed. Hence Jock's interpretation of the signal which specified the date and time for us to report to the Admiralty.

We duly presented ourselves at the Admiralty early one morning, boarded a coach and were taken towards the south coast. A few miles north of Portsmouth the coach veered off the main road and drove through the gates of a manor house lying in extensive grounds. It was still early enough for dew to be lying on the lush lawns and notices strictly forbade us to walk on them in case a large number of footprints could be detected from hypothetical German reconnaissance planes. This was an indication of the thoroughness of pre-D-Day security.

Only now were we informed that we were about to take part in Operation *Fabius*. I thought, if there were any significance in such a title, then this could not be the massive operation which landing on Hitler's

---

[61] Formerly on the staff of the London *Evening Standard.*

Fortress Europe would require. For wasn't Fabius the Roman general who wore down Hannibal with his hit-and-run tactics, Fabius Cunctator (The Delayer)? Surely this was not going to be another Dieppe raid of horrendous memory? My misgivings were soon put at rest: *Fabius* was neither going to be the invasion nor a raid; it was to be a *rehearsal* for the invasion.

After the briefing we carried on westwards and in due course, at somewhere I didn't recognise but probably in Dorset, I embarked on a landing craft together with another Official Naval Reporter. Familiar as everyone would become with flat-bottomed landing craft capable of running ashore through the shallowest of waters, it takes an effort now to realise that I could have been surprised at seeing hundreds of them awaiting the order to proceed. I was only familiar with north-eastern ports and anchorages where not one of these craft were to be seen. For the first time I was aboard an LCT. The tank landing craft had been so-called in the early days of Combined Operations but now it was Landing Craft (Tank) to conform to US military terminology. I thought I had seen most naval craft but this was an entirely new family and I was amazed at the variety as one of the LCT's crew patiently pointed out the types in sight and their functions: LCAs (Assault), LCFs (Flak or anti-aircraft), LCH (headquarters) and so on.

While waiting for our LCT to get under way, I was still puzzled by what looked like big square boxes floating on the sea, apparently made of canvas. I turned to a tall Canadian colonel who happened to be standing beside me and, pointing, inquired: 'What are those craft, sir?'

'Craaft!' he mimicked with transatlantic emphasis on the vowel and registering a degree of scorn at my ignorance. 'Those ain't craaft. They're tanks.' And noting my blank incomprehension, he explained more genially that they were DD (Duplex Drive) Sherman tanks and he had heard that they had been invented by a Hungarian refugee who had been working on their prototype in a London garage. Whether any credence can be given to the colonel's informant, posterity has given Major-General Hobart the credit for the invention. Whatever its origin, the idea was that they could be launched from landing craft while still offshore and make their own way to the enemy beach. There they would drop their canvas covering and Sherman tanks would emerge to give immediate fire-support to assaulting infantry. If the colonel had any misgivings about this innovation, he certainly did not voice them. In the choppy seas of D-Day itself many would founder with their luckless crews. Admiral

Ramsay would record: 'Conditions could not have been less ideal for this novel weapon' and Admiral Vian's laconic comment was that they were 'something of a disappointment'. Nevertheless, there were places where these 'swimming tanks' both made the shore and rendered vital support to the infantry. A total of thirty-four out of forty landed on the British *Sword* sector and cleared the beaches before the infantry landed and fourteen out of nineteen reached the sea wall at Courseulles in support of Canadian troops sheltering from enemy fire.

Operation *Fabius*, during which we forged forty miles into the Channel, turned about and 'invaded' our own coast, was something of an anti-climax after keying ourselves up for the 'real thing' but was nevertheless an invaluable experience, as it was intended to be. At least I would no longer be surprised by the 'new' types of craft.

I was surprised to hear my fellow ONR say: 'I don't like the look of it' and had to conceal my amazement when he added he did not want any repeat experience. It was a wish that would be fulfilled and meant that I would be the only ONR to be in a craft that beached on D-Day. Only a low wooden partition had separated me from the office in which this colleague had worked before the war and I had often seen him then from a distance of a few yards. I knew that in order to report on Sir Oswald Mosley's Blackshirts, he had joined them. It was only after their brutal attacks on hecklers at their Olympia rally in June 1934 that his paper's proprietor had repudiated the aims and policy of the British Union of Fascists. Inevitably, on hearing his reaction to *Fabius*, the thought passed through my mind that possibly he was less prepared to face whatever the future operation entailed because of residual political inclinations. I may have been entirely mistaken and he cannot have been the only one to have had qualms about what was to come. Survivors of another 'rehearsal', Operation *Tiger* in which 1,000 American troops died off Slapton Sands, Devon, must have had similar misgivings. Other such exercises were codenamed *Duck* and *Beaver*.

~~

A few weeks after Operation *Fabius,* almost identical signals in the last week of May instructed us to report at the Admiralty once more. This, surely, could not be another dummy run. In the Admiralty I was handed a sheet of paper with an order in violet typescript headed TOP SECRET from the Office of the Allied Naval Commander, Expeditionary Force

(ANCXF), Vice-Admiral Sir Bertram Ramsay (whose headquarters were in the manor at which we had been briefed about Operation *Fabius* and which I now know was Southwick House). The order was signed in light-blue ink by Cdr John Dillon-Robinson, Staff Press Liaison Officer. I had to report on Friday 2 June to the CO of LCT (Veh) 903 'for duty as already instructed'. In fact, I had been given no instructions other than what was on this piece of paper. Nor would I be further enlightened by the Press Division as to how I was supposed to get my story back in time for it to be released at approximately the same time as the hundreds of stories from the war correspondents in off-shore ships equipped with the machinery for transmitting them.

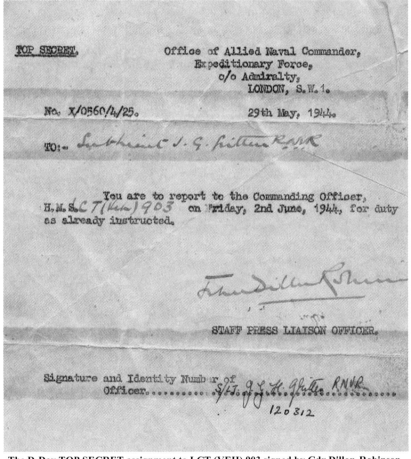

The D-Day TOP SECRET assignment to LCT (VEH) 903 signed by Cdr Dillon-Robinson, RN. Note: No. 1 has been metamorphosed into 120312.

Nor as far as I know had my fellow Official Naval Reporter, Sub-Lieut Raymond Playfoot, been given any briefing before he joined one of the 300 minesweepers which swept the area ahead of the armada. This hazardous operation was successfully completed just off the French coast while it was still daylight, yet undetected by the enemy. It is a measure of the splendid work of these sweepers that only one LST and one destroyer would be sunk by mines in the Channel on D-Day itself.

Playfoot and I were the only ONRs to cover what Admiral Ramsay was to call the 'biggest amphibious operation in history'. Each of the national dailies and the BBC had its own naval war correspondent who had been placed by the Admiralty on board the biggest ships. I gather that more than a few grumbled at not having seen the actual landings at all or only through binoculars.

I found Squadron U49 in Southampton Water and went aboard LCT 903 on Friday 2 June. It was an indication of the youthfulness of the officers in Combined Operations that its CO, Sub-Lieut L. G. Metcalf, in peacetime a bank cashier, was not only the same rank as myself but was four years my junior. The average age of the crew of 903 was twenty.

The next day hundreds of Naval officers crowded into a large covered space in the docks for a briefing. It was lined with extraordinarily detailed maps, evidently of some part of northern France yet to be revealed. There were also silhouette or profile photographs taken at sea level showing coastal buildings, German minefields and gun emplacements, as well as aerial photographs of the terrain behind. Admiral Ramsay and high-ranking officers of the three services were present.

Twenty days earlier, Ramsay's counterpart, General Sir Bernard Montgomery, in overall command of the land forces, had presented the grand invasion plan in the lecture theatre of St Paul's School, Hammersmith, where he himself had been a pupil and where I used to sit as a maths teacher's most obtuse student. We would have been astounded if some prophet had foretold that one day the King and Prime Minister would be sitting together with the top brass from the Allied services in this same lecture theatre listening to Monty unfolding the invasion plans.

Now, in this Southampton dockside warehouse, it was our turn to be given the most closely guarded details which had been entrusted to that distinguished St Paul's audience. First, we were given the code-name of the overall invasion: Operation *Overlord*. The preliminary Naval phase was Operation *Neptune*.

The timing terminology now became common knowledge for the first time among those of us who had not been involved in Combined Ops. 'D' stood for day and 'H' for hour, so, with D-Day indicating the day of the actual first landings in France, D-minus was like BC and D-plus like AD. The time of the actual intended disembarking on the beaches would be designated for each unit as H-Hour or H-Hour plus so many minutes.

Then came the moment for the great revelation of the best-kept secret of the war: the actual part of France's Channel coast which we intended to invade. Elaborate deceptions had been and were still being made to keep the German High Command under von Runstedt and Rommel (responsible for repelling a possible invasion between Holland and Brittany) guessing as to whether we would cross from the Kent coast or from Sussex or Hampshire or from even further west. Because the War Office maps and photographs were on such a large scale they had given me no clue. Now, we were told at last that the landings were to be made along a forty-mile strip of the Normandy coast between the mouth of the River Orne in the Bay of the Seine in the east, and the Cotentin Peninsula in the west. To reach this strip, over ninety miles of the Channel would have to be crossed.

Some 90,000 men, we were told, were to be landed in the first phase: 20,000 airborne and 70,000 by sea. In fact, over the next two months some two million men from twelve nations would be landed in France. Our military planners had divided this forty-mile stretch of coast into code-named sectors: *Sword, Juno* and *Gold* where three divisions of the British 2nd Army under the overall command of Lt-General Sir Miles Dempsey were to be put ashore. The Americans were to land in the western sectors, to be called *Utah* and *Omaha*.

Each sector was to be further broken down into code-named beaches: our LCT 903 was to land its vehicles and their crews at H+90, that is ninety minutes after the first wave had gone in at 07.45 hours, on *King Red* beach in the *Gold* sector. This was about midway between the little towns of Courseulles and Arromanches (to which the fantastic portable harbour code-named Mulberry was to be towed in sections). We would be part of the Naval Force J under the command of Cdr R. E. D. Ryder who had won the VC for leading the raid on St Nazaire in 1942. The Navy and commandos had blocked the Normandy dock so that it could not be used by the *Tirpitz*, the most powerful battleship in either the German or

British navies. Little did I know that in five months' time I would be in very close proximity to this St Nazaire VC.

The first day's objective for the Army in the British sector was the city of Caen, some eight miles inland from the beaches. In fact, this would not be achieved for another month after a tough slogging match with the Germans.

We were told about the air strikes and the paratroop drops—some troops were to be glider-borne—planned for the two wings of the invasion front, as well as such details as the composition of the beaches. Months before, men had been landed from midget submarines in the dark to collect samples of sand and clay, almost from under the enemy's feet. Such information was vital for assessing what would happen to tanks and other vehicles when they disembarked.

To my surprise the whole of the naval force allocated to the British or eastern sector of Neptune was to be under the overall command of Rear-Admiral Sir Philip Vian,[62] flying his flag in the cruiser *Scylla*. He was originally to have been the deputy to an American naval c-in-c before the decision was made to give this command to Admiral Ramsay. Since I had last seen him, Vian had survived the torpedoing of the cruiser *Naiad* in the Mediterranean by sliding painfully over her barnacle-encrusted side. *Scylla* would strike a mine on D-Day and a bracket would fall on his head knocking his teeth through his lower lip.

According to my notes at the briefing, this eastern arm of the Naval force under Vian was to comprise a bombardment group consisting of the battleships *Warspite*, *Nelson* and *Ramilles* and even that floating battery, the old monitor *Lord Roberts*. In addition there would be the cruisers *Glasgow*, *Belfast* (which I had last seen four years earlier in Rosyth with her stern blown off), *Enterprise*, *Mauritius* and *Orion* as well as the destroyers *Saumarez*, *Onslow* (whose boilers I had helped to clean on the Humber), and the Tribals *Algonquin* and *Sioux*. The Americans would have a similar naval force covering the western sectors.

The grim lesson of the Dieppe raid of 1942—that it is fatal to put forces ashore without a preliminary bombardment—had evidently been learned. To reduce the German coastal defences some 600 Naval guns, varying from four to 16-inch, were to hurl shells equivalent to about 2,000 tons of explosive shorewards in any ten minutes. In addition, 7,500 fighter planes would take part in *Overlord* either as direct cover or to

---

[62] Chapter 6 left him steaming out of Namsen Fjord on 3 May 1940 as *Afridi*'s captain.

strafe targets ahead of the invading troops, as well as 3,500 bombers to disrupt communications in France and carry out diversionary strategic raids within Germany.

We were told that 75 per cent of the warships taking part in *Neptune* were British. Of the total number of all kinds of craft, 6,900 or 60 per cent would be British. The rest would be American although many of our own craft had been built in American shipyards. Hundreds of Merchant Navy ships were included in this total.

But now came the most fateful moment of all: the decision had to be taken as to whether or not to launch this vast undertaking on the scheduled date so that the Normandy landings would start on the morning of Monday, 5 June. The decision depended entirely on the one factor that no mortal could control, not Admiral Ramsay, not even the Supreme Allied Commander, General Eisenhower: the weather.

Eisenhower had chosen the date on the advice of his meteorological experts because on only three days in the lunar month would the tide make possible the landing of troops and their vehicles on the French beaches from flat-bottomed craft in water that was not too deep yet, it was hoped, giving them just enough clearance of the German beach obstacles. For maximum surprise effect on the enemy these conditions had to obtain forty minutes after first light.

However, because flat-bottomed craft, unlike vessels with a keel, cannot ride even moderately rough seas without danger of being swamped, the wind would not have to be above Force 4 on the Beaufort scale, that is between 13 and 18 mph. The third factor was that the cloud ceiling had to be just right so that the bombers softening up the enemy's defences could see their targets.

The dreadful dilemma facing Eisenhower on Saturday 3 June was that the weather prophets told him the bright conditions and relatively calm seas that we could see on the south coast would soon change. As we subsequently learned, those sections of the invasion armada that had already set forth from Scottish, Welsh and west coast bases ran into westerly winds too strong for them and they had to take shelter. The meteorologists in the Admiralty were saying it was the worst June weather for thirty years.

It was 04.15 on Sunday, 4 June, that Eisenhower made his shattering but unavoidable decision: D-Day would be postponed. One group of landing craft failed to get the postponement signal and a destroyer had to be sent after them to chase them back to port.

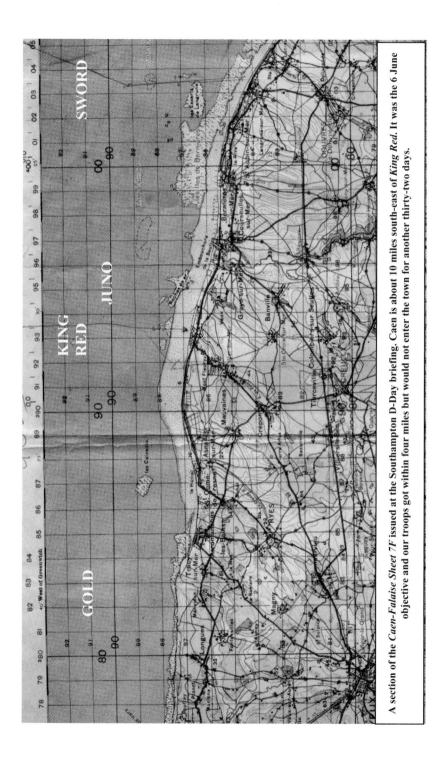

A section of the *Caen-Falaise Sheet 7F* issued at the Southampton D-Day briefing. Caen is about 10 miles south-east of *King Red*. It was the 6 June objective and our troops got within four miles but would not enter the town for another thirty-two days.

For those in overall command there followed hours of agonising frustration and anxiety. They knew that postponement of this mammoth operation for another three weeks when tidal conditions would again be suitable would increase the chance of the enemy getting to know where we intended to land.

It was a trying time for everyone involved in *Overlord* right down to the lowest-ranking squaddy or matelot. In LCT 903's cramped apology for a wardroom some of the Army officers sought relief in poker while some of their men, crowded among their vehicles on the LCT's open deck, played bingo. Other Army officers were concealing their anxiety by studying a report on actual samples of *King Red* beach where they would land. A Naval officer and a major in the Corps of Royal Engineers had scooped up the samples by swimming ashore from a submarine only a few weeks earlier. Still others were poring over the War Office maps and photographs of *King Red* which showed that it was west of a village marked La Rivière.

The nagging anxiety lasted twenty-four hours. The Admiralty weather prophets had been able to predict by 21.00 on Sunday that conditions would improve sufficiently for the crossing to be made on Monday night and in the early hours of Tuesday, 6 June, even though the wind would still be uncomfortably strong and the waves might reach the limits at which the smaller craft could remain buoyant when launched miles off the beaches. At 04.00 on Monday Eisenhower gave the go-ahead.

A sou'-westerly was still blowing at daylight on Monday morning and the sea was too choppy for heavily-loaded landing craft. It was still touch-and-go. But there was no second cancellation.

There follows the minute-by-minute notes I made on the bridge of LCT 903 from the moment we set off at 12.30 on Monday 5 June until just before we pulled away from the French beach and 903 nearly foundered. They were supplemented by details I recalled when writing-up my story for the Admiralty that evening. The time gaps, between 15.45 and 20.00 on 5 June and between 01.30 and 05.20 on D-Day for example, reflect the steady progress towards France without any incident worth noting.

Though the experts had advised against flat-bottomed craft tackling anything above a Force 4 breeze, I noted that when we set off it was Force 5, 'a fresh breeze' according to Beaufort. Eisenhower and his staff were certainly taking a big risk. In one respect, however, this weather was to our advantage in that the German navy had failed to go out on patrol because it was thought we would never launch an invasion in such conditions. That is why the minesweepers had been undetected.

MONDAY 5 JUNE

12.30   Aboard LCT 903 (Veh). Still lowering clouds beneath overcast sky. Fairly high wind: Force 5. The show's on again. Our CO speaks quietly down the voice-pipe to the engine-room: 'Half astern together!' We're under way at last. *Jacta alea est*. What would Caesar have thought of this lot?

Soldiers, packed among vehicles on deck, in high spirits. Our CO to LCT alongside: 'See you later, George!' as if he were catching the 8.40 Richmond to Waterloo on a normal peacetime working day.

Thousands of craft spring to life and the parade begins. Scores of LCTs like us have their personnel and precious cargoes covered by camouflage netting, obscuring them from even their own bridges.

Two Spits [63] zoom overhead. The horizon is ringed with ships. We pass LSIs (Infantry Landing Ships) of 8,000 tons and more, some of them peacetime cargo boats now painted battleship grey. LCAs (Assault Landing Craft) hang from davits—they will be lowered into the sea crammed with troops, make for the shore under their own power and run up onto the beach.

'Greatest 'op in history, sir!' says Signalman David Davies (18) from Barry Docks, Glam. [A phrase Admiral Ramsay himself had used.] Beside me on the bridge, Davies speaks with the self-assurance of someone who has worked in a mill, as a Merchant Navy seaman and as a messenger in Denham film studios.

Sea topped with white horses, spray flying over our ramp, drenching the soldiers: Eighth Army men—how does this compare with North Africa? Our craft shudders and whips. The workmanship of 903's dockyard shipbuilders is being tested to the full.

13.15   Signals flash from Aldis lamps … We're passing a huge, grey-painted American LSI. Long line of escort vessels: corvettes and frigates, two of them French. The whole convoy is protected from low-flying enemy aircraft by silver balloons moored to craft.

---

[63] Spitfire fighter planes.

13.30   Escorting ML (Motor Launch) exercising her sheepdog role. She signals: 'Increase speed!' We have been slightly falling astern of our position in the convoy.

13.55   Another ML overhauls us from astern, this one with a placard TRAFFIC CONTROL. Visual signal from LCT ahead: 'Good luck!' From Squadron Commander. He is Lieut Cdr Roberts on board a LCH (Landing Craft Headquarters). We pass the message by Aldis down the line to LCT astern. Two brand-new destroyers pass us—what class?

14.00   Our squadron re-forms into two columns.

14.25   Passing The Needles on the port beam. Before altering course for France, together with other squadrons, U49 has to rendezvous at a control point approximately 15 miles south-east of The Needles. Low cloud still. Short, heavy swell. We are shipping seas. Two soldiers get a dousing and the CO shouts to them to get under cover.

15.45   Wind abated. But 903 still has sluggish roll.

20.00   About five miles on the starboard beam, two battleships and nine cruisers are silhouetted against grey skies in line-ahead formation. One of the cruisers detaches and comes to inspect our two columns. Sixteen Spits and a number of Lightnings fly overhead.

20.45   Now proceeding south-west in line-ahead formation. Drawing ahead to port is a bombardment force of six USN cruisers.

21.20   A little Greek corvette races past us from astern.

22.15   Count 56 Lightnings as they pass overhead from the south-east, presumably returning after raid over France.

23.00   About eight flashes to port but too far away for detonations to be heard.

TUESDAY 6 JUNE

01.30   Have entered the swept channel marked by buoys laid down by our sweepers. Faint moonlight, enough to see craft ahead about Green One-O. [According to Admiral Vian in his memoirs it was not until after 03.00 that the German naval forces were alerted although the paratroop drops east of the River Orne had started at 01.30. The Allied air bombing started at 03.30. The Naval bombardment began at 05.15 with two battleships, a monitor, five cruisers (including Vian's flagship, *Scylla*) and fifteen destroyers hurling their shells on shore.]

05.20   Dawn. One LCF (Flak) takes up position on our port beam.

05.35   Our Number One, Lieut J. L. Guthrie, a Londoner, says he can see gun flashes ahead. At every point of the skyline there are warships.

05.45   Deep roar of aircraft going south but hidden by cloud bank. Roar continues intermittently for 25 minutes but no sight of aircraft though their trails can be seen through the clouds. We were told at the briefing there are 10,000 aircraft in this show … Seas green and foam-flecked. Still a heavy roll. 'Amazing weather for Glorious June,' remarks the CO.

06.20   Eighteen aircraft fly over in tight formation at about 6,000 feet, followed by another 16 flying south-west.

06.35   Four widely separated red flashes to the south.

06.40   The sun breaking through the heavy cloud bank, the craft on the horizon silhouetted in its rays.

06.50   From the bridge I can see the soldiers removing the camouflage netting and trying to dodge the spray. They're stowing away their beds in lorries, ambulances and Bren-gun carriers. One man is combing his hair—Spartan before Thermopylae.

07.15   Grey LSIs with LCAs slung outboard, probably manned already, appear to starboard and cross our bows. They are still six miles from the shore where there are now repeated flashes—some definitely bombs.

07.20   Red flashes ashore. They must be huge—give the illusion of being detached from the ground.

07.35   The cruiser (probably *Scylla*) escorting the LSIs belches orange flame as she fires four salvoes. The FO (Flag Officer) is signalling to us: 'Utmost speed!' (Our scheduled landing on *King Red* is H-Hour plus 90 minutes—in 10 minutes!) Typhoons roar overhead, flying south. Another cruiser opens fire. Still no land in sight.

08.00   Reach our waiting position about one and a half miles offshore. Now our LCTs are on their own—no escort. Shore visible though much obscured by smoke. German batteries still firing.

08.25   White Verey light shoots up on shore opposite us, signalling capture of a battery. Heavy lowering cloud.

08.35   Two cruisers bombard shore from our starboard stern quarter.

08.40   Slow ahead. Lightnings still bombing shore.

08.50   Shells bursting all along the shore as we approach. Two French (numbered L35 and L78) and a Polish destroyer (L115) as they cross our bows pound away with 4.7s on targets invisible to us. Houses along the coast—a shambles. Germans still firing.

09.10 Four shells burst on the starboard quarter of our leading LCT. More shells bursting among the LCTs ahead from a battery still holding out in La Rivière. But we proceed inshore.

09.15 Shells fall short of us or whine overhead to plop and spout to starboard more or less in the same spot, throwing up miniature geysers. 'My first birthday presents!' quips the CO. It's Metcalf's 21st.

09.20 Destroyers opening up on batteries again. Dense smoke ashore. On left there are the remains of the village of La Rivière. The lighthouse is still standing but with gaping holes in it. About half a mile inland there's another village (probably Mont Fleury) also a shambles.

09.23 Dark red burst and a billow of smoke as an LCT to starboard is hit. As we pass her we can see a jagged hole for'ard of the bridge as if it had been opened up with a tin-opener. One of our flotilla. But she makes it to the beach and offloads 17-pounders. There must be casualties on board.

09.35 Double explosion in LCT immediately to port. [The Germans had planted stakes and iron girders in the beaches, some with shells attached, others with *teller* (plate) mines. Now, at high tide, these were just submerged, invisible, and exploded on impact.] Jagged hole in the LCT's side. Second explosion was under her ramp. She is beaching. But can she lower her ramp?

09.37 We are taking a turn about because the water's edge is jam-packed with craft disgorging troops, transport and armour. We scrape through the stakes and tripods of railway sleepers.

09.40 We're through—beached. We have edged between two other LCTs and lowered the ramp in about two feet of water. Troops are disembarking and vehicles trundle off at intervals whenever a gap appears in the crush ashore. Call it a beach? With the tide now well up there's only a five-yard ribbon of shingle, chock-a-block with men, guns and vehicles. Beyond that, a field with skull-and-crossbones notices marked: ACHTUNG MINEN! Along this narrow ribbon men and vehicles crawl along at a snail's pace, turning inland ahead, past the minefield, along the road that climbs a hill towards Mont Fleury A bulldozer appears as if from nowhere and rapidly clears a passage through sand and pebbles so as to speed up the evacuation of the beach.

Time not specified: Destroyers still firing but shells now fall beyond the hill on which there is what is left of Mt Fleury—presumably laying a barrage in front of the advancing troops who now must be over a mile inland. As soon as they trundle ashore from the LCTs, the tanks add their firepower to the Naval barrage. I can just see a line of armoured cars going along the road towards Caen.

A minefield the other side of the narrow ribbon of beach on which 903's men and vehicles landed.

My notes on what I had observed from LCT 903's bridge ended here. But what had happened before our own run-in to this beach? Mainly from later interviews in Normandy some small pieces of this part of the *Gold* sector mosaic can be added.

While it is indisputable that the Americans on *Omaha* suffered worse than the assault forces on any of the other four sectors—3,000 casualties out of the 40,000 who landed—there is the possibility that, such was the stark realism of the film *Saving Private Ryan*, viewers may have thought the exploits and price paid on other sectors was insignificant. According to Max Hastings in *Overlord: D-Day and the Battle of Normandy*: 'There were moments on the British beaches as shattering as anything that happened on *Omaha*. Although their experience was much less terrible in scale than that of the Americans, in kind it was equally deadly.'[64] In our *Gold* sector the ratio of casualties to men landed was 1,000 to just under 25,000. The Green Howards, whose 1st Battalion had fought in Norway and was evacuated from Åndalsnes, 2 May 1940, met stiff resistance from a battery at Mont Fleury (which I mentioned in my notes at 09.20). It was here that Sergeant-Major Stan Hollis performed the first of a series of exploits that earned him the Victoria Cross. About two miles to the east of *King Red* the Canadians suffered heavy casualties at Graye-sur-Mer and Courseulles. Many, like the Americans on *Omaha*, were forced to seek the 'cover' of beach obstacles or lie in the surf.

The first to land at La Rivière, about three hours before LCT 903 managed to get its troops and vehicles ashore, had been frogmen engineers. Under fire, they started dealing with the *teller* mines and booby traps attached to the partly submerged obstacles intended to rip open the landing craft. Then came the first infantrymen, a battalion of the East Yorkshire Regiment who met stiff resistance and suffered many casualties.

They had been brought ashore from at least one infantry landing ship in LCAs manned by Royal Marines. The coxswain of one of these assault craft gave me a detailed description of the exploit which would win him the Distinguished Service Medal for his outstanding initiative and endurance. At the request of my ONP colleague, he posed on the stern of an LSA to give some idea of what he had done in the choppy sea on D-Day. He was Corporal George E. Tandy of Charleston, London, whose job it was to carry thirty-two of the East Yorks troops to the beachhead at La Rivière in LCA 7906 of 539 Flotilla. This assault craft was launched seven miles off the coast from the LSI. Unfortunately, the hook at the end of the for'ard fall (hoisting rope) struck the LCA's steering wheel which was carried away. Coxswain Tandy tried using the engines to steer the craft but the swell was too great. So he set the engines at FULL AHEAD, then climbed over the stern and stood on the guard-rail of the port rudder, which he then 'steered' with his foot for the seven miles inshore. He had only a cleat to hold onto and he told me that one minute he would be high above the water, the next he was plunged into it up to his chest. As the LCA approached the shore, it came under fire but Tandy managed to get

---

[64] Simultaneously with the announcement in the 2001 New Year's Honours List of an honorary knighthood to *Saving Private Ryan*'s American director, Stephen Spielberg, a wartime British Naval officer drew the Prime Minister's attention to the fact that Royal Navy assault craft were among those which landed the first American troops on *Omaha* and suffered casualties and that Spielberg had been misinformed when he stated that there was no British involvement in *Omaha*.

it through the obstacles and touch down on the correct beach.

Another coxswain, not of an LCA but in an LCT which had beached close to La Rivière, described as 'like two beetles' two mines the craft was sitting on when the tide went out. These were the third and fourth mines they had encountered. When she was first nosing her way into the beach the LCT fouled a teller mine which wounded in the foot her No. 1, Sub-Lieut H. P. Dowell from South Yardley. He later had a toe amputated but for two hours he stuck to his post and the crew did not know that he had even been hurt until be became too weak from loss of blood to carry on. Only a few minutes after striking the first mine, a second blew a large hole through the bottom of the craft and ripped open the plates on the well-deck. But the CO, Sub-Lieut A. Curry whose home was in London's Belgravia, pushed on through the remaining upturned stakes although shells were dropping all around and the craft astern was hit. After the troops, tanks and bulldozers had got ashore and the LCT pulled away from the beach to make room for others, it was discovered that the stern was punctured like a pepper-pot. The water poured in and Motor Mechanic R. Haynes, a Harrow butcher in peacetime, worked frantically to keep the engines and pumps running. But the water kept gaining on the pumps and the LCT had to beach a second time. It was after that that they discovered she was stranded on top of the two mines. Coxswain P. H. Barnes, a Barnet plumber, told me what happened then:

> We sat over them all night scarcely daring to move in case they went off. Royal engineers removed them the next day. Only then could we make a proper inspection of the damage. Apart from the two big gashes for'ard, we counted forty-eight holes in the stern where we had fouled the obstacles. We filled the little holes with blacking brushes, hairbrushes, hammer handles and wooden pegs. The galley was out of action so we cooked by lighting a fire in a bucket.

Despite the big rents in the well-deck, the LCT remained afloat at high tide and she was eventually towed home across the Channel.

The crews were eager to tell me of such incidents which were evidence of the durability of these craft as well of their own dogged determination to fulfil their D-Day tasks. Most of them were Hostilities Only men coming from every kind of peacetime occupation. The officers were RNVR. Unlike their professional RN brethren they had only done a crash-course of naval warfare in the last year or two and certainly had never in peacetime handled flat-bottomed craft.

Typical was the former manager of a big Cardiff hotel (although he was a Dubliner), Sub-Lieut D. A. McCaughley, who was now CO of LCT 921 (54th Flotilla) which was carrying fourteen vehicles—six light American tanks, two half-tracks, three lorries and three trailers—with their American drivers. He was scheduled to land them on one of the American beaches but it proved so crowded that there was no room even to wedge in another craft. So, he waited offshore until D-Day+1.

Here is what then happened as McCaughley related it:

> During the night some bombs fell between us and a cruiser riding at anchor about 200 yards away. We added the fire of our little Oerlikon guns to the heavy ack-ack of the cruiser.
>
> The plane fell out of the darkness in flames. In the morning our flotilla of LCTs landed our 'cargo', the first reinforcements after the initial assault in this sector. Shells were still falling on the beach, where the receding tide left us high and dry for six hours. The crew did some valuable work during that time, carrying wounded soldiers down the beach to a smaller landing craft which took them out to one of the ships. Ignoring the fact that the beaches were still mined and that there was sporadic shell-fire, my men carried fifteen wounded soldiers down to the craft, including a German who had been hit in the foot. A heavy gun, firing from about four miles inland, sent over a salvo as we moved away from the shore on the high tide. We heard it whining towards us and we all ducked as one man. It dropped thirty yards off the port bow and was followed by others just astern until we got out of range.
>
> At 01.15 I actually saw a torpedo coming straight for us on the port beam, hopping along the surface of the water like a dolphin. I also saw the dark shape of the E-boat that fired it.

Sub-Lieut D. H. Longden of Sheffield, a former railway clerk, took up the story:

> The tin-fish hit us under the bridge with a crash that momentarily stunned us. Lieut McCaughley was knocked out

when the compass toppled over and hit him on the forehead. The convoy proceeded on its way according to orders and we thought the E-boat would return to give us the knock-out blow. But having wasted a torpedo on a mere LCT she probably thought that that was enough. The port engine stopped and we proceeded on one screw. But, by a great effort on the part of our two motor mechanics, the port engine spluttered into action again after a few hours. They had had to repair the pipes broken by the explosion, working in the dark. Only a few plates on the starboard side kept our craft from breaking in two and even these were fractured. The only way we could keep afloat was going FULL AHEAD. Otherwise the sea would have rushed through the gaping hole too fast for us to control it.

~~

The moment the last vehicle had been driven ashore from our LCT 903, it was up-ramp, engines half-astern and we pulled out to make way for another landing craft to wedge her way into the vacant space and offload while the now ebbing tide permitted.

I was reckoning that once the beaches were out of sight and there was nothing more to record, I could settle down and write my story for the Press Division. It had taken nineteen hours to cross the Channel and I presumed it would not take much less to get back. Fate, in the form of the enemy's beach obstacles, decreed otherwise. We had scarcely gone half a mile after turning northwards when the diesel engines started to choke and 903 began to settle lower in the water. The pumps were started but it soon became evident that they could not cope with the inrush of water. The engines gurgled to a complete stop and soon the seas were slopping over the gunwale. 903 was foundering. Her bottom had evidently been ripped open by the underwater obstacles, probably as we withdrew on the ebbing tide in water that was not deep enough to carry us over them unscathed.

The CO ordered ABANDON SHIP and the majority of 903's complement scrambled aboard another craft that came alongside. We were taken in tow and for the second time that day 903 beached on *King Red*. When the tide ebbed further and we were left high and dry we could assess the damage: one very large hole beneath the water line and one smaller one. This was more than the Naval beach parties could cope with. Whatever might be LCT 903's ultimate fate, at least she had accomplished the principal job for which she had been built and her egg-box multi-watertight-compartments construction had kept her afloat, as it had so many similar craft. For instance, the LCT that I saw discharge her cargo of guns and men after being holed at 09.23 managed to pull away from the beach which was jammed with craft so as to make way for others waiting their turn to unload. Once in deeper water she began to fill rapidly and slowly heel over to starboard. Yet she refused to sink and remained on the surface with a 40° list.

Another survivor was the LCT alongside our own 903 which at 09.35 fouled one of the barely submerged teller mines attached to stakes or sleepers. After the deep red flash and roar of the explosion, the yellow fumes lifted to reveal the jagged top of a hole, the rest of it beneath the water line. I saw an officer, probably the first lieutenant, lean over the gunwale to ascertain the damage and moments later there was a second explosion under her ramp. She did manage to beach, however, and disgorge fieldguns and vehicles. When the tide went out she, too, was left high and dry. In the afternoon a Naval repair party welded a plate over the hole and she floated off on the next tide.

~~

It was now mid-afternoon, the beaches were clear of troops and I was walking on the soil of liberated Europe for the first time. Only parties of Royal Navy and Royal Marines were detaching *teller* mines from the top of the stakes and other obstacles that sprouted in endless rows along the shore. The first giant Channel-spanning step had been taken towards fulfilling what had seemed little better than a brave hope after the collapse of 1940: that one day we would return to the Continent, reverse the trauma of Dunkirk and, instead of having to brace ourselves against news of retreats, withdrawals and defeats in Greece, Crete and, at first, in North Africa and Russia, we would drive the Nazis back.

Over five decades later, do I imagine the sun actually shining that afternoon as I trudged through the shingle looking for any craft which would give me a lift back to the UK? Or is it only an impression of sunlight, reflecting a buoyancy I certainly felt at the time despite the evidence of war's wreckage, pain and deaths which would multiply until the Nazis capitulated? A recurring thought was how much more intense must be the feelings of the Free French troops and the men in the French warships on returning to their native soil and home waters. I was not to know that of the nearly forty divisions of Allied troops assigned to *Overlord* only one was Free French and that did not land on D-Day itself. I have had confirmation that, after the morning's mainly grey skies, the sun did shine on the Normandy seashore that Tuesday afternoon.

It was early in the evening before I found a craft which was ferrying materials from a ship offshore and returning. I decided that this was probably my only chance that day of getting at least one stage along the return trip. From this craft I saw the first 300 German prisoners captured on this particular sector on the invasion coast. They had been lined up on the shingle about seven deep awaiting embarkation to prisoner-of-war cages in England. A north wind, very cold for this time of the year, was blowing in from the sea, obviously penetrating their grey-green uniforms. They were huddling together and stamping their feet. Many had their boots removed, no doubt Tommy's precaution against them doing a runner. One of them was trouserless, his tunic barely covering his underpants as he sheltered from the wind among his fellows. It was a scene on a miniature scale bringing to mind the photographs and newsreels we had seen of endless lines of German PoWs in the Russian snow, shuffling and shivering in uniforms totally inadequate for the bitter cold of the steppes, victims of Hitler's illusion that he could get to Moscow before the winter of 1941. After a while, guarded by Royal Marines with rifles, these men were shepherded aboard a Jumbo motor craft which conveyed them to an LSI lying offshore.

Light was fading as the LCT in which I was taking passage drew away from the shore but I could just see through binoculars another batch of German prisoners coming back down the road which in the morning had been jammed with our troops and vehicles pushing towards Caen.

That was my last D-Day impression of this toehold in a forty-mile strip of liberated France.

Still going on. White Very lights goes
up. .... as, meaning ....
? battery. Heavy lowering cloud.
continuous lightnings .

8.35. 2 Cruisers bombard shore from
stbd stern quarters .

8.40. Slow ahead. Lightning; still striking
Now.

8.50. Shells bursting all along shore as
we approach. Destroyers pounding
shore as they pass along coast across our
bows.   L.35 & Polish destroyer [L.45]
[L.78]
flares along coast & shrapnel.
9 shells burst near L.CT. on stbd sides.
shells firing among LCTs fords. but we
proceed inshore . 9.15. shells seen to fall in
same short, and short. destroyers along
shore sunk,
Pass L.C.T. with bows ablaze in port stbd side, belong
to our flotilla

A page of notes scribbled shortly before LCT 903 beached on *King Red*.

Chapter 10

Mixed Cargo

I have been given reports from both the American and Canadian fronts of women snipers, wives of German officers, who fired on Allied troops and as a result were themselves shot.

General Montgomery at a press conference on 12 June 1944.

The next group of German prisoners-of-war I would meet were of another category and of very different appearance. They were a group of Wehrmacht officers in immaculate great coats in pastel shades of green and blue with high-crowned caps, some monocled, waiting for disembarkation from an infantry landing ship in a Southampton dock six days after D-Day. They were standing apart from 300 German other-ranks who, watched by US General Lee, Rear-Admiral Pipon, Flag Officer in charge, Southampton, and Admiral Sir Charles Little, C-in-C Portsmouth, were going ashore under guard to a PoW cage.

A school friend who became an Eighth Army officer told me after the war that, knowing that the enemy had endured exactly the same rigours in the desert as he and his comrades, he felt no resentment or enmity towards Rommel's Afrika Corps prisoners. For him the common denominator of violent deaths, wounds and daily hardships experienced by men on both sides cancelled out unremitting awareness that the enemy were representatives of an egregious ethos under the command of an enthusiastic Nazi. Perhaps because my experience had been so different, my feelings towards this batch of German officers were not so magnanimous. Even that shivering bunch of PoWs on the evening of D-Day I had only seen through binoculars and, before that, the enemy had only been invisible pilots and bomber crews. In six years of war, these officers on the LSI would be the closest I would be to 'the enemy'. The nearest the Navy would get to the kind of fellow feeling my Eighth Army friend described would be on those very rare occasions when our crews would pick up survivors from a stricken German warship. That had not come within my experience. The only time I had felt sympathy for our adversaries was when we thought men had been trapped in that U-boat off the east coast of Scotland in the winter of 1939–40.[65]

I confess I did not share my friend's 'objectivity' and, even if some German officers were by now coming around to the view that their First World War corporal was leading them to disaster, these specimens of the *Herrenvolk* as they chatted and chuckled, appeared self-assured, even jaunty, certainly quite unbowed. On principle, one should not condemn individuals for the sins of their peer group without evidence of their specific guilt. However, by mid-1944 we were well aware of the slaughter of civilians in territories which peers of these officers had overrun, the horrors of Lidice and Oradour and in hundreds of villages and towns in Russia. Even if these officers were not directly implicated, it is extremely doubtful whether any of them would have been critical of these acts of inhumanity. I was 'unprincipled' enough to the extent of having not an iota of sympathy for them in defeat. My reactions would have been even more intolerant if I had known then of the shooting of British PoWs which would be revealed after the war.

Yet in the next few months, indeed, within the hour, I would come across various examples of the pitfalls of generalisations to individual cases. In a war atmosphere hasty interpretations of human motivation are more likely to be black or white with no allowance for shades of grey. I was about to meet situations where there were more question marks than certainties.

~~

As my Official Naval Photographer colleague, Lieut Allen, and I moved further inboard we could not have imagined that our efforts that morning to find stories for the Press Division would lead to questions being asked

---

[65] See pp. 49–53.

in the House of Commons. Apart from ascertaining that the LSI's commanding officer was Lieut Cdr P. R. Brown, RNR, our further inquiries had no strictly Naval connection. But, call them prisoners or 'passengers' on this vessel, they proved increasingly interesting, and, from the media reaction to our stories and pictures, the press evidently thought so too.

We had only gone a few steps away from the German officers when somebody informed us that there were thirteen civilians among this batch brought over from Normandy and a search on the crowded mess-decks brought us to a group who were not in uniform. One was a tall man with Mongolian features and close-cropped hair, wearing an old, patched boiler-suit, a lone figure looking a bit bewildered, possibly apprehensive. I tried speaking to him in English and French but with no response.

Seeing my problem, a small, middle-aged man in a French beret came up, introduced himself in fluent English as Samuel Dorfmann and offered his services as interpreter. He spoke Russian, and that was the language the tall man spoke. As it turned out, he was not Russian but before the war had lived a nomadic life in the mountainous Kirghiz Soviet Republic. He had been conscripted in 1940 into the Red Army. Although he had survived the biggest set battle of the war, on the Kursk salient in July 1943, and taken part in the recapture of the Ukrainian capital, Kiev, in November, he had had the misfortune to be captured at Krivoi Rog about 225 miles to the south-east the same month. The Germans had sent him immediately, like so many other Red Army prisoners, to Hitler's so-called 'Atlantic Wall' on the French Channel coast, where he had been obliged to work for the Wehrmacht. And here was that day's first question mark: while his American captors claimed he had been sniping at them, he maintained he had been deliberately firing over their heads. Nobody was ever going to find out the truth or know what happened to this man who had lived a thousand miles east of the Caspian Sea. We would only know after the war that many of the Red Army men like him who had become German PoWs were executed under Stalin.

Samuel Dorfmann himself then gave me his own story. He was a Russian who had emigrated to France in 1920. Later he had come to London to start a tailoring business in Soho but after a while returned to Paris to set up another branch. When the Nazis invaded he had been unable to escape but, he said with a wry smile, they never discovered he was a Jew. When he learned of the Allied invasion he had made his way to the coast with the help of the French and had hitched this cross-Channel trip in the LSI so that he could get in touch with his wife, Sarah, and his sons, Louis and Maurice, whom he thought had joined the British Army. I would never know whether the reunion took place.

While Samuel was telling me his story, a small, elderly woman kept trying to intervene. At last she succeeded and started speaking volubly in heavily-accented French. Again with the help of Samuel, I gathered that she also was Jewish, having at some time hailed from Constantinople. While tongue-lashing the Nazis for their anti-Semitic persecution, she kept pointing an accusing finger at another woman on the other side of the deck. With a pushing-away movement of her outstretched hands she indicated she was glad to be as far removed from this person as possible. Since they were the only women we had seen on the ship and the object of her distaste appeared to be under guard by a GI corporal with an automatic rifle, I was intrigued, thanked Samuel for his help and crossed over the deck to ask the corporal what he knew about his prisoner.

> I was told to be very wary of this prisoner, sir. The guards who handed her over said that she had been taken at St Mère Eglise after firing on our soldiers. She would smile at them and, when they approached her, pull a gun on them. She had winged a few that way.

The woman was dressed in a brown overcoat of ersatz lamb's wool, brown stockings and imitation lizard-skin shoes (bought not in France but in Upper Silesia, she would tell me), and she carried a deerskin handbag. Her brown hair was 'bobbed' (to use the contemporary description of a neck-length coiffure), her eyes were blue and she had a broad, tanned face. She could make herself understood in English but at least she made no attempt to smile at *me*.

Her name, she said, was Myra Speilmann, born twenty-nine years before in Rawicz, which was on the Polish side of the frontier with Germany up to 1939 but was incorporated into the Third Reich under the Nazi-Soviet carve-up of Poland in August of that year. Today, Rawicz is about seventy miles inside Poland. But she had left Poland many years ago. 'That's why I cannot speak Polish,' she said. She had settled in Hamburg and in 1931 married a German who had been killed in Belgium in 1940.

I had no means of knowing how much of this was true. Accused of sniping at the Americans, she must have felt some alarm at her situation. If I had been in her position, I would have tried to convince my interlocutor of my innocence and gain his sympathy. I assumed she was doing just that. She was in the dark as to the purpose of my questioning and may well have thought that this was a preliminary interrogation by an intelligence officer.

As for myself, it was droll that after nearly five years of war against Nazi Germany, the first 'enemy' I should be talking to was a civilian and a woman. But she had been firing a gun, hadn't she? 'I have only been cooking for the Germans,' she insisted, adding hastily 'and also for the American wounded.' She did not explain why she had left Germany the previous December. Had she volunteered or been directed to work in Normandy? Had she taken the first opportunity to get away from the bombing of Hamburg? 'It was worse than Hell,' she said. Was she trying to elicit sympathy or was it her attempt to justify her shooting at the Americans, getting a bit of her own back for the bombing of her city? In view of the Luftwaffe's blitzes on our cities—Hull was particularly in my mind—she could have saved her breath.

What I didn't know then was that Myra was referring to what her fellow citizens would call *die Katastrophe*, the night of 27–28 July 1943 when the word *feuersturm* would be coined and 40,000 people died, most of them incinerated or asphyxiated. The RAF Bomber Command under Air Marshal Harris had been experimenting with incendiary raids over Hamburg for weeks. It culminated on this particular night with a qualitative difference: the hundreds of separate fires joined up to create a fire storm with winds exceeding 100 mph, burning at 800°C and a vortex into which the oxygen was sucked, stifling thousands in their shelters. Another 3,000 tons of bombs were dropped on Hamburg three months before D-Day. 'Carpet bombing' and even the targeting of civilians was deliberate policy 'to make them feel the weight of war,' to use a War Cabinet phrase.[66] A few voices were raised against the combined immorality and futility of the 'bomb 'em into surrender' policy but at that time the protests were generally scoffed at and even today there are those who attempt to justify the indiscriminate bombing of cities like Hamburg and Dresden.

When Myra Spielmann said she had a child who was blind and was

---

[66] Compare Government bombardment instructions early in the war, p.108.

in a 'home' in France, was I to believe or disbelieve her? Was she playing for sympathy on genuine or spurious grounds? Her answer to the question 'Did she think the Germans would still win the war?' was a model of discretion: 'Those are weighty military matters, not for me.'

What was to follow is an example of how the wartime press could blow up a story which really had the minimum of verifiable facts, elaborate on them and produce a flamboyant piece of propaganda.

Our story and pictures, after the usual Admiralty and MoI processing, were first picked up by the London evenings. One of them showed Myra being led away by a policewoman and the story was headlined: 'THIS GERMAN GIRL SNIPER SHOT MEN WITH A SMILE'. By the morning it was the turn of the national dailies. *The Daily Mirror* devoted its centre page spread to: 'WOMEN AT WAR' with a page-length picture on the left of Myra and on the right the story and picture of Lieut Margaret Standfil from Missouri, a nurse. Among other stories on these pages was one about two young French women who had died in Normandy after shooting at Germans. *Mirror* readers were told: 'Here is the story of five women at war—of Myra, the German Delilah who smiled at our men in Normandy and shot them dead, of Margaret, ready to tend the wounded, friend and foe alike … '

~~~

I had not quoted the American corporal guarding Myra as saying she 'shot them dead'. He had actually said: 'She winged a few' and a dictionary definition of winged is 'to wound in a wing or arm.' And though in the *Mirror* version and in the press generally she was referred to as 'Myra the Sniper', there was no mention of her sniping in my story. The corporal had said she 'pulled a gun' on the paras. Another tabloid, which chose to change her name to Erna, said the Americans would have been justified in 'shooting her out of hand'. Even a national daily like the *News Chronicle*, with a reputation for moderation and tolerance, under the headline: 'WILL THE GIRL SNIPER BE EXECUTED?' reported she had been landed in this country 'wearing no uniform or insignia' and told its readers:

> The fate of a *franc-tireur* is normally death and by the laws of war, the American soldiers who captured her would have been justified in shooting her.

WOM...

HUNS THOUGHT ODETTE AND MADELEINE JUST PRETTY AND DUMB

Yesterday Hilde Marchant told you of the French woman sniper who killed our men. Today she tells another story, of two more women of France, and of how they, too, shot to kill. It was not our men they shot. . . .

THERE were two women of France, Odette and Madeleine. They were young, and they passed their adolescence under German occupation, in a small Normandy village.

It was a centre of resistance. Information passed out of the village, but pretty girls, with the face and figure of Odette and Madeleine, are not politically alert.

They were the daughters of a farmer, pretty but dumb.

When the Germans started moving out of the area on D-Day, they found they were being sniped at from the windows of a farm.

They shot the farmer, but they could not kill the other two snipers.

The snipers went on firing, killing forty-nine Germans in retreat with the ease that all farmers' daughters learn when they are shooting rabbits or rats.

It was Odette and Madeleine.

Ammunition Gave Out

They had given the information, they had hoarded ammunition and guns, they had seen their father killed.

They went on shooting until their ammunition gave out, until they could no longer hold the rifles because they had lost so much blood from their wounds.

British paratroops took over the village found two young

How the *Daily Mirror* (15 June 1944) presented the Myra Spielmann interview. Myra becomes 'the German Delilah' contrasted with sister of mercy … →

EN AT WAR

HERE is the story of five women at war — of Myra, the German Delilah, who smiled at our men in Normandy and shot them dead, of Margaret and her mission of mercy, of Odette and Madeleine, and of Lesley, of the ATS.

Myra, pistol-packing for Hitler, had no mercy. Margaret came 4,000 miles to help our men on the Normandy beaches. Odette and Madeleine lost their father to the Huns, but they were revenged. Lesley, heroine of the Ilford train crash, has been killed on duty.

Look at Myra in the big picture on the left. She has reached England in a tank landing ship. Even the men told off to guard her were warned she was a tigress.

But she had a tale to move to pity the people she despised for pity. "Her blind child . . . the horror she endured in the Hamburg raids." Her questioners think she is something of a liar, too.

Then look right, at smiling Margaret — Lieutenant Margaret Stanfill, Allied nurse from Hyti, in Missouri, U.S.A., ready to tend the wounded, friend and foe alike.

She was there on the very first day of invasion, when nobody knew what was in store. Her friends say she was the first woman to land in Normandy.

She says nothing; merely keeps her smile honest, for Ally or German. Mercy, like justice, does not discriminate.

But when Myra, the sniper, landed here an American corporal stood by, with an automatic rifle, ready for tricks. "I was told to be very wary of this prisoner," he said.

"The guards who handed her over to us said that her method was to smile at our soldiers and pull a gun on them when they approached her. She winged a few of them that way, so I am taking no chances."

Dressed in an overcoat of ersatz lamb's wool, brown stockings, imitation lizard skin shoes —which she said she had bought in Upper Silesia—and carrying a deerskin handbag, she was given a wide berth by her fellow collaborationists.

Captured at St. Mere Eglise, on the Cherbourg Peninsula, the woman said she was 29.

She protested she was really a Pole and had been merely cooking for the Germans for the last six months.

She even tried to elicit sympathy by talking about her blind child whom she had left in a home in France.

Train sma[

L ESLEY, 24-year-old ATS heroine of last January's Ilford train smash, was a dispatch rider. It was as a dispatch rider with a convoy that she died.

Her real name was Private Mrs. Madge Evelyn Hocking. She had not seen her husband since he was sent to India two months after her marriage in 1942.

It was while she was waiting

The smile of mercy

→ ... American nurse Lieutenant Margaret Stanfill from Hyti, Missouri, and with a Normandy farmer's two daughters who shot at Germans on D-Day.

Whereas one paper reported that Myra Spielmann was 'under a decision reached late last night to be treated as a prisoner-of-war', the next day another report stated that she would not be treated as a PoW but as an enemy alien.

Five days later, Major Sir Jocelyn Lucas Bt, Conservative MP for Portsmouth South, asked the Under-Secretary of State for Foreign Affairs, George Hall, whether 'women in civilian clothes without brassards or distinguishing marks caught sniping at Allied troops were to be treated as PoWs or as *franc-tireurs*?' Hall answered that only one woman had so far been landed in this country who had been engaged in active hostilities against the Allies in France. He added:

> There is no evidence available so far to show whether or not any other woman was so engaged or whether or not she was wearing any uniform or other distinguishable marks at the time of capture. This woman is being detained in this country as a civilian.

The implication that she could have been in uniform was odd. Why should she have been taken out of it and put into the civvies in which we found her including the shoes 'I bought in Silesia'? The redoubtable Sir Jocelyn (who according to *Who's Who* had 'hunted several packs of hounds') was not satisfied with Hall's answer and pursued his quarry: 'If evidence is proved that she was shooting, will she be tried and can an assurance be given that women will not be protected by reason of their sex?' The Under-Secretary replied: 'We must wait to obtain evidence before any decision can be arrived at.'

A Labour Member (wounded twice in the First World War but with a German-born wife) asked for an assurance that there was no widespread use of *franc-tireurs* 'as has been indicated in a wide section of the press'. Hall agreed: 'we have no evidence to support the allegation … '

The public were to hear no more of Myra Spielmann. She was forgotten in the new menace from the air. The first four flying-bombs fell on South-East England only a few hours after I had been interviewing her. There was the continuing news of the war in France to report; the hammer blows against the Nazis in Russia; the attempt on the life on Hitler and so on.

If she had survived until today, an octogenarian Myra might have been persuaded to give us the answers to whether she spent the rest of the war in the Isle of Man or in a PoW cage, whether she was actually gun-toting on D-Day, whether she 'winged' or 'shot dead' any GIs, whether her blind child existed and, if she did, how long it was before they were reunited, and a host of other questions.

Though news of Myra faded, the stories of women with guns still cropped up. On board the British hospital ship *Naushon*, also in Southampton after crossing the Channel from the American sector, Corporal Leo Dalpe from Albany, NY told me about one of his patients, a thirty-one-year-old French woman who said she had been living for four years in a house on the Normandy coast occupied by German troops. She maintained the Germans were 'bribing' French women to snipe at Allied troops though she protested she had not been one of them. The sceptical corporal remarked dryly: 'I reckon she didn't get hit in the legs, both arms and the buttocks if she was sitting at home knitting.'

His buddy, First Sergeant in the Medical Department L. W. Marzecki from Perth Amboy, NJ volunteered: 'A Ranger told me two snipers had given him and his men a lot of trouble until they were silenced. They turned out to be French girls aged fourteen.' In contrast, two of the *Mirror*'s 'five women at war' were daughters of a Normandy farmer who were badly wounded after firing on Germans moving out of their area on D-Day.

Doubts about Myra Spielmann's veracity were revived when Marzecki, himself of Polish origin, said many of the wounded German PoWs claimed they were Poles because they thought they would get better treatment from their captors.

A further twist to the story was given on 20 June when a spokesman at General Eisenhower's HQ told the press that there was considerable doubt as to whether there had been any women snipers. It was possible that they were German troops trying to escape dressed as women. It was an ingenious explanation which conformed to the policy of appeasing General De Gaulle and playing down the current stories about *collaboratrices* and the Normans' alleged lack of enthusiasm for *Le Débarquement*. However, a German soldier dressed as a woman trying to escape must have been irresistibly trigger-happy to have risked exposing his disguise by taking unprovoked pot shots at those from whom he was escaping. Pull the other one, as the saying goes.

Chapter 11

Vive la France Libérée!

In some places, of course, résistants went beyond sabotage in aid of the Allies and took matters directly into their own hands ... [In Brittany] the Allies met virtually no opposition until they reached the U-boat bases at Brest, Lorient and Saint-Nazaire.

Occupation, The Ordeal of France 1940–1944: Ian Ousby

The officers I interviewed were eager to relate their bizarre experiences with Hitler's newfangled weaponry. This was neo-Nelsonic close-encounter sea warfare, unprecedented in the current conflict, at least on this scale. Not till now had I heard phrases like:

> Running alongside we tossed hand grenades at him ...
> We came across a survivor screaming 'Kamarad!'
> I poked my head inside and managed to neutralise the self-exploding device ...
> As proud as peacocks we began to tow her ... there was a vivid flash ... she disintegrated into a shower of debris.
> She looked long and white, like an Eskimo kayak ... we left her a burning hulk.
> We rubbed our eyes ... it was a Messerschmidt fighter on top of a Junkers 88 bomber ...

It was a pity the censors' blue pencils prevented a doodle-bug-shocked public learning about these stimulating stories.

I had returned to France in the second week of July as the Normandy beachhead's Press Liaison Officer, to cater for visiting naval correspondents sent out by their newspapers, in addition to my role as Official Naval Reporter. When compared with the RAF's PR set-up in Normandy, a large well-equipped and well-manned unit which I once visited, my one-man effort was pathetic. In the event, in over two months I would have only two correspondents as my protégés.

I was based at Courseulles, a seaside town a little to the east of where I landed on D-Day. This was the headquarters of Rear-Admiral J. W. Rivett-Carnac, Flag Officer, British Assault Area. As on the Bitter Lakes and in Kenya, I shared a tent and ate in a marquee. My 'office' was a table in a hut on the other side of a partition where fellow Naval officers plotted various activities of a clandestine nature. In August I would inadvertently hear that some of these hush-hush gentlemen had been in touch with the FFI (*Forces Françaises de l'Intérieur*) in still German-occupied Paris. (It would be the FFI which would begin the uprising before General Leclerc's Free French Second Armoured Division completed the liberation of the capital.) Why Royal Navy officers should have been in any way involved 100 miles inland I never discovered, although I would spend a night in November 1944 in a chateau just outside Paris commandeered by the RN, presumably for liaison with the French Navy.

When I arrived I was told Courseulles was shelled sporadically by an 11-inch gun mounted on a railway bogie miles along the coast. The Germans would trundle it out of a tunnel, fire a high-velocity shell and then shunt it back again, making it a very frustrating target. An officer in another tent woke up one morning to find a jagged piece of shrapnel beside his pillow.

At least with the 'Myra the Sniper' story there was some satisfaction in seeing the results of one's work in the press. There now followed a phase in which I was working not only on my own, without a photographer, but anything I wrote went into the limbo of censorland. Only later did I learn that a few of the stories had been released for publication and had appeared in print. Of the three services, RN censorship was the toughest and some disasters were kept secret for years such as the sinking in 1942 of our cruiser, the *Curaçao*, by the

Queen Mary, a liner turned troopship. This information was not released until May 1945.

Although the Allies had succeeded in getting their forces ashore, the struggle not only to prevent us being thrown back into the sea but to advance, with Germany being the far-distant goal, was to prove arduous and bloody. The Allied armies moving south and east would be dependent for the next five months on reinforcements of materials and men being landed on the Normandy coast. It was, therefore, top priority to protect the beachhead from seaborne enemy attacks by either E-boats, U-boats or more unconventional weapons against cross-Channel traffic. German intelligence would be on the alert for evidence of the effects of such attacks. This made the beachhead a highly sensitive area and the Press Division, or more precisely its censorship department, had to balance publicity for the Navy against the overriding criterion of security.

I expected the stories I sent to the Press Division about Hitler's latest 'secret' sea weapons would be blue-pencilled. But it was not for me to decide their sensitivity. My job was to report and when one day the security ban would be lifted, these stories could have a niche in the history of the Normandy beachhead. In any case, just then disclosures about unmanned explosive motorboats on the other side of the English Channel were hardly newsworthy compared with the terrifying unmanned aircraft. These were variously dubbed flying-bombs, buzz-bombs or doodle-bugs or given their actual German designation, V1s, which from 13 June 1944 to the end of March 1945 were dropping on the southern counties, 2,400 on London alone, at the rate of seventy a day in July and August. It was only disclosed after the war that they killed 6,200 people and injured 18,000 others. They would be followed in September by the V2 rockets, nine-tenths of which fell on London, which killed another 2,800 and seriously injured 6,500.

Nevertheless, had Hitler's secret weapons been as successful as he had hoped, with massive destruction of the shipping in the artificial Mulberry harbour and off the beaches, a serious setback could have been in store for the Allied armies.

The Germans had experimented, unsuccessfully, with human torpedoes off the Anzio beachhead in Italy in June. The first mass attack on the Normandy beachhead was launched eight weeks after D-Day on the night of 2 August. I wrote that, though the Germans had been using human torpedoes on their own in the Channel since 5 July (when nine were sunk) and on 8–9 July (when all twenty-one were destroyed), it was not until the night of 2 August that packs of them were launched supported by explosive motor boats (EMBs). To these the Germans gave the odd code-name *Linsen* (lentils). E-boats (equivalent to our MTBs or motor torpedo boats) were also present in order to divert attention from this attack by what I called these 'freak weapons'. Again it proved a fiasco and from the figures I obtained from the Flag Officer's staff, I listed their destruction: twenty-one human torpedoes definitely destroyed, three probably destroyed and eleven possibly sunk; thirty-two EMBs definitely destroyed, two probably destroyed and one possibly sunk; one E-boat destroyed and two badly damaged.

Our MTBs and MLs (Motor Launches) of Light Coastal Forces, the frigate HMS *Duff* and the minesweeper *Gateshead* accounted for most of the bag. But RAF Spitfires also claimed four definite kills and fourteen possible kills.

From descriptions given to me at the time, the 'lentils' were sixteen feet long, had a beam of six feet, a speed of 30 knots and a crew of two. They were driven close to and aimed at the ship to be attacked. A switch was then turned on and the crews would jump overboard and take to rubber dinghies.

Seventeen years later, Captain Roskill in *The War at Sea*, gave details slightly at variance with my description which was based on knowledge gained in the early stages of these attacks. He explained that for every two EMBs there was one control boat. As I have stated, the pilot in the EMB aimed it at its target and jumped overboard. But, according to Roskill, the pilot was supposed to be picked up by the control boat which then radio-controlled the lentil to the target. Moreover, he maintained that the 300-lb. explosive charge was in the stern and he made no mention of explosive bumpers around the bows, as described to me by those who tackled them.

According to this post-war information, during the 2–3 August raid, twenty EMBs with twelve control craft and fifty-eight one-man torpedoes were launched. The E-boats carried new long-range circling torpedoes. Forty one-man torpedoes [67] out of the fifty-eight were sunk and one captured intact. Only ten of the EMBs, that is half, returned to base. As far as the human torpedoes were concerned, the Flag Officer's total of thirty-five (twenty-one definitely sunk and fourteen 'possibles') is modest

---

[67] The Germans gave them the code-name *marder* (martens, the weasel-like animals with valuable fur) but they were also known as *negers* (negroes).

compared to Roskill's forty-one sunk. The FO's figures for the EMBs (thirty-two sunk and three 'possibles') apparently varies widely from Roskill's 'ten sunk', unless one adds the twelve 'control craft' which would bring his total sunk to twenty-two. As will be seen below, one witness alone claimed he actually saw seventeen destroyed.

From interrogation of captured crews (one of the interrogators at least worked the other side of my 'office' partition) we discovered that, except for the officers, the crew had no idea of the task that was expected of them until they had climbed aboard these explosive motor boats and were about to embark on the operation. They were trained in Germany, ostensibly for air-sea rescue. The address they were allowed to use in letters to their families was Air-Sea Rescue, Berlin. They travelled with their boats by road and rail from Germany via Paris to the launching port in Normandy, probably Le Havre or Dieppe. During the forty-eight hours in which the crews rested in a camp after their journey, unknown to them, explosive charges were placed in their craft. Just before zero hour they were told there was going to be a big attack on Allied shipping by human torpedoes and their task was to pick up survivors. Otherwise, they were to launch their craft at the biggest ship within range, turn a switch and jump overboard. That was the information gathered from captured crews and as retold to me.

Lieut T. H. Barker,[68] in peacetime a pharmacist in Hull, who commanded MTB 649, gave me this version of an encounter that night with two human torpedoes:

> My coxswain pointed to port and asked: 'What is that bow-wave, sir?' At first I thought he was seeing things but the next second I made out a human torpedo which became entirely invisible every time it plunged into a wave. We immediately went in pursuit and, running alongside, we tossed hand grenades at him. He was a tough customer and this method of attack didn't appear to shake him. About seven minutes later we sighted another one, haring for home. I had just put my cigarette to the fuse of a 5-lb. charge when the coxswain told me its occupant seemed to be struggling to remove the perspex cupola. But the fuse was already burning and, rather than blow myself up, I hurled the charge at the target. Luckily for the

---

[68] All officers in this chapter are RNVR (Royal Naval Volunteer Reserve) unless otherwise stated.

German, it fell just aft of his torpedo. Also badly shaken, he surrendered. He proved to be an officer who recovered sufficiently to tell us he was 'sick as Hell of the war'. But by the time we landed him he had become the typical truculent Nazi.'

I was able to inspect the captured *marten* Roskill had mentioned which lay for a few days on the beach, a perspex dome over the pilot's cockpit. It was then taken back to England.

ML 185 blew up two EMBs and captured two prisoners. This description of the action was given to me by Australian Lieut G. A. Ramsay, RANVR, a Sydney audit clerk before the war:

The after lookout reported a suspicious object crossing our stern. We turned the ship around to bring all guns to bear and, together with *Gateshead*, we pumped everything we had into it. After a few minutes of this it began to glow and rapidly grew into a fierce fire. It burned for a few minutes then blew up with a mighty roar, showering our ship with burning debris. We picked up one survivor who was nearly drowned. He wasn't a sailor but turned out to be an army corporal.

A few minutes later we opened fire with all our guns on another EMB. The gunners kept pressing the triggers until the target was blazing fiercely. It, too, blew up with a tremendous explosion, flinging debris high into the air. About half an hour later we came across a survivor screaming 'Kamerad! Kamerad!' and in a terrible panic. We had great difficulty fishing him out of the drink and my First Lieutenant had to go into the water to help him on board. He was an officer who told us his craft had a crew of two.

There were some hairy but abortive attempts to capture an explosive motorboat. A Hull fisherman, Lieut S. N. Orum was aboard ML 146 when one was spotted lying stopped about twenty yards away, undamaged. It had been abandoned for reasons that could only be guessed at. Orum thought it was an ideal opportunity to capture one for investigation by RN experts. He and the ML's first lieutenant paddled out to the EMB in a Carley float which was attached to the ML by a rope. They managed to get a heaving line around the EMB's rudder post, paddled cautiously back to the ML and, proceeding dead slow, towed it for fifteen minutes before the tow rope broke.

A second time they paddled out to the EMB, boarded her and shackled a wire strap to a ring-bolt in her deck. The EMB was being taken in tow a second time when the officers noticed their Carley float— the only means of getting back to the ML—had started to drift away. However, the ML risked coming close to the explosive motorboat and the First Lieutenant made a flying leap onto its deck. At this point the Carley float drifted alongside and Orum, grasping his prize with one arm, got his feet onto the boat and asked the ML's CO to pull it into the side of his craft. Orum then described his further efforts:

> I hung onto the EMB with all my strength. It was surprising how heavy she was. It seemed as if my arm would be pulled out of its socket as I stood on the Carley float between the ML and the EMB and slowly drew them together. The crew managed to pass me a rope and, getting back aboard the EMB, I made her secure. I then heard a regular purring sound coming from the cockpit, so I poked my head inside and managed to neutralise the self-exploding device. When I got back on board the ML we proceeded very cautiously to take her in tow once more. But fate was against us: the ring-bolt ripped out of the flimsy deck and the EMB started to sink by the stern until her bows were sticking perpendicularly out of the water.

Although he believed an explosive-packed bumper ran around the EMB's bows, for the third time that night Orum lowered himself over the side and, clutching the ML with one hand, with the other he pushed a rope around the rail on the bows of the EMB. But, while a seaman was trying to secure the other end of the rope with a boat-hook, the EMB gradually slipped beneath the surface and finally sank.

On the same night (2–3 August) another abandoned EMB was discovered by ML 131. This vessel held the record for operating off Normandy longer than any other of the Light Coastal Forces: for thirty-three days after D-Day the crew of this very small craft never went ashore. Later that night, after ML 131 had depth-charged a human torpedo, the red and green lights of the EMB were spotted. The CO, Lieut J. P. Fullerton from Ardrossan, also had to solve the problem of taking her in tow without blowing up his own craft. He told me:

> The sea was calm enough but that didn't prevent both of us bobbing up and down. Sure enough, while Number One (Lieut R. E. Greiner from Twickenham) was trying to secure her with a rope, we gave the bumper two rapid knocks. My heart jumped into my mouth but, thank goodness, she didn't explode.

Lieut Fullerton was the second officer to refer to an explosive bumper. Greiner carried on with the story:

> The captain first of all brought the ML around to the stern of the EMB and I managed to sling a rope over the standard of the red rear lamp. But it wasn't strong enough and was torn away. We stooged around looking for some other means of securing the EMB and that was when we bumped her. Finally, by leaning over the side, I managed to get the eye of the rope over a cleat on her deck and made her fast. Feeling as proud as peacocks, we began to tow her at a steady four knots. She followed like a lamb, shoving her nose well down into the water, probably because of the weight of the explosive.[69] We had travelled a fair distance when, without warning, there was a vivid flash, a terrific detonation and, amid clouds of black smoke, she disintegrated into a shower of debris. Only one of our crew received a superficial wound.

An LCF (flak) which witnessed seventeen EMBs destroyed in two hours during the 2–3 August attack picked up thirteen prisoners out of the sea. Lieut G. C. Carlton of Gerards Cross recalled how they were blowing whistles to draw attention to themselves in the water 'but were very arrogant once they were safely on board'. His craft had spent seventy-four days since D-Day within range of the German shore batteries and they were often shelled and bombed. But Carlton claimed his LCF's chief claim to fame was having shot down one of the German 'pick-a-back' aircraft.

> We rubbed our eyes when we saw it—but not for long. We opened up with our Oerlikons and pom-poms and brought it

---

[69] Greiner also evidently thought this was in the bow not the stern.

down with only a few bursts—a very cheap kill. It was the usual type: a Messerschmidt fighter on top of a Junkers 88 bomber.

A second mass attack by EMBs was launched against Allied shipping on the night of 8–9 August.[70] Caen had at last been taken a month before and on this particular night Polish and Canadian armour was battling against stiff resistance near St Sylvain, about five miles south-east of Caen. But the Germans still occupied the coast east of the mouth of the River Orne so that star shells from an artillery duel ashore lit up at least one action at sea that night involving our craft and EMBs. According to Lieut P. Vanneck RN, commanding HM Gunboat 696, which sank four of them in company with MTB 714 (Lieut Ian Lyall):

> The Army were putting up a wizard show on shore, exchanging salvoes with the Germans on our eastern flank. Starshells were hanging in the sky and, with the help of bright moonlight, we spotted a number of EMBs approaching. As a result of our combined efforts one of them blew up with a terrific crash and a vivid orange flash.

Two more were similarly despatched but the fourth had to be chased at full speed until she suddenly stopped and was caught in 714's searchlight. Vanneck explained: 'She looked long and white, like an Eskimo kayak. As she crossed our bows she was silhouetted against the moon. We gave her everything we had and left her a burning hulk.'

I had no idea what damage these 'freak weapons' had caused. After the war it was disclosed that we lost the destroyer *Quorn* and the trawler *Gairsay*. A landing craft and two transports were damaged in the 2–3 August mass attack by the *Linsen* explosive boats which were part of what the Germans called Small Battle Unit Flotilla 211 under a Lt Cdr Bastian. We sustained no losses in the 8–9 August attack. There was a further attack on either 15–16 August or 17–18 August (which I did not record) by forty-two one-man torpedoes of which only sixteen returned to their base. It was the last time they were used in Normandy. In spite of these heavy losses for comparatively little damage achieved, the Germans mounted similar attacks with similar results against the Allied landings in

---

[70] Roskill records that 16 *lentils* with 12 control craft had set out from near Honfleur; all of the former and four of the latter were destroyed.

the south of France in September and against our shipping in the Scheldt in March 1945.

~~

At least two of the Light Coastal Forces' officers had spoken, probably with justification, of the 'Nazi truculence' of men they had fished out of the drink. From my unofficial liaison with Naval and Royal Marine Commando PoW interrogators, I found corroboration of this but also an example of the 'pitfalls of oversimplification' which I mentioned in the last chapter. Nazi conditioning had been thorough and if there were doubts among some of Hitler's generals about the outcome of the war, there were still plenty of *Herrenvolk* fanatics, especially among the Hitler Youth incorporated into the services, who either still believed in the Führer's invincibility or deliberately dispelled any misgivings.

An example of someone who apparently fitted into this category was provided by one of the interrogators, red-bearded Lieut Brian Connell who, after the war, was presenter of ITV's *This Week* current affairs programme and later programme adviser for Anglia Television. Brian confided one day that he had just interrogated one of these prisoners for no less than eleven hours—keeping him standing for most of that time—before the man cracked and gave away the information we required. It was important to discover operational details about these 'secret' craft and what plans the Germans had for their future use.

On the other hand, there was the experience of Lieut David X who was a perfumery company's salesman before the war, operating mainly in Germany. He told me how his interrogating of a certain prisoner who was still on board one of our ships after a *marten* or lentil mass attack had become rather aggressive. As a Jew, Lieut X had every reason for finding it difficult to contain his impatience with what he perceived was the stubbornness of another specimen of the Nazi anti-Semitic assassins. His hectoring reached a certain point where the prisoner suddenly spat at him. Lieut X assumed that this was the prisoner's Nazi-conditioned reaction to being questioned by someone who appeared to fit his stereotyped perception of a Jew. The lieutenant's own reaction was spontaneous: he slapped the prisoner hard. The only effect was to make the man, if possible, even more recalcitrant, so the former salesman of seductive perfumes decided to change his approach: he would try sweet reasonableness. It worked. The German claimed he was not a Nazi and that if the lieutenant had treated him considerately from the beginning, the sooner he would have cooperated. Unfortunately for Lieut X, the slapping incident had been witnessed by a padre who must have reported it. In spite of the ultimate success of the interrogation, he was reprimanded.

I went on a night patrol in an MTB in the hope that I would see some action at first hand and report on how the crew performed. But though we went as far as the E-boat lair of Dieppe and hovered off the coast in the moonlight, no enemy in any shape picked up the gauntlet. Neither was there any correspondent in the offing needing my attention. It was time I looked further afield for stories.

~~

With the most powerful components of the German army in Normandy engaged by the British and Canadians in the east, the Americans under General Collins were able to clear the Cotentin Peninsula in the west and on 27 June capture the port of Cherbourg. This had been a major objective of *Overlord*, made even more important by the destruction of the American *Mulberry* artificial harbour by a five-day-long unseasonable gale which also damaged the British one. But unfortunately, before he surrendered, General ('Fight to the last bullet') von Schlieben was able to wreck the port facilities and mine and block the harbour. This was a considerable setback despite the prodigious quantities of men and materials that continued to be landed on the beaches. It would be late September before the port would be fully operational.

In the second week of August I decided I should pay Cherbourg a visit. Again, my stories never got past the censor. The frustration of war correspondents can be gauged from the comment in the *Daily Telegraph* that 'strict censorship bans discussion of the tasks undertaken to restore Cherbourg to maximum working order.'

I shared that frustration but sent my stories into the void notwithstanding. On 19 August I went aboard HMS *Esmeralda*, the first ship to sail directly from England into Cherbourg after its liberation. A veteran of mine-clearance operations, 50 per cent of the ship's company had been decorated including her CO, Lieut-Cdr C. D. Callieu, who had been awarded the DSC. With Petty Officer M. Aldridge BEM I shared experiences of Namsos: he had been aboard the sloop *Bittern* when it was bombed and sunk in the fjord. Two Australian officers had been awarded the George Cross and the George Medal and an incident in Cherbourg harbour involving a third Australian George Medallist, Lieut L. V. Goldsworthy, was described to me by Cdr Freedman Ashe Lincoln:

> I was standing on the *Esmeralda*'s upper deck when Lieut Goldsworthy who was on the seabed sent up a message by telephone that he had found a mine. He shackled a line onto it before he came to the surface to report that he estimated that it weighed about a ton. After clambering aboard and getting out of his diving suit he directed a crane on the quay to haul the mine up very gingerly until it was just beneath the surface. He then ordered it to be swung slowly away from the ship's side and from the quay and lowered to within a foot of the ground. When it had stopped revolving, it was lowered inch by inch onto the quay where Goldsworthy and Callieu rendered it safe—and I breathed freely again. But to these officers it was all in the day's work.

In fact, Ashe Lincoln himself (a barrister who would become a judge after the war) was no stranger to German underwater death-dealing devices. Since early in the war he had worked in the Directorate of Torpedoes and Mining (Investigation) working out, largely from deduction, the nature of the underwater weapons that had caused our vessels to sink, and whether there were characteristics they had in common. They then tried to recover specimens of the weapons themselves so that autopsies could be performed and antidotes developed. The dismantling was always a highly perilous undertaking because the Germans were continually developing new kinds of booby-traps and inevitably there were fatalities among the DTM (I) staff. This was Ashe Lincoln's 'speciality' which, he told me, he sometimes carried out on one of the little islands in the middle of the lake in London's St James's Park where he would not harm anybody but himself if they exploded. He did not mention this in his thrilling memoirs: *Secret Naval Investigator*. For his part in recovering one of the first magnetic mines, Ashe Lincoln was awarded the King's Commendation for Bravery. He was also mentioned in dispatches for his discovery and analysis of a new type of mine and he rendered safe the torpedoes of the first U-boat to be captured intact, which was recommissioned as HMS *Graph*.

~~

Without impugning any reputations, I can reveal that in Cherbourg I met several war correspondents, including the Marquess of Donegall, in a brothel—correction: *un ancien bordel*. The house had been taken over by the British as somewhere for war correspondents to work in, probably in all innocence despite the vivid floral wallpaper. Madame had allowed time for the officers to settle in, then had come around to inquire if she could provide the same facilities as the German officers had enjoyed. When this offer was somewhat brusquely rejected, Madame was indignant. She had had no complaints from the Wehrmacht officers, so surely? But the new occupants were adamant. Madame retired, uncomprehending. 'Ah, ces Anglais, ils sont incroyables!'

~~

Undue credit was given at the time to the spectacular American sweep into Brittany at the end of July and early August by General George ('Old Blood and Guts') Patton, the 'posturing general' as he has been called, considering most of it had been liberated by the Breton Resistance, the *maquisards*, to whom General Eisenhower himself paid tribute. Rennes fell on 3 August. I was there about ten days later on my way to the Brittany coast. The towns and villages were relatively unscathed compared with the depressing piles of rubble to which so many Normandy villages and towns I passed through had been reduced. For their inhabitants liberation had meant devastation which tended to blight enthusiasm for their liberators. Moreover, at that stage of the war, for all they could tell, the Allies might still be forced to do another Dunkirk. As my Royal Marine corporal drove our jeep westwards, the more frequently we received a friendly wave or were offered fruit by the locals. I was surprised and moved. The Bretons had not only been more recently liberated but must have seen thousands of German prisoners going in the reverse direction, a fairly reliable sign that liberation was for good. It was a pity that we had to spoil our reputation by running over a dog. At least I insisted we stop and the driver gave the poor beast the *coup de grâce* with a tyre lever.

In Rennes itself I had another reminder of Norway. Years later, I would regret having lost my note of the name of the gentleman drinking a *vin blanc* at a table outside a brasserie who, the moment he saw the ROYAL NAVY shoulder flash on my khaki battledress, greeted me in faultless English. He introduced himself as Capitaine … and was soon telling me that he had been the French naval attaché in Oslo before the war. He maintained he had been instrumental in informing his British opposite number of the position of the *Altmark* which had led to her being intercepted by Vian's *Cossack* and the subsequent release of the British Merchant Navy prisoners.[71] When I happened, some forty years later, to meet the family of our assistant press attaché in Oslo in 1940, there was no recollection of individual contacts with the French embassy in the normal diplomatic socialising. But if I had been able to recall the name of Monsieur le Capitaine it might have rung a bell and at least verified his presence there. He had returned to France, he went on to tell me, worked in the underground movement for four years and claimed he had carried out 'some very useful work for the Allies'. Now that France was in the process of being liberated he was looking forward to returning to his family and vineyards near Toulon and still hoped to get command of a French ship to continue the fight against the Germans.

What had conditions been like in Rennes during the occupation? Immediately after our adieux I noted his reply:

> The Gestapo ruled Rennes. They had a veritable garrison here. Their *Sicherheitsdienst* (Security Service HQ), as they called it, was in what used to be the students' quarters of the university. It was beautifully furnished but the Gestapo stripped it completely before they left, even taking away the carpets. Perhaps they were trying to cover up what went on there. People were continually being spirited away or openly shot. There were very few collaborators but, over there, you can see the offices of the *Croix de Feu*, the fascists.

Correspondents who were shown over the Gestapo headquarters shortly after Rennes was liberated described the torture weapons used against captured members of the Resistance, and interviewed a British medical orderly PoW who had tended two Frenchmen before they died from their Gestapo-inflicted beatings.

~~

I was sitting on a seat in a little square when an elderly gentleman, well-

---

[71] See p. 72

dressed in a light grey suit and Panama hat and carrying a cane, stopped in front of me, looked with interest at my battledress and naval cap and was overjoyed when he read the ROYAL NAVY flash. 'You are the very first Englishman I have met in over four years, the very first,' he emphasised. That was not surprising since Rennes was in the American Third Army zone. He had been working for British intelligence, he soon let me know. 'What another?' I was thinking. Was this just coincidence that the two men with whom I first conversed in this city should tell me of their clandestine connections with the British? My, perhaps not surprising, first reaction was to wonder how much was fact and how much, for reasons best known to themselves, was a wish to please. Then, on second thoughts, it seemed churlish to disbelieve, on no evidence either way, men who, if what they told me were true, had certainly run appalling risks. As early as September 1940 a man had been executed in Rennes for sabotage. It was generally known by 1944 that contact between Britain and the French underground had been established over the years and that the Resistance in Brittany during the recent Allied advance, sabotaging the railways and fighting pitched battles with the Germans (as Ian Ousby points out in *Occupation*), was testimony to its having been long organised.

Panama Hat introduced himself as Monsieur Legrand and even gave me his address in Paris: 49 rue Lacépède. I listened to his story: how his friends and fellow conspirators had been caught red-handed and how he himself, though the Germans could pin nothing definite on him, had been put in a concentration camp:

> The conditions were terrible. We lived on soup, ersatz coffee and black bread most of the time. Many became very ill and I contracted bronchial pneumonia. For some reason the German Kommandant took a liking to me—perhaps because of my age—and when my fellow prisoners were about to be sent to Smolensk he gave me the tip and I managed to escape. I have a brother in your Pioneer Corps in Egypt. His wife and family are in England. I am myself a refugee from Paris. My wife is still there. When do you think Paris will be liberated?

~~

Passing through the village of Dol on the way to St Malo, our jeep was hailed by a little group standing with their baggage and bundles at the side of the road. I told the driver to stop. They were refugees from St Malo and had been staying in Dol until it was safe to return. The RM corporal helped to sling their baggage aboard and they climbed in themselves: an old man in the washed-blue two-piece and peaked cap of a former generation of French peasantry, his wife in a black bonnet and white lace, and their married daughter.

Granny sat beside the driver; the rest of us sat on top of the baggage in the back of the roofless jeep and as we rolled along with many a jolt, Grandad, a seventy-three-year-old who was very lucky to be alive, related an extraordinary story. Every now and then his wife turned around and gave her hero an approving nod as he told how he had seen a German soldier maltreating a child in St Malo and got so indignant that, despite his age, he had intervened. The soldier merely laughed at him and when Grandfather had continued to protest, raised his fist to strike him. Still nimble and his fury lending him additional strength, he struck the soldier with the spade he was carrying. Perhaps taking his age into consideration and to make a show of leniency he was given thirteen months in a concentration camp instead of being shot as others had been who had allegedly struck German soldiers merely with their fists.

~~

When I got to St Malo, a peacetime seaside and yachting resort on the northern coast of Brittany, it was the worse for having been shelled for over a week. The Americans had entered the outskirts on 10 August but, in spite of the use of flamethrowers in the street fighting, it did not fall until 16th and they were still shelling the offshore Ile de Cézembre at the mouth of the River Rance.

There were several stories going the rounds about the 'fanatical' monocled Nazi commander, Colonel von Auloch, and the reasons why he was still holding out in a fort on this islet. Refugees from St Malo had claimed that he had refused to surrender when the town was being reduced to ruins out of spite because his wife and two children had been killed in a recent Allied raid on Berlin. Another rumour was that he had been informed by the German High Command that he would be relieved, was convinced the Germans had retaken Avranches and boasted that St Malo would become 'a little Stalingrad'. Indeed, Hitler, after dismissing General von Runstedt, ordered his successor General Gunther von Kluge to counterattack, which he did at Mortain on 7 August. This failed. Von Kluge got caught in the so-called Falaise Gap and lost 60,000 men, captured or killed.

The most bizarre of these von Auloch stories was that in order to induce him and his little island garrison to surrender he had been offered an escorted ride in an American jeep for a hundred miles in any direction to prove to him that the Allies were in control. Presumably this did not apply to the U-boat bases of Brest, which did not fall until 19 September, nor to Lorient and St Nazaire, which were bottled up but not liberated until the end of the war in Europe the following May. Part of the 'deal', so ran the rumour I heard, was that von Auloch could also spend the night with his alleged mistress in St Malo. There was confirmation of at least the first part from another source which maintained the Americans had indeed offered him safe conduct to travel around Avranches, Mortain, Domfront and Chartres and then to return him to St Malo Citadel just to show him that the Allies had occupied all these towns. The colonel (unlike in the version given to me) did not accept the offer but, after a further bombing raid, surrendered nevertheless. Whichever way it happened, when von Auloch did eventually surrender, he was heard shouting 'Heil Hitler!' to a group of officers among his 560 fellow PoWs.

On the way back to Normandy I stopped in the town of Vire, on the margin between the American and British sectors, one of the first towns to fall when the Allies' trap began to close around the Falaise pocket. In what I called a 'skeleton town', which was all that was left after the fighting had passed on, a cluster of about a dozen people poured out their tales of German atrocities during the Occupation. The curé's sister had lost her life in an air raid and the Germans had broken open her coffin to cut off her finger and steal her bejewelled gold ring. In another case, the people pointed to the spot in the road where a seven-year-old boy had been shot. These were just two of the legion of unverifiable stories that become local legend in occupied territories anywhere and in all ages and which certainly did in Occupied France. Again, as in Rennes, I wondered what was the motivation behind the gratuitous and unsolicited recounting of these stories to a British officer in transit through their town.

Further along that road back, we stopped to inspect a burned-out German tank. Lying on a caterpillar tread was a hand—detached, whole but black and calcified. That at any rate was indisputable evidence of the atrocity that is war.

~~

I would be a witness to a further example soon after my return to the British Assault Area headquarters. The Allies, while advancing eastwards, had for the most part by-passed the French Channel ports, leaving intact the garrisons which Hitler had ordered to hold out in the vain hope they would divert and pin down Allied forces. These ports would eventually capitulate to the Canadians. One of them was Le Havre which, from a cliff-top between Trouville and Honfleur on the southern jaw of the mouth of the Seine, I watched being bombarded by our warships and bombed by wave after wave of RAF bombers. It was 'an atrocity of war' in that there must have been hundreds of victims among the people we had come to liberate. Such was the destruction that most of Le Havre had to be rebuilt and today tourism brochures advertise it as 'France's only twentieth century city'. Neither then nor now could I judge whether bombardment on such a scale was necessary to destroy the concrete shelters used by E-boats.

After the war we would learn that the Germans' circling long-range torpedoes, which they had intended to use in combination with their explosive motorboat attacks, were put out of action. I was with my first naval war correspondent 'customer', George Edinger, commissioned to write a feature for the *News Chronicle*. A sensitive and compassionate journalist, George felt for those French civilians, as I did, as we watched dense black smoke rising from the town. It was the first urban air raid either of us had witnessed without ourselves being in the target area.[72] Though we had come to report the bombardment, we hit upon another story, again unverifiable. Local people maintained that in 1940 when the Nazis were planning Operation *Sealion*, the invasion of England, Austrian troops had been stationed in the area. German officers in command of an invasion rehearsal were apparently able to persuade these troops from a landlocked Central European state that the coastline they could see on the other side of the mouth of the Seine was England. They were not even told that this was only an exercise but believed that it was the invasion proper. Already unnerved by the

---

[72] I am uncertain of the date of this particular attack on Le Havre of which there were several between June and the capitulation of the German garrison on 12 September. These included, according to French sources, a 350 carpet-bombing raid by Lancasters in which a tunnel converted by the Germans into a civilian shelter was hit with over 320 killed and a bombardment by the monitor *Erebus* and the old battleship *Warspite* in which there were over 2,050 casualties.

unfamiliar boisterous seas, the Austrians, so the story went, had to be hyped up with some drug before embarking. Fact or fiction? It was evidently considered a good propaganda story, was passed by the Admiralty censors and actually appeared in at least one of the national dailies.

~~

It was an eerie sensation driving cautiously through the streets of Rouen strewn with rubble and the bloated corpses of horses, without the faintest idea of how close the enemy might be. This was the first of two occasions I would set out (with another jeep driver) to find the Royal Marines Fourth Special Service Brigade (as the RM Commandos, the 'Green Berets', were properly designated). All I knew was that they were fighting somewhere east of the Seine. My Press Division brief was to cover stories not only about Naval but also Royal Marine personnel.

Until he was wounded on D-Day+6, the flamboyant Brigadier Lord Lovat commanded the First Commando Brigade which consisted of elements drawn from nearly eighty regiments and corps including No. 45 Commando. The Brigade fulfilled its D-Day task: landing in the *Sword* sector to the east of Ouistreham, the port on the Caen Canal at the mouth of the River Orne, fighting its way inland and joining up with two glider and parachute brigades dropped overnight. Other RM commandos were in the Fourth Commando Brigade, consisting of Nos. 48 and 41 (which had suffered severely when it landed to the west of the First Brigade between Lion sur Mer and Courseulles), and No. 47 which also suffered losses through its craft striking mines further still to the west, between Arromanches and Port en Bessein.

The First Commando valiantly and effectively held the area east of the River Orne against German counterattacks. In spite of being decimated and without casualties being replaced, it was not reinforced by the Fourth Commando Brigade until D+5 and even then the First was not actually withdrawn from Normandy until it reached the Seine on D+83 (28 August), having lost 967 men killed, wounded or taken prisoner.

Lord Lovat would record in his memoirs [73] (referring specifically to No. 45 Commando before D-Day): 'They had not yet seen any enemy action. But those young Marines carried the traditions of the famous

---

[73] *March Past: A Memoir* (Weidenfeld & Nicholson).

Corps. If they lacked experience and cunning, they had done well enough in training and there was a fine discipline at every level.'

When I did eventually catch up with No. 45 Commando I was given graphic accounts of what had happened on D-Day and since. No. 45 was in the second flight of craft, half an hour after the first had landed on the beach just east of Ouistreham. This was the easternmost flank of the bridgehead where parachutists and glider-borne troops in an early morning assault had captured the Orne bridges and the commandos had to link up with them. When No. 45 were landing, the beaches were still being shelled and one of the LCIs received two direct hits. There was very stiff fighting inland as they fought their way across the canal and the river towards Franceville Plage. As a lifelong cycle-touring enthusiast I was particularly interested to learn that the commandos used bicycles as a means of transport but had found them awkward when they had to manhandle them over ditches. There was heavy fighting until the end of D-Day+2 when they had been without rest or food for thirty-six hours. This was when there had been the greatest number of casualties: 190 out of 450 men. They were billeted in a church for the night.

The brigade's Naval Roman Catholic chaplain, Father Costello, who had served in two Tribal destroyers, *Tartar* and *Eskimo,* explained how the commandos had only been equipped, mentally as well as logistically—for their initial task: to hold the bridgehead across the Orne with the airborne troops. They had become extremely tired after fighting for seventy days. Men had dozed off for seconds while marching and every man had a tale to tell of near-shaves from snipers' bullets. His own allotted task when in action, said Costello, was to make for the nearest casualty clearing point and minister to the wounded. He was regarded by the men as a general factotum who would lend a sympathetic ear to their needs, however trivial. At the village of Dozulé, for instance, he had been asked to look after a puppy which had been left behind by the Germans. At Sallenelles he had held a mass only 200 yards from where the Germans were mortaring and shelling. This was inside a battered church, in one of its walls a gaping hole. He had gathered his 'congregation' in a corner which seemed to give a little more protection but the shelling had got too hot and they had to make a dash for a slit trench. 'That', said Father Costello, 'gave me quite a kick.'

The seventy days had expanded and these 'one task' Royal Marine Commandos had crossed another four rivers after the Orne, the Dives, Toucques, Risle and now the Seine, and they were still in Normandy after ninety days. But once they had crossed the Seine, as their CO, Brigadier B. W. Leicester, RM, put it, they had little with which to contend except 'a battle of flowers' with the grateful Seine-Maritimers.

~~

My first attempt to find these Fourth Brigade commandos was made at the beginning of September. With my Royal Marine driver I got as far as this almost deserted city of Rouen without knowing that it had only been captured by the commandos on 30 August, but there were no signs of its liberators. It was already late afternoon. I decided that to go on looking for the Green Berets, even if it were possible to cross the Seine—all the bridges we had seen so far had been destroyed—without knowing their location or even the whereabouts of the Germans would be folly. So we drove what was not far short (with diversions) of the hundred miles back to Courseulles.

Having made this preliminary reccy, I invited my second 'customer', Jimmy Southcott of the London *Evening Star* newspaper, to accompany me the following morning on my search for the Green Berets. I explained we might be going on a wild goose chase and there was even the possibility of capture. Jimmy, a veteran of the First World War, treated the prospect lightly.

When we got to Rouen my fear that all the bridges had been bombed by the Allies or demolished by the retreating Germans seemed to be confirmed. However, there was a railway bridge to the south of the city in a suburb called Sotteville which presented possibilities. Though the middle of it was sagging into the Seine, the railway lines—still attached to sleepers, were bridging the gap a few feet above the water. Regarding this as a challenge to the ingenuity and resourcefulness of the Royal Corps, our redoubtable driver decided: 'Let's have a go, sir!' and go we did, the jeep being metamorphosed into a locomotive, albeit with not quite the right gauge. We jolted over the first part of the inclining tracks, slowing down when we got to the middle. I offered up a silent prayer for the blessing of Niagara Falls tightrope walker Blondin as we bumped over the swaying sleepers with nothing but the flowing water beneath us. The jeep seemed to take an interminable time covering those few yards of metal and wood before it revved up to mount the other half of the bridge and emerge triumphantly onto the other side. As imperturbable as a London cabby, our driver showed no alteration of expression.

Leaving Rouen, we pointed the jeep sharp north-west, keeping the looping Seine away on our left and assuming from our scant information that the Green Berets were making for the coast. We had no radio in the jeep and I doubt whether we were aware during our cross-country meanderings of the up-to-date details of the lightning advance of the Allies after the German débâcle at Falaise. Montgomery's British and Canadians had taken Amiens, due north of Paris (itself liberated on 2 August) the day after Rouen had fallen; Brussels was next, on 3 September, and Antwerp the day after. It was these Channel coastal pockets that had still to be mopped up and our destination must have been somewhere between Le Havre and Dieppe.

There now began for us the same welcoming experiences the victorious Marines had already enjoyed, a hundred times more deservedly, when passing through territory they had liberated and which was unscarred. I felt something of an impostor as a non-combatant who wielded nothing more liberating than a pen and in the uniform of a service which did not normally operate on land. These Seine Maritime Normans ran into the road in the villages and even between them to greet us with smiles and sometimes with tears, slowing down or actually stopping us to embrace or offer us apples, camembert, cider or flowers. 'R ... o ... y ... a ... l ...e ... N ... a ... v ... e ...e ... ' they would pronounce slowly as they deciphered my shoulder flash and there would be more hugging and back-slapping. At one little hamlet a man who said he was a ship's chandler in Fécamp produced a bottle of Bénédictine and we drank a toast to *La France libérée*. In one place a young woman, her eyes brimming with tears, brought me her baby insisting I should kiss 'it'. 'My father was Irish. We have been waiting so long, so very long,' she sobbed.

~~

I had already noted the different reactions to liberation in areas from which the enemy had been expelled weeks before. Now, in the next few days, I would be struck by the varied, even contrasting, emotional responses of those to whom liberation had happened only a few hours previously: elation and sorrow; gratitude and resentment; euphoria and dread.

A Royal Marine drum major gave me a graphic example of these contrasts when we finally caught up with the Green Berets at Yvetot, a town about twenty miles south-east of Fécamp. Two officers and fifteen men from each commando in the Fourth Brigade had taken part in the march-past in Paris after its liberation less than a week before. Drum Major Thomas Cooke from Brighton gave me two instances of the different ways the same piece of music had affected different people.

> As we marched down the Place de la Concorde we played *Tipperary*. The Parisians were wildly excited and sang with gusto the old 1914–18 song their fathers had learned from the Tommies. The following night we played to the people of Caen, a city of ruins where the civilians must have had a terrible time. Tipperary was one of the pieces which were part of a pot pourri we played and I had expected the people of Caen to join in just as the Parisians had done. But they didn't sing. When they heard the first few bars, men and women wept instead. Being the drummer, I was at the back of the band and the crowd was close around me. One elderly woman actually leant her head on my shoulder, tears streaming down her face.

Strolling through Yvetot after interviewing the Marines we met *Monsieur le Directeur de l'École,* Henri Cahan, who insisted we should come home with him. But the headteacher wanted to show us something first. He took us to a crossroads almost at the gate of his house and pointed to a splodge of dried blood on the gravel. He explained:

> This morning a German motorcycle despatch rider screeched to a halt just here, his engines still running, and shouted to me: 'Which way to Caudebec?' I shook my head. Caudebec is only the next village a few kilometres down the road but I wasn't going to tell him and I began to turn away. He swung his gun around at me. Whether he intended to shoot or merely to threaten me I'll never know for the next moment there was a burst of automatic fire and he collapsed, his motorbike on top of him. The FFI had shot him. Boche he might be but we gave him a decent burial.

The *Forces Françaises de l'Intérieur* were an amalgamation of various resistance movements which had grown, gradually at first after the initial shocks of the Occupation and Pétain-Laval collaboration with the conquerors, into a figure one estimate put at 30,000 in 1944. This swiftly swelled after an Allied victory seemed certain. When the BBC gave the 'mobilise' signal it was reckoned some 200,000 troops were raised, their arms supplied largely by Allied airdrops.

Inside *chez* Cahan, Jimmy Southcott, our RM driver and I were introduced to his wife and family. Neighbours began to come in, too. When his wife started setting the wine glasses on the table, *Monsieur le Directeur de l'École* held up a restraining hand. 'Wait', he said. He had a surprise for which different glasses would be needed. He went out of the room and came back with a pair of stepladders, placed them alongside a wall cupboard, climbed up and opened a pair of doors at the top. He rummaged inside for a while, then: 'Eureka!' he exclaimed and descended gingerly with a couple of small dark brown bottles with labels which even at a distance seemed familiar. He announced triumphantly: 'I have kept these for four years. They were in the stores your Army left behind at St Valéry in 1940. I got there before the Germans took everything away and vowed to keep these until you came back again. *Et voilà!*'

With that, off came the metal caps of the bottles and he poured the four-year old Guinness into our glasses. If it had retained its head it would have qualified for the Guinness Book of Records; if it had been like vinegar, we would have still drunk it to show our appreciation of such faith in our return, such optimism conceived in France's darkest hour. A considerable proportion of his compatriots, however, had for a long time regarded Britain as the traditional *Albion perfide* responsible for the *pagaille* in which they found themselves and who had then 'abandoned' them.

Henri Cahan proved a past-master of ceremonies, with a nice feeling for the dramatic. Out came another bottle which had been kept for such a day, a rare old port. The ancient gramophone was cranked up and as we drank to *La France libérée* the four-note motto theme with which Beethoven's Fifth Symphony opens crashed out full volume, its notes escaping freely through the open windows into the street. This was the most significant illustration which anybody could have devised in the circumstances that this portion of France, at least, was free from the detested Nazi yoke and that the rest soon would be. Had this schoolmaster been brooding for years on just how such a day should be celebrated? As every wartime adult knows, in Britain and on the Continent, that four-note motto corresponded to the three short dots and a dash of the Morse code's letter V—and V stood for Victory. The repeated: Boom ... boom ... boom ... BOOM call-sign preceded the BBC's broadcasts to Nazi-occupied Europe. Those who dared to tune-in had to keep the volume to a barely audible minimum in case collaborators, the police or the Germans themselves heard it. That would mean a visit from the Gestapo or their French stooges, with some kind of hell to follow. Hence the significance of it now being played full blast.

When the glasses had been refilled, *Tipperary* came into its own again, a song of a vintage even older than the port. It had been top of the pops over a quarter of a century before. Now its nostalgia was transferred from a British Tommy yearning to get away from France back to the sweetest girl he knew, to these people around the table who had been longing to be freed from a foreign tyranny. They, and the millions who had been singing it down the years, were unconscious of the irony that Tommy, for all his yearning for his colleen in Tipperary, had probably been engaged (or at least some of his comrades must have been) in the bloody suppression of an attempt by her country to win its independence: the Dublin rising of Easter 1916. To these French people and all like them, *Tipperary* represented the dual association with their anti-Boches ally of 1914–18 and anti-Nazi ally of the current war.

~~

That night, in a Rembrandtesque setting, I was witness to how the two liberators in this area, the FFI and the British, met to discuss mutual assistance. M. Cahan's school was like the rest of Yvetot, without electric light. In one corner of a large room candles had been placed on a table. Under the flickering light, Brigadier Leicester and his Green Beret officers stooped over a map, together with members of the FFI who were pointing out enemy locations and planning when and where they should be attacked. The immediate objective was the fishing port of Fécamp. I slept on the schoolroom floor that night.

In the morning, I noticed considerable activity in the streets leading to *la mairie*. I was informed that there were nearly ninety women inside the town hall but that the number was not quite complete for the next act in a drama that was taking place all over liberated France but of which I was unaware. From the open door I could just see them sitting facing each other on two long benches. These, it was explained to me, were the *collabos horizontales*, the ladies of Yvetot who had shared their beds with the Germans, at some time or regularly, during the last four years. They were awaiting punishment for this fall from grace: their heads would be shaved.

The temptation to 'collaborate' in this way must have been very strong, and for some evidently irresistible, with so many of their countrymen absent. There were two million PoWs in 1940 and in 1942 there were still 1,500,000. With Laval's 'relief' bargain with the Germans, the exchange of PoWs for volunteer labour, thousands of men went to Germany. This was inevitably followed in 1943 by forced labour so that in 1944 there were hundreds of thousands of Frenchmen either in Germany or building the 'Atlantic Wall' for the Todt Organisation. Nevertheless, these women must have been resented, scorned and even hated by others with a political, civic or patriotic conscience which imposed its own discipline, who found it impossible to treat the Germans in any other way than as conquerors of their country. A hundred women in a small town like Yvetot having allegedly 'collaborated' was quite a high proportion who were not all that discriminating.

This human dilemma was sensitively portrayed by Vercors, the pseudonym used by Jean Bruller, in his novel *Le Silence de la Mer* where there is mutual attraction between a young German officer billeted on a Normandy family and his host's daughter. But the young woman, fully aware of the Nazis' record, maintains an unexceptionable silence in the presence of the officer. Notwithstanding this continual rebuff, he keeps talking to her and is forced by her very silence to expose his innermost thoughts. When it appeared in 1942 it was the first major French clandestine novel. I had read it and been impressed with the stoicism of the French girl. I doubt if I spared a thought for the temptation consequent on the absence of French menfolk and certainly had no knowledge of the scale of it. My oversimplification of the problem did not allow for much sympathy for these victims of the barbers' clippers. Their hair would grow again, the millions of the Nazis' victims—it was only a fortnight before British newspapers would carry accounts of the extermination ovens at Maidenik in Poland—had no heads or bodies left on which hair could grow.

~~~

From the little town of Cany Barville to Fécamp the country road was thronged with peasant families who must have come miles to give the Green Berets an emotional welcome. We could see some of them who had not got to the road in time, waving and running towards us from afar across the fields. At some point progress was held up as the commandos were bombarded with dahlias and chrysanthemums, mobbed and kissed. Although we were in the rear we had our share of all this euphoria and, as before, I felt I was undeservedly basking in it. I countered with an attempt at rationalisation: even if I had not fought with the commandos along the hundred miles from the beachhead and suffered their grief for fallen comrades, nevertheless, in the previous four years I had added my grain of war effort, culminating in this day's liberation of the countryside I could see around me. So, why not enjoy the welcome without reservations?

Besides, I had another, very personal reason to be elated: by coincidence I was about to participate in the liberation of the only town in France that I had been in prior to D-Day. As an eight-year-old I had spent a holiday in Fécamp with my parents but had never again visited our neighbours across La Manche. I was looking forward to seeing the abbey, La Trinité, and checking on why my child's awe of its enormous nave had left such a lasting impression. It is one of the longest in France, only just short of that in Notre-Dame, Paris. And would the footprint in stone still be there, claimed to be that of the angel Gabriel? Or the ruined tower opposite the abbey where my father had laid his five foot ten full length in an embrasure to demonstrate the thickness of the twelfth-century wall? Or the Bénédictine 'monastery', actually a distillery which produced the famous sweet, amber liqueur and where I remembered a room where the walls were covered by hundreds of bottles with counterfeit 'Bénédictine' labels?

The further we got into Fécamp itself, the slower the progress. There was small-arms fire ahead and within a few more minutes our jeep was completely jammed behind troops and trucks in a narrow street. We happened to be outside a butcher's and this worthy insisted we park our jeep in his yard, that we should come in and meet his family and, of course, celebrate *La Libération*.

So, once again, as in Yvetot, little Jimmy Southcott was sitting at one end of a table, this time in a room gleaming with copper pots and pans and thronged with exulting Normans. Our halting French matched the even scantier English of our hosts and produced banalities which didn't matter a damn because it was only the spirit in which they were expressed that counted. Not only did the wine flow, but in no time a splendid dinner was conjured up. What better luck could have befallen us than that our jeep had got snarled up outside a butcher's? Never did beef taste so succulent. It was a joyous and unforgettable occasion.

It was not so joyous, however, for some others of Fécamp's inhabitants. Replete, we dragged ourselves away from our hospitable hosts and since progress was now possible we drove through streets where sobbing women clutching scarves over their invisibly bald heads were running the gauntlet of their fellow citizens' curses and ribaldry.

Some of the shooting we had heard may not necessarily have been an exchange of fire between the commandos and remnants of the Wehrmacht. More likely it was the FFI meting out retribution to collaborators. One German they made sure did not get away and summarily shot was the Gestapo chief. He had ordered punishments for the people who had dared to place a flag on the graves of British soldiers who had fallen during the 1940 evacuation. The people of Fécamp had persisted in putting flowers on these graves which were now carpeted in blooms.

We made our way to the central square, the Place Thiers, where the crowd were singing what I had by now come to realise was for the French our national anthem: *Tipperary, mais évidemment*! When the last echoes had died away, the mayor appeared on the balcony of the *mairie* and in well-phrased English addressed the Royal Marines below. He expressed the gratitude his townspeople felt not only for the progressive liberation that had begun on 6 June and now at last had reached Fécamp, but also for the sacrifices British soldiers had made in 1940 and to which their graves testified.

~~

The next day I wandered around on my own trying to locate landmarks I remembered from my boyhood visit: Madame Wariquet's *pension* (no luck there); the café where I had been allowed a few sips of *vin blanc et fraises* (also just a memory); but, yes, the abbey was there, solid and unscathed, and of course the Bénédictine distillery. The docks, too, were recognisable. I went further afield and inspected how the Germans had fortified this part of the Atlantic Wall, an unlikely choice for an invasion from the sea since Fécamp snuggles between high cliffs. I presumed the FFI had already inspected this recently-vacated dugout system but, in retrospect, I was acting in foolhardy oblivion of possible booby-traps. My snooping netted a number of photographs which the troops had left behind. Some of these were of wives and children, some of girlfriends, whether German or French who could tell? More interesting were those that showed a crowd of Wehrmacht and naval top brass, one of them giving the Nazi salute, on a Fécamp quay alongside a vessel on which other soldiers were standing. It was presumably a high-level inspection. In another it looked as if a steel-helmeted soldier was searching a handcart as a woman, its owner probably, watched him. In other snaps, three *Feldgendarmerie* were posing, sitting on a parapet wall in their polished knee-high boots and carrying gloves. There were eagle emblems and swastikas on their uniforms. Is it the same three who appeared at a distance in the background on Fécamp's pebbly beach on which sat two girls, one attractive but looking at the picture-snapper unsmiling and her companion covering her face with her hand? There were also pictures of Cologne cathedral and panorama shots of the city, possibly a clue as to where these military police hailed from.

Other photographs showed a cemetery with hundreds of identical white tombstones—obviously war graves and presumably British or French. There were wrecks of RAF planes, one burning in a field; another with German soldiers or airmen posing in its cockpit. A third which had crashed on the edge of the sea is swarming with soldiers inspecting it. In yet another picture, a corpse lay spread-eagled, lapped by the surf where it had been washed up, only a skull and the bones of a hand visible protruding from a uniform—another British airman? These must have been propaganda pictures to impress the vanquished.

~~

After four days with the Green Berets it was time to leave Fécamp, but not before there occurred one of those deaths that seem all the more tragic because they happen not in the heat of action but haphazardly, when no enemy is active within miles: a Naval lieutenant in a jeep was blown up on a mine by a road just outside the town.

On the outskirts our jeep was hailed by a couple of Tommies with their new French girlfriends. They wanted a lift to the next village and I told them to hop on board. They sat, perched up at the back, singing merrily. A little further on, we were stopped by a British Army officer, probably a colonel, certainly of higher rank than mine, who wanted to know: 'What the Hell is going on here? This is the worst case of a breakdown in discipline I've seen since D-Day. As an officer you should know better. Good thing you're in another service!' Indeed, and I adhered to its silent reputation. The soldiers and their friends jumped out smartly, which saved me from attempting to answer the unanswerable and we drove on.

Lest I give further encouragement to our licentious soldiery, it was evidently time I left France.

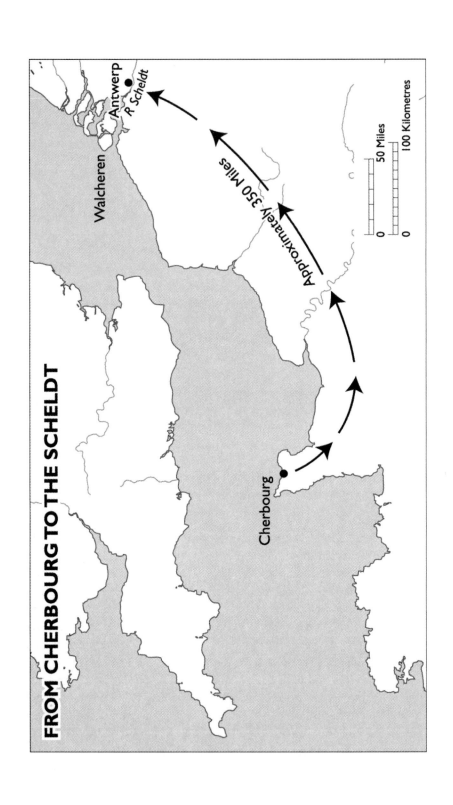

FROM CHERBOURG TO THE SCHELDT

Walcheren

Antwerp

R Scheldt

Approximately 350 Miles

Cherbourg

50 Miles

100 Kilometres

0

0

Chapter 12

A Costly Assault

The cannons have their bowels full of wrath,
And ready mounted are they to spit forth
Their iron indignation

King John Act II Sc. 1: William Shakespeare

The assault on Walcheren will stand for all time as one of the finest episodes
in the long history of the Royal Marines.

The War At Sea: Captain Stephen Roskill DSC, RN

Adieu France! But it was only au revoir to the Green Berets who were again the principal component in my next assignment: the most crucial combined operation since the Normandy landings. It was, of course, hush-hush. The naval war correspondents were usually tolerant and good-humoured about Admiralty smoke screens, realising that thousands of men's lives were at stake if the enemy gathered foreknowledge of impending operations. But sometimes they did find the going hard and patience wore thin.

Towards the end of October 1944, after a lull in naval activities, the correspondents were suddenly told to be at the Admiralty with their razors and toothbrushes at what was, for them, an unearthly hour in the morning. I had been ordered by Cdr Dillon-Robinson to be their PRO, although I was given no clue myself as to what was up. I recall we were brought by coach to a dockyard, where I ran around like a blue-arsed fly trying to find the various craft to which the correspondents had been assigned, while they hung about in the bleak, inhospitable docks. Then I was told it was postponed 'because of fog'. I conveyed Dillon-Robinson's profuse apologies, re-embarked in the coach and landed up in the evening at Manston RAF aerodrome. After dinner, as hearty types with Wing-Co Kite moustaches lubricated their guests, speculation as to the ultimate objective of this operation became more bizarre as the night wore on.

The next morning, fortified by a good breakfast against the sobering chill of a raw autumn morning in this bleak Kent airfield, we set off in our coach, reasonably optimistic that we were getting somewhere at last. And so it seemed as far as Dover. But there we stopped. We sat, seemingly interminably, the correspondents nursing their impatience: I my embarrassment.

A pre-war colleague, 'Binks' Hartin of the *Daily Mail*, in his late forties, gravel-voiced and with a rather prominent Adam's apple, came up with, if not our destination, at least with what he claimed was its code-name. As if he were to let us into a piece of information he alone had been able to ferret out of the Admiralty, he declared: 'The code-name for this lark is Operation *DRAINFU*.'

There was a moment's silence while his colleagues cogitated over this word. Fish or fowl? Someone, less ashamed at showing his ignorance, asked: 'Drainfu, what the Hell's that?'

'Yes, DRAINFU, I assure you that's what it's called,' Binks replied, nodding sagely.

'But what is a drainfu, old boy?' pursued his questioner.
Binks relented to the extent of giving them a clue: 'It's an acronym, old boy.'

But even the crossword enthusiasts were stumped. 'We give up. Do you know yourself what it stands for?'

'Of course.'

'Then spill it for God's sake, old man. We can't stand the strain.'
Binks complied, first pronouncing each letter: 'D R A I N F U stands for Dillon-Robinson's Aimless Inevitable Naval Fuck-Up,' which was greeted with a chorus of good-humoured groans. Although I was the butt by proxy of this witticism, I was glad of the timely light relief. Everyone, including Binks, knew that the weather was to blame and that the hiccups with which this venture had started had nothing to do with the genial commander. Nor did Binks and the others know that behind Dillon-

Robinson's bonhomie there was a rather sad story. Having sailed through the usual RN channels, Osborne and Dartmouth colleges, to becoming an officer, he became a lieutenant, only to be invalided out because of an eyesight problem. For someone devoted to the service this was a cruel blow for which becoming a hop merchant hardly compensated. As his son would tell me one day, Dillon-Robinson was 'no lover of war but being called back was no hardship. It was with a certain amount of sorrow that he was forced to leave again in 1946.'

The actual code-name of the operation, which we would eventually learn was *Infatuate*, was almost as obscure as Binks's fictitious one. We all know what the adjective 'fatuous' means and that 'infatuated' can be a synonym for unrequited love. But the transitive verb to 'infatuate'? That's not exactly in everyday use, especially the meaning my dictionary gives it: 'To affect with extreme folly'. Even if the simpler 'to make foolish or fatuous' was intended to apply to the enemy, Operation *Infatuate* was not very appropriate and the price would be a heavy one, as it had been for our forefathers 135 years before, as we shall see.

~~

I have mentioned earlier that the main thrust of the British and Canadians had reached Antwerp, Belgium, on 4 September, only a day or two after we had been in Fécamp. Unlike at Cherbourg, the Germans were so taken by surprise by the swiftness of the Allied advance, a 250-mile dash by the 11th Armoured Division in five days, that they had no time to demolish the port's installations. This was also due in no small measure to the initiative, resourcefulness and courage of a member of the local Resistance, a civil engineer named Robert Vekemans who managed to discover the Germans' intention to sink five block ships in the harbour. How he managed to contact the British vanguard before they entered the city, showed them how to outwit the Germans and get across the River Scheldt and race through the city to the docks to capture the port intact, was told in the *Guardian* twenty-five years later by its editor, Alastair Hetherington, who had been an officer in the 11th Armoured Division.[74]

I marvelled at the continuous flow of military traffic on the main roads of Northern France. The distances to be covered from Cherbourg lengthened so that by the time the Allies pushed beyond the frontiers of

---

[74] And re-told in Mark-Arnold Foster's *The World At War* (Collins).

France, these arteries supplying the armies' life-blood were stretching for 350 miles. But how much further could the armies advance without a closer source of supply?

The controversy would rage over whether the war would have been shortened if Montgomery had had his way, delivered a left hook with the weight of forty divisions, been able to seize the Ruhr before the winter set in and press on to Berlin. He would always hold firmly to this contention and no doubt it will always have its supporters. So will Eisenhower who, as the Supreme Commander, was able to insist on the adoption of a more cautious strategy, one influenced by fears of the entire advance grinding to a halt if it outran its supplies: the so-called 'advance on a broad front'. Montgomery would scathingly call it 'not an advance on the Rhine on a broad front' but 'on several fronts which were uncoordinated.'

Whatever the long-term merits or drawbacks of these two views, one thing is certain: the Germans took advantage of the fact that it was nearly two months after the capture of Antwerp that attacks were launched to clear the mouth of the River Scheldt, eighty miles away. Montgomery waited ten days before declaring the Canadian Army's first priority to be the clearing of the Germans from the mouth of the river 'to enable full use to be made of the port'. But, with Eisenhower's approval, this was deferred in favour of trying to force the Rhine, including the valiant but abortive attempt to capture Arnhem: the *Bridge Too Far*.

Field Marshal von Runstedt, whom Hitler had reinstated as Commander-in-Chief in place of Model (he committed suicide after the surrender of 320,000 of his troops in the Ruhr), ordered the 80,000 troops trapped in the Pas de Calais to be evacuated by sea across the Scheldt to the island of Walcheren. They could then make a further escape across the causeway linking Walcheren to South Beveland and thence across the isthmus to the Dutch mainland. Runstedt, like Eisenhower, thought Montgomery had reached the end of his supply line.

Yet as late as 5 October, a month and a day after the capture of Antwerp, Montgomery was maintaining that he could take the Ruhr without making use of the port. Eisenhower thought otherwise:

> Until the approaches to the port (Antwerp) were cleared, it was of no value to us. Because the Germans were firmly dug in on the islands of South Beveland and Walcheren, this was going to be a tough and time-consuming operation. The sooner we could set about it the better.

Peter Calvocoressi in *Total War* deals with the differences between the views of Montgomery and Eisenhower and their political motivations. He mentions the capture of Antwerp (without saying the port facilities were intact) and passes onto a detailed description of the Arnhem failure and the Ardennes Battle of the Bulge. What seems extraordinary is that no attention is drawn to the potential logistical value of the capture of Antwerp and there is absolutely no mention of the Walcheren assault to clear the mouth of the Scheldt to exploit this.

On 1 October Eisenhower approved a plan for the bombing of the Walcheren dykes as a preliminary to seaborne landings. At last, on 16 October, the newly-promoted Field Marshal Montgomery once more agreed to give priority to the clearing of the Scheldt mouth—something the Navy had long been pressing for.

The Germans were not only in occupation of the island of Walcheren (Flushing is on its south side) but also the town of Breskens opposite, on the south bank of the West Scheldt. They completely dominated the mouth of the river. They had flooded large parts of the area, which made it very tough going for the Canadians who did not capture Breskens until 22 October and then South Beveland on the 30th and North Beveland on the 31st.

~~

There was a historical precedent for the delay in launching Operation *Infatuate*. As a diversion to help the Austrians' valiant but forlorn attempts to throw off the yoke of Napoleon and after their defeat at Wagram in 1809, what has been described as the largest force that had ever sailed from English harbours—40,000 soldiers in nearly a hundred ships—landed on Walcheren at the end of July after a four months' delay. Although Walcheren and South Beveland were taken, as well as Flushing after a siege and sea bombardment, the French under Marshal Bernadotte heavily fortified the Scheldt approaches to Antwerp and withdrew their fleet up river out of harm's way. While the commanders argued about what to do next, the French let Walcheren's swamp fever take a devastating toll of the British forces, and the survivors withdrew in December. Historian H. W. Wilson summed it up: 'The failure was due to friction between the Army and Navy, the selection of an incompetent general and the despatch of the force at the wrong season of the year.'

It was not until the correspondents had been put on their respective vessels that I reverted to my Official Naval Reporter role, crossed the Channel in an MTB and in Ostend was at last put in the picture. Now I learned that this was Operation *Infatuate* and the aim was to clear the mouth of the Scheldt so that the port facilities of Antwerp could be used by the Allies. The source of the information was a briefing, complete with blackboard, at which details were given by the same Brigadier 'Jumbo' Leicester whom I had last seen talking to the French Resistance by candlelight in Yvetot. Since Fécamp, 41, 47 and 48 Royal Marine Commandos under his command had taken Le Havre and had been withdrawn from the siege of Dunkirk to prepare this operation.

We were told that the Army, despite the difficulties of the flooding of the countryside and stiff resistance by the Germans, had reached the causeway linking Walcheren to South Beveland. Our task was to land the Green Berets at Westkapelle on the west or seaward side. The Army, meanwhile, was to attack Flushing on the south of Walcheren where its artillery would support the landings. The landing craft in which the Marines were to make their assault and the rocket (LCRs) and gun (LCGs) craft covering it were under the command of Cdr K. A. Sellar RN.

~~

On receiving my own sailing orders for *Infatuate* I learned that this time I would not be making any beach landing. I was to have a view of the assault on Westkapelle from the stalls: the bridge of an LCH (Landing Craft Headquarters).

We sailed from Ostend overnight on the last day of the month and, from early on the morning of 1 November 1944, I got the impression that everything was not going according to the plan outlined at the Ostend briefing. With the Army attacking Flushing, the Germans were of course on the alert and the powerful Westkapelle batteries had not been silenced. According to Roskill, there were 'no less than sixteen batteries, mounting between them forty guns, 3-inch to 8.7-inch.' Far too many shells were scoring on our invading armada or sending fountains of water high into the air.

As the batteries seemed to be getting the range of our LCH, which, as its name and amount of communications equipment signified, had a directing and not a front-line role, our CO remarked in the tone of someone saying 'Please pass the sugar' at a vicarage tea party: 'I think we should perhaps move out a teaspoonful,' a view with which Commander R. E. D. Ryder VC, RN,[75] standing beside him, concurred. The appropriate orders were given and we took a turn about to put us out of range. In reality, nothing could have been further removed from the atmosphere of a tea party than the vicissitudes of this operation at that moment. Ryder's stern, weathered features reflected the gravity of the situation: unless the German guns could be silenced they would play havoc with any attempted landing by the Royal Marine Commandos. By this time, the air strike should have taken place but had evidently been held up by the low cloud ceiling. It also seemed an inordinate length of time before the 'heavies' began hurling their 15-inch shells towards the batteries. These were the ancient monitors—themselves floating batteries—*Erebus* and *Lord Roberts,* and the veteran battleship *Warspite*, who was firing her guns in anger for the last time before her final decommissioning. When at last, around 9 a.m., their bombardment bellowed from afar astern of us, although it might have been more accurate if the weather had permitted spotter planes to liaise with the gun-layers, it did seem devastating: a curtain of black smoke tinged with brown hung over the shore, witness to the inferno beneath.

The weather improved enough for the RAF to follow up the Naval bombardment with its own strafing of the shore defences with rockets and bombs. Yet even then the opposition was by no means silenced.

When the turn came for the LCRs, the rocket-firing craft, to shoot their cascades of destruction shorewards, it was my first opportunity to see them in action, although they had been used to effect in support of the Normandy landings. Like other landing craft, an LCR's bridge was aft (asbestos-shielded, I was told) but the whole of the forepart consisted of row upon row of what looked like chopped railway lines upturned at a forward-sloping angle. On each of these was a rocket and the rows could be fired serially so that a given area of beach would be systematically saturated with explosive.

We had been watching the rockets swooshing shorewards and their distant bursts on the beaches, when my attention was drawn to LCRs about a mile astern on our port quarter. I could see a succession of dark red spouts of flame as each row of rockets was fired. But these, instead of bursting on the beaches, were falling short among our own craft. I had heard during my Normandy travels of Allied troops being bombed in

---

[75] Because of his initials, always known as 'Red' Ryder. After the war he would become a true-blue MP for Merton and Morden (1950–55). See p. 165 for reasons for being awarded his Victoria Cross.

error by Allied aircraft and had tried to imagine their consternation. Little did I imagine how near I would come to having a similar own-goal experience.

First one then another of the LCRs' missiles blanketed areas of the sea, miles short of the shore, with lethal results for our vessels. It seemed persistent and unstoppable, like a nightmare from which one longs to escape and cannot, although the whole grim episode was over in minutes.

The last act was a barrage that crept closer and closer to our own LCH. As we watched, each row of explosives sent up spouts of steaming water in inexorably shrinking distances from us. The next craft, less than a hundred yards away to port, was completely enveloped in this devil's cauldron.

At that moment I glanced at Ryder. Did I imagine a slight change of colour? Otherwise, the stern expression was unchanged. We were aware that the moment of our most imminent peril had come. There had been no time for evasive action; we were as much a sitting target as if we had been embedded in concrete. It seemed inevitable that we would be smothered by the next row of bursting rockets as our neighbouring craft had been. But it was not to be. Fatefully for them, mercifully for us, they had been the victims of the LCR's last row of rockets. When the steam and smoke lifted we could only see the surface of the sea as if seconds before nothing had been upon it; the craft and all aboard had disintegrated under the impact and their components sunk without trace.

At the time, the rumoured explanation for this particular unforeseen hiccup, and in the totality of Operation *Infatuate*, as distinct from the human tragedy involved, it was no more than that, was that the Germans on Walcheren by some cunning radar device had been able to deflect or in some way interfere with the range-finding equipment of these particular rogue LCRs. I would eventually learn that the rocket craft were in the wrong position and were also confused when one of their number was hit. As it was slewing around, its rockets were released in the wrong direction.

I have often tried to analyse my reactions in the final seconds of this incident and to compare them with the inability to control my fear when alone in the Queen's Gardens dugout on the first night of the big Hull blitz. Did being in the presence of an apparently imperturbable VC—at St Nazaire, Ryder had been under heavy fire, often at point blank range, for seventy-six minutes—act as a deterrent to the jitters? There were several of us on that bridge and I don't think anybody flinched. Just as mass hysteria is an infection, an example of fortitude or restraint can have a group mirror effect. Our apparent sang-froid—an electrocardiogram might have been more revealing—may only have been the result of the fascination with which our attention was locked-on to the approaching menace, like the hypnosis of the cobra's victim. It could also have been the instantaneous realisation, once the neighbouring craft had been hit, that there was absolutely nothing we could do to save ourselves from the same fate. Infantry have battle courses in which they are conditioned to control instinctive reflexes to danger. In the Navy there could be no similar training and each individual's capacity to control shock had its first test in action, real not simulated. I would have three further such tests—two of them in circumstances verging on the bathetic.

~~

As I viewed the actual run-in of the Green Berets in their assault craft towards beaches crowned with smoke through which a windmill incongruously protruded, my lasting impression was of the exceptionally tall figure of my Official Naval Photographer colleague, Lieut M. H. A. MacNeill, standing up in one of these craft grasping his camera. I was both apprehensive for his safety, since resistance ashore had still not been entirely subdued, and admiring of his courage. When I eventually returned to the Admiralty I was relieved to find he had survived, and brought back his pictures.

Operation *Infatuate* attained its objectives: the Germans were cleared from Walcheren and the whole mouth of the Scheldt was purged of the enemy. The river was swept of mines and by the end of the month (eighty-five days after the capture of Antwerp) the port became operational and supplies flowed in profusion for the Allies' onward push into the wolf's lair. But it had been a costly operation. Apart from the tragic own goals scored by the rogue rocket craft, a hospital ship was hit, though most of its 300 casualties were transferred to a frigate. One estimate claimed we lost 70 per cent of our craft. Subsequent figures revealed that only seven out of the original twenty-seven gun and rocket craft were undamaged and total casualties in the Royal Marine assault force and the Naval personnel in the supporting craft were about 7,700 men.

I came ashore at Breskens and, as on D-Day, I had to find a way back to the UK. The little Dutch town was teeming with soldiers and I hitched a lift, climbing into the back of one of the trucks. By coincidence, in the huddle I found Captain Wilfred Sendall, RM, a pre-war journalist who had also been covering *Infatuate* for the Press Division. Instead of Ostend, where we had expected to find some kind of UK-bound craft, the truck took us to Brussels where the commandeered Hotel Metropole, chock-a-block with mainly British Army officers, had a shortage of beds and Wilfred and I were obliged to share one.

The next evening, in contrast, found me in a handsome flat, the guest of a young officer in the Royal Belgian Navy who had a handle to his name and was connected to the royal family of Brabant. Apart from members of his family, there were other guests at what, considering it was wartime, was an exquisite dinner enhanced by the gaiety of the conversation. Brussels itself had only been liberated weeks before and now the freeing of the Scheldt was a further reason for celebration. After dinner we retired to the drawing room, a most improbable setting for my next test of nerves after the rogue rockets' experience. Suddenly, above the chatter, laughter and clink of glasses, I heard a sound familiar and ominous.

The few days I had spent in London between D-Day and returning to Normandy had been long enough for me to be apprehensive of the sound of an approaching doodlebug. With my brother, on leave from the RAF, I had decided to have lunch in the BBC's Bush House canteen in the Strand. We then changed our minds and went instead for a jug or two in the Red Lion off Fleet Street. We heard a terrific explosion and by the time we had walked back to the corner of Kingsway, a huge slice had been blown out of the upper storeys of the Air Ministry building by a V1 flying bomb. Opposite, rescuers were carrying out people from the Bush House canteen, cut and pierced by slivers of plate glass.

Seconds after hearing the familiar guttural drone of this doodlebug over Brussels my companions heard it too. Being the very first to come over their city, they were filled with curiosity, insisted on putting out the lights, drawing aside the blackout curtains, opening the French windows and crowding onto the balcony to see if they could catch sight of this novel phenomenon. As the doodlebug passed almost overhead, the deep-throated oscillations of its engines made the windows rattle. Then they cut out. That for me was the nerve-testing moment.[76] The louder the sound of the engines had grown the stronger my urge to use the large table in the

---

[76] 'When the engine, after a final cough, suddenly cut out, that was one's cue to take cover,' recalls Norman Longmate in *How We Lived Then* (Arrow Books). He also mentions soldiers in a training course in Islington reacting to the sudden cut-out by 'going to ground' beneath their desks.

middle of the room as a substitute Morrison shelter (the steel construction for inside the home for protection against the debris of a collapsed building which was named after the Home Secretary).

If I had been on my own I would no doubt have done just that, particularly at the moment of accentuated silence when the engine stopped and I knew the infernal machine was going into a downward spiral. No one could tell until it was too late where it would land with its load of destruction. However, to dive under the table while everyone else, including my Royal Belgian Navy blue-blooded host, was eagerly scanning the sky for Hitler's 'secret' weapon, would be plumbing the depths of depravity. So, choosing death to dishonour, I remained erect. The darkness concealed any sign that I was very aware that if the blast were too close we would have every chance of being skewered by slivers of glass from the French windows. I was frankly relieved to hear the explosion in the middle distance. My friends re-entered the room, discussing the event, switched on the lights and, hopefully, my qualms had not been noticed.

~~

The next day I was offered a lift to Paris by Robert Barr who had been a feature writer on the *Daily Mail* and was now attached to SHAEF, Eisenhower's headquarters. Although there was no justification for such a trip the temptation to see the French capital after four years of German occupation was irresistible. Bob was a dynamic Glaswegian, ten years my senior, with a fund of experiences with which he entertained me during an arduous drive. After the war he would write one of the earliest BBC television scripts, about the Allied occupation of Germany, and become a scriptwriter of such popular television series as *Z Cars*, *Maigret*, *Spycatcher*, *Moonstrike* and *Spy Trap*.

I was briefly back in France, but retain only fleeting cameos of that first visit to Paris. In contrast to the spontaneous friendliness of the Bruxellois, three-months after liberation, Parisians seemed tense and preoccupied. I shared what I suppose were the rigours of their rationing in a restaurant where, unable to produce a ration card, they presented me with a single course consisting solely of potatoes. It was an ironic introduction to the gastronomic centre of the universe. One further recollection was staying the night in a chateau occupied by the RN presumably for the staff liaising with La Marine Française, in beautiful grounds, somewhere in the outskirts. Here, I gave my visit to Paris a semblance of legitimacy by taking advantage of the first opportunity I had had to send a Walcheren story to the Admiralty. My European war came to an end when I hitched a flight back to the UK, sitting on the corrugated metal interior of a seatless Dakota. That was the first time I was airborne.

FOURTH TURN–*Bombs*

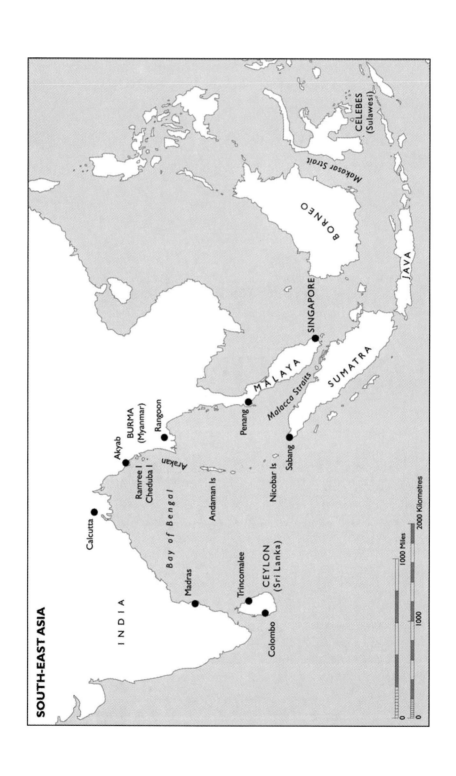

SOUTH-EAST ASIA

INDIA

Calcutta

Madras

Colombo

Trincomalee

CEYLON
(Sri Lanka)

Bay of Bengal

Akyab

Ramree I
Cheduba I

Arakan

BURMA
(Myanmar)

Rangoon

Andaman Is

Nicobar Is

Sabang

Penang

MALAYA

Malacca Straits

SUMATRA

SINGAPORE

JAVA

BORNEO

Makasar Strait

CELEBES
(Sulawesi)

1000 Miles

2000 Kilometres

0   1000

Chapter 13

First Patrol

In the war against Japan, British submarine captains were to repeat the exploits of their predecessors in the First World War, often choosing the gun rather than the torpedo against the small vessels they mostly encountered.

Sea Power: Lord Hill-Norton

Just about the time the troopship *Durban Castle* was landing me in Colombo, Ceylon, in January 1945, together with hundreds of other personnel for duties with SEAC (South East Asia Command), an odd exchange of signals was passing between the commanders of two British submarines in the Indian Ocean a few hundred miles to the east. 'What is your wife's Christian name?' was one of them, made to Lieut David Swanston DSO, DSC and Bar, RN in the first few minutes of the fifth day of the most gruelling experiences that any submariner could have survived. Promoted, with a second wavy gold ring on my sleeve, and appointed as the only British East Indies Fleet Official Naval Reporter, I was privileged to hear this remarkable story from Swanston and his crew when they returned to Trincomalee.

Without any means of calling for assistance for his crippled HM Submarine *Shakespeare*, (her wireless had been shattered) Swanston had set a course which he knew would cross that of a submarine of the same flotilla, the *Stygian*, outward-bound from Trinco. She was commanded by his personal friend (they had been cadets together), Lieut G. S. Clarabut. Sure enough, *Stygian* spotted the Verey lights *Shakespeare* was sending up and realised that her sister sub's other recognition signals were correct. But, wary of Japanese tricks, Clarabut wanted further assurance: hence the question about the name of Swanston's wife. 'Stella. And that is also *your* wife's name,' Swanston added for good measure in the return signal. That was enough and *Stygian* turned about to accompany her sister sub, which had a 7° list, back to Trinco. When it became light, one of *Shakespeare*'s seamen who had died from his wounds was buried at sea and a fol boat was then sent over from *Stygian* with medical supplies, food and a working party. A photograph taken from *Shakespeare*'s conning tower shows the arrival of the fol boat and about fifteen of *Shakespeare*'s crew, most of them stripped to the waist, lining the sub's casing beneath a bravely fluttering White Ensign.

In the afternoon a destroyer met the two subs and, while *Stygian* resumed her patrol, *Shakespeare* was escorted (and eventually towed) back to Trinco where I met her and her courageous ship's company.

~~

On 7 December 1941, simultaneously with Tokyo's declaration of war against the USA, bombers from Japanese aircraft carriers carried out their devastating raid on Pearl Harbor, the American mid-Pacific naval base near Honolulu in the Hawaiian Islands. The following day Britain joined the USA in declaring war on Japan. Hitler, fulfilling an undertaking under the treaty of September 1940, made the fatal mistake four days after Pearl Harbor of declaring war on the USA.

For us, there followed the débâcles of the fall of Hong Kong, Singapore, Malaya and Burma, as well as the sinking of the brand new battleship *Prince of Wales* and battle-cruiser *Repulse*. The British 14th ('The Forgotten') Army battled away in Burma for years trying to stem what seemed like the Japanese aim of invading India. Having crossed the Indian frontier, the Japanese had suffered defeat in July 1944 after protracted and bloody struggles in unsuccessful attempts to capture the town of Imphal and the village of Kohima in the Naga Hills. In September the British—or more precisely the Anglo-Indian-African 14th Army—under General Sir William Slim and the Americans and Chinese under US General Stilwell started their counter-offensive in Burma under the overall command of Vice-Admiral Louis Mountbatten who, in this story, we left in command of the destroyer *Kelly* in Namsen Fjord four years before.

For the war against Japan, the Royal Navy was divided into the BEIF (British East Indies Fleet) and the BPF (British Pacific Fleet) which was working with the Americans in General MacArthur's trans-Pacific island-hopping slogging match with the Japanese. This had progressed from the decisive victory at Midway Island in June 1942, via the ultimate capture of Guadalcanal in the Solomons in February 1943 to that of the Philippines in October 1944.

Even before the end of 1944 the BEIF had won control of the Bay of Bengal to the extent that the Japanese were no longer able to supply their army in Burma through the main Burmese ports. Much of the credit for this went to mine-laying by aircraft and to the BEIF's flotillas of submarines torpedoing or otherwise destroying Japanese merchant shipping, ranging from 5,000-ton freighters to junks. The strategic consequence was that the Japanese were now reduced to trying to supply their land forces through small harbours in southern Burma, Siam, the Malay Peninsula and even the offshore Andaman Islands (from which they would still have to run the gauntlet of our submarines and surface patrols to tranship cargoes to the mainland). In fact, our patrols went as far south-east as Sumatra.

~~

HM Submarine *Shakespeare*, which had only recently joined the BEIF, sailed from Trincomalee before Christmas 1944 on her first patrol—off the Andaman Islands. Early on in the patrol she sank by gunfire a medium-sized merchant ship in convoy and was unscathed by depth-charges when escorting warships attacked her. Then, in Swanston's words:

> Four days later we engaged another merchantman in a gun duel and scored three hits on her. As a Japanese submarine-chaser loomed over the horizon, however, we decided to dive. But our luck was out. A shell from the merchantman tore a hole nine inches by four in the pressure hull before we could submerge. Water poured into the engine-room and other compartments and we were unable to dive.

The submarine's guns were manned again and the duel resumed. Meanwhile, Petty Officer Telegraphist V. G. Harmer and Leading Telegraphist Kenneth Wace, both East Anglians, on their own initiative clambered out of the conning-tower onto the saddle tanks which were awash and began to plug the hole with blankets and hammocks. Four more shells ripped into the *Shakespeare*, the blast from one of them blowing off Harmer's boots. But, clinging to the rails, he continued to hold the blankets in position with his bleeding and blistered feet. He remained in this position for twenty minutes until he was washed off. But *Shakespeare,* on its one still functioning engine, was able to manoeuvre sufficiently to rescue him. After that, Harmer and Wace joined the bucket chain which was trying to keep the water level down. An hour later, Harmer went to the bridge and, although wounded in both feet and in the left arm, remained until nightfall firing an automatic gun at Japanese bombers and fighter-bombers. In Trinco, at the request of my ONP colleague, Lieut Charles Trusler, Harmer posed for a picture with his gun.

After the second duel began, the Japanese merchantman's gun was put out of action and she finally turned away with a list to port. However, the submarine-chaser took up the challenge until Swanston was able to get *Shakespeare* out of range. By now she was being steered solely by a portable compass supported on the knee of the helmsman, Torpedo Gunner's Mate T. Gates, a Scouser. For the next eight hours until darkness fell, *Shakespeare* was attacked almost incessantly from the air. But the gunners, many of them wounded, put up a withering fire. Even when two of them collapsed (and later died) the guns went on firing, the wounded below helping to reload the pans of ammunition.

One seaplane making a low-flying bombing attack was hit by *Shakespeare*'s Vickers gun, fired by the second coxswain, after dropping a bomb which missed by about twenty yards. It crashed about half a mile away. More bombs caused further damage and flooding but the crew maintained they scored hits on four more of the enemy aircraft. The attacks ended soon after sunset and the crew had their first respite after nearly twelve hours' continuous action.

Chief Petty Officer Watcham, a Norwich man who had been eight years in the submarine service, was full of praise for the crew, most of whom were Hostilities Only ratings. 'Many of them were on their first patrol but behaved magnificently' was his tribute to the young men of the eponymous *Shakespeare* who had lived up to The Bard's 'Courage mounteth to the occasion.' Most of the time they were joking, Watcham recalled, 'and they didn't get a hot meal until the third day.' Exposed to machine-gun and rocket fire and flying bomb splinters in twenty-five attacks, casualties there had to be: seventeen wounded, of whom four died.

After Trusler and I were shown the damage, we persuaded the CO, his No. 1, PO Harmer and a couple of stokers to pose for a photograph around a hole about two feet by twenty inches and there were other gaping gashes, much bigger than the original nine by four inches Swanston had mentioned. It was disclosed after the war that *Shakespeare* was never operational again.

By the end of the war Swanston had had a DSO added to his DSC and Bar and carried on in the Submarine Service after it. When he was invalided out of the Navy in 1955 he had already been a Commander for two years. From 1976 to 1981 he was House of Commons Deputy Serjeant at Arms.

~~

My admiration for submariners was unbounded and increased every time I read the reports they made after each patrol. I was permitted to scan these for potential 'stories' for the Press Division or for the broadcasts I used to make about the BEIF's activities over Radio Colombo. If the explosions of *Afridi*'s depth-charges which had shaken the boiler-room plates had quickened my pulse, infinitely greater must have been the effect on submariners at the receiving end of enemy depth-charges. They must have had nerves of steel. I would read accounts of objects leaping into the air or of leaking seams after the impact of a depth-charge near-miss; of a sub suddenly being plunged into darkness; of the crew communicating in whispers as their vessel lay doggo and tracking the sounds of their hunter's engines, wondering whether the next pattern of depth-charges would rock them worse than the previous one or would cause irremediable damage from which the chances of escape were minimal. Even if they reached the surface, capture by the Japanese could mean at least being beaten-up, at worst torture, execution or death by disease or malnutrition in one of the notorious PoW camps which had been the fate of 'survivors' of the submarine *Strategem*.

In addition to their task of sinking enemy shipping, our subs performed other roles such as picking up survivors of ditched aircraft or bringing back to Ceylon for intelligence interrogation selected occupants of small craft which they had intercepted. When junks, manned not by Japanese, but by the indigenes of these Indian Ocean islands or mainland, were stopped by a sub they were examined and, if found to be carrying merchandise, particularly foodstuffs destined for the Japanese garrisons, the crew, whenever circumstances permitted, were allowed to transfer to another small craft or sometimes were put ashore. An explosive charge was placed in the junk and it was blown up. That was the price of being in the wrong place at the wrong time within Japan's so-called Greater East Asia Co-Prosperity Sphere. It was a wartime paradox that this treatment was 'humane' compared with more drastic measures sometimes undertaken, not by submarines, but by the destroyers—as I would discover.

Chapter 14

Rum, Suicide and 'Butchery'

I was beginning to suspect that, in the Japanese spirit, death and life was the ultimate romance: the way one died was more important than how one lived, and even the best of living was not valid until vouched for by the manner of dying. The dead, not the living, were the really happy spirits.

Yet Being Someone Other: Laurens Van Der Post

I wanted to learn more about these mysterious people, to learn why they had behaved as they had. I have found it impossible to be bitter against the Japanese.

The Emperor's Guest: John Fletcher-Cooke

In contrast to my coverage of the Walcheren assault 'from the stalls' (the headquarters craft), I would be landing on a beach again in my first operation with the British East Indies Fleet, as in Normandy. Once more I would be with the Royal Marines, in what has been described by John Winton in *The Forgotten Fleet* as the 'only purely Naval assault landing of the war'. With such a claim to uniqueness it was a pity that it would be something as banal as my 'European' battledress which marked the climax to my contribution to an event which had several elements of *anti*climax.

Operations to clear the Japanese out of the Arakan coast, on the eastern side of the Bay of Bengal, had begun in December 1944 and the re-planning of the assault on Akyab must have been going on about the time I arrived in Colombo. Operation *Lightning*, the unopposed occupation of Akyab, lived up to its name: it was all over in six days and we were in possession of both a valuable airfield and a harbour. There followed the capture of Myebon and, on 22 January 1945, the start of the fight to capture Kangaw, defended by 3,000 Japanese.This developed into a five-day battle, one of the costliest in human life in the whole Burma campaign. It was followed by the largest amphibious operation on the Arakan, the capture of Ramree Island with its harbour at Kyaukpyu and the airfield, invaluable for supplying the 14th Army in its drive southwards and from where I would embark for the recapture of Rangoon four months later.

Soon afterwards the Fleet's Official Naval Photographer, Lieut Charles Trusler, and I were given orders to join the cruiser HMS *Newcastle* in Trincomalee for Operation *Sankey*, the assault and capture of the smaller island of Cheduba to the west of Ramree. For this, 500 Marines had been brought together from BEIF cruisers and a battleship to form the assault force. They had been training in jungle warfare in Ceylon but had never been in action as a body on land before. They were commanded by a colonel with a double-barrelled name but who was always being referred to as Colonel So-and-so 'Hiccups'. I never discovered whether he was aware of the nickname, nor how he had earned it.

I occupied the time as we steamed north-east across the Indian Ocean interviewing members of *Newcastle*'s ship's company, including two sets of brothers and a father and son. These were surely exceptions to the wartime rule not to put members of the same family on the same ship so as to reduce the chance of a double bereavement.

In due course we arrived at our appointed position with the low-lying island of Cheduba in sight. There was the now familiar preliminary bombardment of the enemy beach as well as the terrain behind by *Newcastle*'s 6-inch guns and those of her sister cruisers, the *Kenya* and *Nigeria* and those of their escorting destroyers. This was followed by strafing and bombing by Naval aircraft from the escort carrier *Ameer*. As soon as the bombardment and bombing stopped, my first surprise was to see the Marines in their bottle-green battledress clambering with their arms and equipment, not into the flat-bottomed, welded-steel landing craft with ramps which had been used on D-Day and at Walcheren but into open wooden longboats which were then lowered into the sea from the cruiser.

No one in Colombo had provided me with the same jungle battledress as the Marines were wearing. I was still in the khaki uniform with the ROYAL NAVY flash on the shoulder with which I had been issued for the ops in Europe. A minor detail, I thought. I would learn in due course that that was not Colonel 'Hiccups's' opinion.

I climbed into one of the longboats already packed with leathernecks and as we chugged shorewards I felt as uncomfortably exposed as that lofty photographer, Lieut MacNeill, had seemed at the Westkapelle run-in. Armed as usual with notebook and pen, I wondered what I was supposed to do if Emperor Hirohito's fanatics were still giving us a warm reception when we hit the beach.

As our motor-propelled longboat chugged towards the shore there came the morning's second surprise: each man was offered a tot of rum. My last tot had been on leaving the *Danae* in Mombasa and giving a sailor's farewell to the Lower Deck. I have never heard or read of rum being issued while the tens of thousands of troops were making the run-in to the Normandy beaches and, unless I was too preoccupied, I certainly had not noticed any being given to the men on LCT 903. This must surely have been the doughty colonel's initiative, perhaps to commemorate this all-Naval show with a traditional pusser's tot (though 8 a.m. was hardly the traditional time for 'Up Spirits'). If it was his idea of instilling Dutch courage, as far as I was concerned it had a double-edged effect: while the inward glow made me feel marginally less exposed, the mere fact of it being doled out seemed to emphasise the magnitude of the peril ahead.

We drew closer and closer to the palm-fringed shore. I began to wonder why no flak seemed to be coming our way, recalling that at Walcheren 15-inch shelling, bombing, strafing and rocket saturation of the beaches had failed completely to silence the opposition. Now, there were no shells splashing in the drink around us, not a bullet whining, no arcing tracer. When the longboats finally crunched into the sand and the Marines scrambled ashore, not even a blowpipe opposed us. Were we being led into some fiendish Oriental trap?

Swiftly, the Marines sped across the beach and dived among the palms and undergrowth. I, too, jumped ashore, by now fairly convinced the Japanese had pulled out of Cheduba altogether before we arrived. I had just crossed the beach to the first fringe of palms and seen the corpse of an unfortunate Cheduba indigene doubled up in a salaam to death in a shell or bomb crater when I heard the colonel's indignant roar from about one hundred yards further inland: 'What the Hell is that man doing not in jungle battledress? He'll give away our position to the enemy. See that he returns to the boats immediately.' I realised I was 'that man' and summoning all my reserves of dignity strolled back to the boat. Recalling the episode in the jeep outside Fécamp, I began to think I was destined to fall foul of colonels.

Sure enough, the enemy had pulled out of the island. But only just; we had apparently disturbed their breakfast: the Marines found eggs ready for cooking beside a fire at their headquarters in the village.

~~

From bathos to pathos in the space of eight weeks: if an item of uniform had been the focus of this episode, it was another, a Naval officer's cap, that imposed on me a fraught mission which I would only fulfil by proxy.

A hefty and handsome young Canadian gunnery officer whom I got to know on the *Durban Castle* trooper began a shipboard romance with one of the scores of Wrens who were also on passage to Colombo. This blossomed after our arrival and I believe they actually got engaged. She worked in the BEIF headquarters on the staff of the commander-in-chief, Admiral Sir Arthur Power, and he joined the destroyer HMS *Rapid*. In March, in company with two other destroyers, *Rapid*, on her second operation with the BEIF, had entered Stewart Sound in the Andamans. She steamed into a bay which revealed no signs of the enemy but when she was well within range of a concealed shore battery, it opened fire and scored a direct hit on one of *Rapid*'s pom-poms. My Canadian friend was literally blown to pieces and ten ratings were also killed in the action. *Rapid* limped back to Akyab. In Trinco I was taken aside by an officer of a sister destroyer and handed the Canadian's cap, with the request that it should be given to his Wren friend or fiancée with the information, intended to give her a modicum of relief in her bereavement, that he never knew what had hit him. I had never spoken to her and had to find a way of delivering this pathetic relic. I managed to contact the only resident of the Colombo Wrennery with whom I had exchanged a few words on the *Durban Castle* and passed on the cap with the verbal message. The intermediary who fulfilled this distressing task would one day become my wife.

~~

Four men were in the sea either treading water or clinging to the floating wreckage of their ship. They were Japanese who had survived a battle with four BEIF destroyers and our Liberator bombers and were photographed by someone aboard one of the four destroyers. Two officers described what happened when they were lowered in a boat to pick up survivors. According to New Zealander Lieut-Cdr J. Lennox-King:

> We managed to haul five badly wounded Japanese on board although one of them tried to swim away. We then came across two more on a Carley float. On seeing us approaching, one held out at arm's length a sword bayonet about three feet long and after three attempts succeeded in plunging the point into his throat.

Gunner E. W. M. Peters DSM, RN from Pitsea, Essex, took up the story:

> Another Japanese dived under the water when he saw us coming and a big air bubble was the last sign we had of him. We came across two more who were shamming dead with their faces in the water and their mouths to one side. When they thought we were not looking they quickly turned their heads. Another man was lashed to the mast to make sure he went down with his ship.

After a prodigious expenditure of ammunition, the destroyers' guns as well as torpedoes and the Liberators' bombs had sent to the bottom one 1,500-ton freighter, another of 400 tons and two submarine-chasers. The merchantmen had been carrying about six months' supply of rice for some garrison troops.

An officer described for me another bizarre incident after one of the submarine-chasers had been tin-fished and sank within minutes.

> One of the survivors in the water began to batter the side of our ship with a pom-pom shell. He expected to blow a hole in our side and blow himself up too. He must have known very little about pom-pom shells because no matter how hard they are knocked, they won't explode. This man was bald, half out of the water, clinging to the rescue net. I hung onto a guard-rail

stanchion with one arm, leant over the side and hit him over the head with my pistol. He dropped the shell and swam away.

~~

This and similar phenomena, including the kamikaze attacks on our warships and American ones in the Pacific, must have been discussed in wardrooms and on mess-decks throughout the fleet and no doubt there were a few better versed in the Japanese psyche who made intelligent efforts to explain why so many Japanese chose death to captivity. But to me, these destroyer officers merely recounted events as they had observed them. However puzzled they were at such behaviour, they gave the impression that it deserved only their contempt. If any of them for one moment thought there was anything noble or heroic in such antics, I never heard them express it. How could they feel otherwise? In their attempts to rescue these men, admittedly not exclusively for humane reasons, for prisoners were always needed for intelligence purposes, they had exposed themselves to danger and their stationary ships were at risk of being torpedoed by a lurking submarine. Yet their efforts had been spurned by the men in the water who preferred to die rather than be taken prisoner.

What impelled the bald man to hammer with that shell against the ship which had just sunk his own? Hatred, a blind impulse for revenge? A sworn fighting man of the God-Emperor, was it a compulsive sense of duty that impelled him to devote the last moments of his life to attempting to destroy Hirohito's enemies, a fanatic's act of self-sacrifice? (When our own countrymen chose certain death to attack an enemy we did not call them fanatics but awarded them the Victoria Cross.)

And how important an element—if present at all in these men in the sea—was the conviction that 'death and life was the ultimate romance', a national, religion-inspired characteristic which Van Der Post thought he had discovered? Or was it something more mundane: the fear of family and social ostracism or possible punishment when they ultimately returned to their homeland after being made prisoners?

Perhaps there was some of all these motivations in their conduct. If the attitude towards them of our own fighting men was uncomprehending and dismissive, it was because, in the daily process of prosecuting the war, there was scant opportunity for philosophising or to probe an enemy's deeper motivation. It would not be until a month after hostilities had ceased that the SEAC Supremo, Admiral Mountbatten, would explain in his Order of the Day to all under his command:

> You will find that there are many Japanese who are no more taken-in by the preposterous claims of the militarists than you are yourselves. The Japanese, as a nation, had no say whatsoever in their own government, and were perhaps less responsible than any other people for their government's decision to go to war. Many of them therefore have had little desire for a long time now to continue the fight and are only too thankful that it is all over.

But even some of those for whom it was all over and who found themselves well-treated by their captors did not want to live. They either thought that there was some ulterior motive behind such treatment or that it would not last, presumably because of the abominable treatment generally meted out to their own prisoners. Or some of the motivations just mentioned may have been responsible for their persisting in the death wish. An example was given to me by the CO of a Burma RNVR motor launch, part of a flotilla blockading the Japanese escape route from the island of Ramree. These craft were entirely manned by Burmese: Arakanese, Sino-Burmans, Karens and Anglo-Burmans. The officers were both Burman and European peacetime expatriates. He recalled:

> After the Japanese discovered the impossibility of running the blockade by boat, some of them made attempts to swim the channel. One of them, when he was certain he had been detected, screamed out in English: 'Hullo! Help me!' at the top of his voice. We lowered our dinghy and caught him before he could reach the opposite bank. He turned out to be a very scared Japanese officer, convinced that he was going to be executed. But when we treated him as an officer, allowing him the use of the wardroom, he appeared to regain his confidence. He was a well-educated man who had a university degree and had been some kind of higher civil servant in Tokyo. He agreed to appeal over our loud hailer system to his comrades to give themselves up. Unable to escape by sea, they had been wandering in the mangroves for days without food or water. But presumably because of the denseness of the mangroves preventing those

even a few yards inland from hearing his appeals, the attempt was abortive. Later, he was handed over to the authorities on shore and placed temporarily in a hut. I was amazed to learn that, here, he turned to his guard, pulled open his shirt and said: 'Now shoot me!' The astonished guard called an officer and it transpired that, unconvinced by our correct treatment, he still thought he was to be executed. And that was the mentality of an educated Japanese officer!

Or did his captors misunderstand him? Perhaps the man who had yelled for help and then collaborated with his enemy by appealing to his compatriots to surrender had been overcome with remorse and genuinely wanted to be shot.

There were a few exceptional people like Van Der Post and Sir John Fletcher-Cooke who had experienced the horror of PoW camps but who had the moral stamina to differentiate and to isolate the brutality of individual Japanese without making blanket racial condemnations. They wished to seek out the positive elements in Japanese traditions and culture on which a peaceful post-war Japan could begin to rebuild.

Even in the Andaman Sea episode, not all the Japanese had preferred death to capture: forty-six men allowed themselves to be rescued. In the pictures taken on board one of the destroyers some of them can be seen on deck dhobeying in buckets. Whether they were doing their own 'smalls' or their captors' is a matter for conjecture. All are wearing gleaming white sun helmets. Where did they come from and why are they wearing them?

The Japanese had one need shared by troops the world over but their means of satisfying it was indefensible. On board the larger of the two freighters there had been eighteen women, presumably at least a proportion of them in transit to be 'comforts for the troops' on the Andamans and more than likely press-ganged and abducted. Of these, only seven were rescued and in one of the pictures there are four of them sitting on the destroyer's deck in what are almost certainly men's trousers several sizes too big and rolled up from the ankles. They were probably given to them by the crew as makeshift covering after being fished out of the sea. They look pretty disconsolate after their experience. One of the seven was said to be pregnant and another showed off perhaps her only scrap of English: 'Kiss me quick!'

Up to 200,000 women became 'sex slaves'. Apart from Indonesians, there were Koreans, Chinese, Dutch and Filipina—and for years those who have survived have been campaigning for compensation. Some sued the Japanese government which maintained that compensation claims were settled in the San Francisco Peace Treaty of 1952 and in bilateral treaties. At that time these 'comfort women' were not officially recognised as having existed. Only forty years later did the government release records proving that the Imperial Army had indeed press-ganged these foreign women into sex slavery.

~~

In Operation *Sunfish* two things were dramatically brought home to me: first the extreme risks Fleet Air Arm pilots ran even when no enemy was involved and, second, that war, however morally justified we may believe it to be, will sometimes oblige a protagonist, on either side, to commit morally unjustified acts in which civilians are the victims.

I was aboard a destroyer, one of two groups of five which sailed from Trincomalee on 8 April together with the battleships *Queen Elizabeth* and the French navy's *Richelieu*, the cruiser *London*[77] and two aircraft carriers. This was Force 63 under Vice Admiral H. T. C. Walker, the BEIF's Second-in-Command, flying his flag in *Queen Elizabeth*.

On the first day I was shocked to see, away on the starboard beam, a Fleet Air Arm aircraft which, while attempting to land on the carrier *Khedive,* hit her stern instead and plunged into the sea in flames. I would learn afterwards that it was a Hellcat and the pilot was killed. Two days later, as I happened to be watching through binoculars, the arrester wires on the same carrier failed to stop a landing aircraft and it crashed into another plane already on the deck and pushed it over the side. Four were killed.

Several days later, the two battleships and *London* bombarded the island of Sabang at the extreme north-western tip of Sumatra although there was apparently no shipping in the harbour, and three destroyers (not ours) bombarded a town on the mainland. This was at the entrance to the Malacca Strait, the approach from the Andaman Sea to Singapore at the tip of the Malay Peninsula. We, however, were ordered to proceed further south to search and destroy shipping along the north-western coast of Sumatra.

---

[77] The ship in which I had taken passage from Alexandria to the Clyde in 1943.

~~

We lost the distant prospect of blue-hazed mountains as we steamed close inshore through narrow channels between small islands, luxuriant with often vivid green foliage growing down to the fringe of sand between jungle and sea. This was Conrad's *Lord Jim* country. Occasionally, brown roofs of villages could be seen through the huge leaves and giant ferns. It was a peaceful tropical scene into which we erupted with gunfire, blowing to bits high-sterned junks and little fishing craft, the very means of livelihood for the local fisherfolk.

I will give our destroyer the 'no names, no pack drill' treatment used by Jack whenever prudence called for anonymity. One unhappy recollection was of her steaming up to what looked like the dead end of a creek where there was a village with a miniature bamboo jetty. Alongside this was a fishing craft which could not have been much more than 15 feet long. We fired a shot, presumably to warn the crew and any curious villagers to vacate the area promptly. The next moment one of our shells snapped the little vessel's mast and it came toppling down on a man who had not been quick enough to make himself scarce. Further shells sent splinters soaring among the palm fronds.

This was the strangest 'warfare' I had come across in six years. Did we really have to do this? Was it credible that by destroying these little wooden fishing craft we were somehow depriving some unseen Japanese outpost of sustenance?

Atrocities committed by the Japanese military were common knowledge by now. In 1942 a civilian cousin of mine was thrown into Changi Jail, Singapore, and tortured in an attempt to find out which of his friends were making home-made radios. Such was his condition on his release at the Japanese surrender in 1945 that his own brother failed to recognise him. Much more prevalent than the tolerant attitude of a Van Der Post or Fletcher-Cooke was that of Tristan Jones in *Heart of Oak*:

> I felt sick to my stomach that anything that pretended to be human could treat its fellows so. I know there were decent Japanese, kindly and civilised and cultured … But I didn't want to know them … I could not forgive them for the tiny corner in my heart which had nothing but hatred for them.

But did this knowledge justify attacking anything and anybody which or who might be useful to their troops? The victims included those who themselves had been exploited by the Japanese.

'Orders is orders' and we proceeded with our sweep to within about a hundred miles north of Padang, shooting up anything that floated. We were about to reach the nadir of our part in this dismal operation of 16 April 1945. We were steaming offshore in line-ahead, our sister destroyer astern, when we sighted not even a junk but a canoe. It was being paddled by brown-skinned men, presumably Sumatrans. It seemed incredible, and afterwards I learned that was not only my view, but the order was given by the CO to open fire. There were two single-turret 4.7s for'ard on this class of destroyer and several rounds were fired from them. Each shell sent up a fountain of water well wide of the canoe, its occupants still paddling away for dear life as we steamed past them.

I turned to see what our sister ship would do, dreading that I might have to be the spectator of senseless slaughter. She did not open fire, which I interpreted as a tacit criticism of our own action.

A little later, I was standing close to the crew of one of the guns that had been ordered to fire. There was an argument going on in which a Glaswegian voice announced: 'If we ha' hit those poorr basstids I'd ne'er look m'mither in the face again.' As for the officers, I got the impression that some of them were embarrassed by what had been done that day and particularly by the last incident.

~~

There are some puzzling features about these events, which were described laconically in a SEAC communiqué: 'Our destroyers sank off the coast of Sumatra six small supply vessels between outlying islands and the mainland.'

First, Sumatra before its occupation by the Japanese was part of the Dutch East Indies and whatever criticisms there were in some British quarters of Dutch colonial administration, which they considered inferior to ours, it was assumed at this time that the Dutch would return once the Japanese were defeated. At the same time we must have been aware of the strong nationalist movement which would eventually prevail and result in the formation of the new entity to be called Indonesia. In retrospect, it would seem to have been counterproductive to have alienated gratuitously the Sumatrans still further by such incidents. Were commanding officers, when given orders to make such anti-shipping sweeps, told to use their discretion, to weigh the possibility of these native craft and their owners being pressed into the service of the Japanese, against the certainty of an exacerbation of anti-European feeling if their craft were destroyed and loss of life incurred?

Second, the CO of the destroyer on which I was aboard wrote a letter twenty-four years later in which he claimed that Admiral Walker himself had called the sinking of these junks 'butchery'. But without knowing the context in which the admiral is said to have used the epithet, it is impossible to tell whether he meant that he regretted having given the order which led to the 'butchery' or whether he was merely being critical of the CO for having interpreted his order too literally. There is, again, the possibility that the admiral, sensing some degree of remorse on the CO's part, was using 'butchery' tongue in cheek. Nor can one judge from the letter whether the CO himself was indignant at the Admiral's choice of the word 'butchery', considering he was only obeying his superior's orders, or whether he agreed with the admiral's censure (if such it was) and was being honest enough to draw attention to it.

Third, there is the anomaly as to why this particular commander did interpret his orders so literally. He was a Quaker, a sect with strong pacifist views and humanitarian outlook. Surely there is a contradiction between being a pacifist and a professional sailor who must be prepared to go to war and to kill? During the First World War many Quakers courageously registered as conscientious objectors, suffering social ostracism and imprisonment. In the Second World War I believe most Quakers reluctantly acknowledged that the beastliness of fascism had to be confronted by armed force, though some found non-combatant ways of helping the anti-fascist struggle. But it would be interesting to know how a Quaker rationalised making the armed forces his career in peacetime.

This commander had followed the long Naval tradition of his family and had at least one namesake who had been an admiral. One can only guess as to whether there was also a family Quaker tradition and that this apparent contradiction had long been resolved. But this commander, whom I only met when formally welcomed on board his ship, was later described to me as 'a teetotaller, terribly upright and correct and would never dream of doing anything to bring discredit on the Navy.' Or to his religion?

As it happened, exactly one month after this operation he brought considerable credit to the service and to his ship when she was the first to make radar contact with a Japanese heavy cruiser at the extreme range of thirty-eight miles and, after engaging the enemy in the company of three sister destroyers, fired a total of eight torpedoes at her, delivering the *coup de grâce* with the last two.

Though this shipping sweep and the canoe episode was minuscule compared with the horrors inflicted on civilians in the Second World War and since, it still deviated from the precept that, when there are ways of avoiding or containing the suffering of civilians caught up in war, care should be taken to do so. The submariners tried to take off the crews of small craft before sinking them. Why not the commanders of surface vessels?

Chapter 15

Sibling Rivalry

'Sir!' said King Riance, 'I came hither by a hard adventure.'
'Who won you?' said King Arthur.
'Sir!' said the King, 'the Knight With The Two Swords and his brother which
are two marvellous knights of prowess.'

Morte d'Arthur: Sir Thomas Malory

Before I introduce Leopold and the celluloid image of his brother and relate the circumstances of their apparent prowess and rivalry, I must set the stage onto which Leopold's massive bulk strode one day prior to my next sea-going operation. It will be for the reader to judge whether there are fascinating aspects to Leopold's story as he recounted it to me, or whether he will come to the same conclusion as his peers: that he was the prince of bores.

If in mid-1945 you were to travel by bike (as I did daily in temperatures of over 90° F) or by rickshaw or taxi from the centre of Colombo along the coastal Galle Road you might notice lying back on the right a two-storey colonial-type building set in partially palm-shaded grounds that sloped gently towards the beach. This housed the sleeping quarters and wardroom for junior Naval officers, most of whom worked in the British East Indies Fleet headquarters in the capital of Ceylon, as well as some sea-going types awaiting posting to a ship or enjoying a spell ashore while their ship was undergoing a refit. In the grounds were bandas, wooden huts with palm-plaited roofs which served as sleeping quarters.

In the wardroom of an evening, officers relaxed in cane chairs, sipping their duty-free gins-and-orange or liqueurs. Big fans rotated silently in a slow rhythm above our heads and, as silently, 'boys'—that patronising label applied by the British Raj to waiters and servants irrespective of their age—dressed in spotless dotis padded on bare feet balancing trays laden with glasses of Van de Hum, Curaçoa or 'Starboard Light' (absinthe). Most of these officers were only in their twenties, fewer in their thirties and fewer still, perhaps a sprinkling, of two-and-a-half ringers, in their early forties.

Imagine then everyone's tactfully concealed curiosity when into this youthful fraternity ambled one evening a man who must have first seen daylight some six decades before. There may have been a recalled admiral or two of about his age still on active service but this man was only a Wavy Navy two-ringer. How come?

His age was only one of the odd aspects about him. Immediately striking was his Himalayan height and massive build, then the fleshy nose, hammocks under the eyes, Michelin jowls and—most extraordinary of all—in his right eye a monocle. In white drill shorts, he kept a fountain pen clipped to the top of his white stockings and whenever he left the wardroom, even to go to his banda, he sported a silver-topped Malacca cane.

After the first evening I noted this distinctly one-off character in conversation with first one, then another of his fellow officers but never the same one again. By the end of the week, whenever his bulk loomed on the horizon, occupants of the wardroom became ostentatiously absorbed in the contents of their glasses or their newspapers.

On inquiry I learned that his name was McLaglen, Lieut Sydney Leopold McLaglen, RNVR, a sufficiently unusual surname for me to associate with, and see a resemblance to, the raucous sergeant in *Gunga Din*, the roaring *Beloved Brute* or, again, that pugilist's mug surmounted by a Foreign Legionnaire's kepi in *Under Two Flags*, all Hollywood films that had thrilled pre-war movie fans. Could there be a connection? The physique was similar. And the face? Surely I was not imagining a resemblance in those rubicund, fleshy features a few yards away across the wardroom to those I had seen only on the silver screen: those of Victor McLaglen, Hollywood's epitome of machismo, the inveterate tough guy, the John Wayne or Gene Hackman of the Thirties and Forties.

Confirmation came soon enough. Shunned by everyone else, Leopold lowered his huge frame into the cane chair beside me and we began by exchanging information about our current war efforts. His, apparently, included training the Ceylon police in unarmed combat. This struck me as somewhat irrelevant considering there was not the remotest possibility of the Japanese invading Ceylon now that they were on the run in far-away Burma. And, even if there had been, I doubt whether the Colombo cops would have had either the will or the opportunity to try out their newly acquired skills in unarmed combat against fully armed invaders who had conquered about two-thirds of Asia.

There had been an invasion scare in Ceylon two days after Pearl Harbor in December 1941 when the battleship *Prince of Wales* and the battle-cruiser *Repulse* had been sunk and when the Japanese aircraft-carrier force struck in April 1942, sinking two heavy cruisers, the *Cornwall* and *Dorsetshire*, and bombing Colombo and Trincomalee, where they sank the aircraft carrier *Hermes*. It was not known at that time that the Japanese had reached the westernmost limit of their conquests.

If Leo noticed he had been shunned, did he have any inkling why? I doubt whether it ever occurred to him that the Silent Service eschewed the line-shoot, considered in the RN officers' code the next most heinous crime after treason. However, blissful in his ignorance of this taboo, when he heard that my current duty was to give publicity to the operations and personnel of the BEIF, he had absolutely no inhibitions about launching into an account of the redoubtable exploits of Leopold McLaglen.

His confirmation that he was indeed the brother or, more accurately, one of the eight brothers of Victor McLaglen was made with a certain diffidence which was at first open to several interpretations: modesty, perhaps, at being so closely associated with a name known to millions of film-goers? That didn't seem to square with what appeared on short acquaintance to be the bombastic character of Leopold McLaglen. On the contrary, did he have reasons for not wanting to be associated with Victor?

Having at last found a sympathetic ear, Leopold's verbal flow, which even initially needed little prompting, turned into a veritable spate of reminiscing. In due course I came to the conclusion that the tone in which he had attested to his relationship to Victor was meant to imply:

> Yes, I'm the brother of the famous Victor McLaglen all right but don't imagine for a minute, young man, that I'm not every inch as worthy of such fame as he's won, even if until now

you've never heard of me.

As he cornered me on several subsequent evenings, I began to realise that something more than the roulette wheel of coincidence must have accounted for the remarkable similarities in the careers of these two brothers.

In everything Leopold recounted about his own deeds he implied or expressly stated that he had gone at least one better than Victor. On the other hand, Victor was the younger by one year so that possibly it was he who from childhood had been trying to emulate and surpass the exploits of Leopold, the eldest of nine sons of the Revd Dr McLaglen, one-time Bishop of Clermont near Cape Town.[78] There was no doubt, however, that Leopold (who was sixty-two at the time of our encounter) was intent on shrinking the stature of little brother Victor (who was a mere six foot three inches and weighed only fifteen stone to Leopold's six foot six and sixteen stone.) 'I'm very proud of the fact that I've held three commissions signed by three monarchs: King Edward VII, George V and now George VI.' His voice boomed above the wardroom's subdued conversational hum. 'Not bad, eh? And what's more I've served in each of Their Majesties' three armed services.'

'Really? And how did that come about?' I enquired—not that our Leo needed any encouragement.

'Well, I started soldiering in 1900. Just a lad of er, let me see—sixteen. I left home—we were in Bromley, Kent by then—and joined up in the Imperial Light Horse in South Africa. I got my commission when I was eighteen and served throughout the Boer War under Generals Babington, Shackleton and Brocklehurst ... ' He made these names rumble like a military drum roll.

Brother Victor, he let it be known, had enlisted in the Life Guards at fourteen so as to serve in the same Boer War but somehow landed up in Windsor Castle, the nearest he ever got to Spion Kop or Mafeking. So that was Round One to Leo.

After regaling me with some of his Boer War experiences, he jumped to 1914. Sniffing war in the air, the young Leopold had sailed 17,000 miles from Australia where he had settled down in the meantime. He was commissioned for the second time one month after the start of the war in September 1914:

---

[78] As Victor died (aged 72) in 1949 it is impossible to get his version or to assess to what extent sibling rivalry played a part in his climb to fame.

> Yes, m'boy, at Chatham I trained all the officers and men of the warships *Vindictive*, *Daffodil* and *Hindustan* in armed and unarmed combat. That was for the raid on Zeebrugge, in 1915—the first commando raid of modern times, y'know.

The Sinhalese messboy padded in silently with another gin and orange, as Leo recalled how he had served on the Somme, then in East Africa where he was wounded. Later, as Staff Captain Leopold McLaglen, he became Military Landing Officer at Calais in 1918.

And what was brother Victor doing meanwhile? He had joined the Irish Fusiliers, got both knifed and poisoned in Mespot[79] and ended his war as Assistant Provost Marshal in Baghdad, a mere three-pip captain. Leopold, on the other hand, took his leave of the Army as a major. He was still leading on points.

Adolf Hitler gave Leo, at fifty-five, his third chance to play war games but not this time as a soldier. In 1939 he became Pilot Officer Leopold McLaglen RAF and was shortly promoted to squadron leader. With the Nazi juggernaut gearing up for Operation *Sealion*, our island was apparently in imminent peril from invasion. But no need for England to tremble. Squadron Leader L. McLaglen was at hand organising the defence of certain important airfields, he confided with a nod and a wink from which I was supposed to understand that he had laid some ingeniously unpleasant surprises for Adolf's paratroopers.

There was a gap in the Leopold Story that he never got around to filling: what had transpired to make him leave the RAF and join the RNVR, dropping rank from a two-and-a-half ring squadron leader to a two-ring lieutenant in the Wavy Navy? His own explanation was: 'I wanted to get to grips with the Japs, m'boy.'

Apart from telling me that he was in the battleship *King George V* when she bombarded the Germans on the Isle of Melos north of Crete in 1944, I learned little of what he had been doing in the Navy before he turned up in Colombo training the island's police in unarmed combat. This was a phase that somehow got overlooked when he decided to get in another sly dig at Little Brother Victor: 'He can do his fighting on the screen. As for me, I don't consider I'm too ancient to do my bit for the Old Country.'

---

[79] Mesopotamia, now part of Iraq.

I reckon Leo lost a point there, for hitting below the belt. Victor could hardly put his body at the disposal of the Old Country even if for no other reason than that he was already a citizen of the USA.

On another evening, Leo invited me into his banda to inspect his 'inventions'. First of these was his Heath Robinson booby trap to deter uninvited guests. This consisted of strands of cotton stretched across the window (unglazed and always open because of the heat), the ends tied to a collection of gin bottles high up on the shelves. 'Don't trust these natives, m'boy. Any of 'em come sneaking through that window when I'm asleep, that little contrivance will wake me up instantly—and give 'em a shock into the bargain!' A mirthless belly chuckle came out of the gathering gloom inside the banda.

Leo then dived into the black trunk which he pulled from under his bed. After rummaging around he pulled out another of his inventions, a knuckle-duster with a vicious spike sticking out at right angles. Leopold extolled its assets: 'If you're engaging an assailant in front of you and some bastard comes at you from behind you just swing your arm back, like this … ' and, swoosh, went the leg-o'-mutton arm tipped by the spiked knuckle-duster in a backward sweep … 'and you cop him with the knife like that. Dainty little toy, eh?'

I appeased him with a nod and a grin but in truth felt much safer when he was comfortably seated, reminiscing. So I led him back to filling the peacetime gaps in his story.

Peace was evidently just a barely tolerable interlude while Mars had forty winks and Leo had to take special precautions against softening up before the next bout of war games, so he devoted the non-belligerent years to perfecting his own system of unarmed combat and travelled the world instructing police forces in jujitsu. More than 15,000 London policemen, he assured me, had passed through his hands. He had also set up a jujitsu club at Oxford University. 'The ladies of Somerville College and Lady Margaret Hall joined the club as well. D'yer know something? I reckon I was the first man to put women athletes on an equal footing with men.'

~~

I was, of course, already struck by the patent similarity in the careers of the two brothers and was curious to discover if Leopold's obsession with unarmed combat had any parallel in Victor's repertoire. I made a tactful enquiry. 'Well, yes,' Leo admitted, 'he did a bit of professional wrestling. Boxing, too. In fact, he became boxing champion of Eastern Canada. What's more, he went six rounds with Jack Johnson.' Victor must have been no mean dab with his dukes if he had survived six rounds with the fabulous Negro world heavyweight. However, Leopold's tribute to his brother's prowess was evidently grudging, judging by his reaction, not only to the interest I showed when he told me about it, but also to the clanger I then proceeded to drop. 'And did you do any professional wrestling yourself?' I asked in all innocence. There was a moment's awful silence as the monocled eye swivelled around to transfix me with a reproachful glare. 'D'yer mean to tell me, m'boy, that you didn't know that I became jujitsu champion of the world in 1907? And that I retained the title in more than forty contests?'

He was only appeased by this lamentable gap in my education to the extent that he was able to seize the opportunity of filling it by recalling incidents in his wrestling career. These were calculated to put the six-round dispute between Little Brother Victor and Jack Johnson, if not in the shade, then at least into perspective. Leo, it seemed, had 'got to grips with the Japs' in a far more literal sense than he was ever destined to do in wartime:

> The Japanese jujitsu champion from whom I wrested the title in 1907 was a Professor Kanada—that was his title anyhow. The little bugger declared before the match that he would rather die on the mat than be defeated at the hands of an Englishman. By God, it was only by the skin of his teeth that he didn't. The contest was in front of 30,000 people in New Westminster, British Columbia, 14,000 of 'em Kanada's own compatriots. The Prof was so stubborn it lasted one hour and thirty-eight minutes and at the end of it he was almost totally paralysed. The Chief Sheriff of New Westminster was acting as referee and declared me world champion.

Macabre though it was, he recounted this with evident relish. But I was not to be let off with the paralysing of this hapless Japanese wrestler. Leo, who incidentally claimed that he too had been in Hollywood in the Thirties, acting as technical adviser on certain films and had himself appeared on the screen, was determined to show that he was not lacking in a sense of theatre. This Thousand and One Nights tale was moving to its dénouement.

Leo fished around again in his black trunk and brought out a sheaf of cuttings which he shuffled through. Then, he exclaimed triumphantly:

> There you are! It was all in the papers at the time. That's it: 913, when I took on two Japs at the same time, m'boy. How well I remember it! The Belvedere Palace in Calcutta, home of Warren Hastings the Empire-builder.[80] In fact, our match took place on a carpet that had belonged to Warren Hastings himself, valued at £10,000. Stubborn, m'boy, blind stubborn the Japs. D'yer know? These little buggers wouldn't quit until I'd broken the wrist of one of 'em and bust the other's arm

I suppose even Hollywood was not big enough for two McLaglens. Otherwise, Victor's fame based on appearing in fifty films might not have eclipsed Leopold's—and this bizarre sibling rivalry might have produced yet another twist.

~~

A suitably abridged and edited version of the Leopold story was given the Navy's official imprimatur by passing through the usual censorship and issued to the British media by the Chief of the Department of Naval Information (the Press Division having changed its title). It also happened to be published in the *Times of Ceylon* and so was seen by some of our wardroom colleagues. One of them—I think he commanded a Light Coastal Forces flotilla—was furious. 'Are you responsible for that?' he demanded without raising his voice but holding up the offending article. I confessed I was. 'You should be ashamed. It's a disgrace to the Service,' he censured me with restrained, cool acerbity. I had broken the unwritten code, perpetrated the unforgivable, by abetting Lieut Leopold McLaglen RNVR's personal line-shoot.

---

[80] Warren Hastings (1732–1818) became the first Governor-General of India after making a large fortune in the East India Company. He retired after making a second fortune, was impeached for murder and extortion but was acquitted after a seven-year trial in Westminster Hall but was left impoverished and discredited.

Chapter 16

Dracula Unslaked

The Japanese began the campaign [for Imphal and Kohima] *with an army of 85,000 men; in it they lost 53,000. The British and Indian casualties amounted to 16,700. The result ... was terrible, wasteful, ignominious defeat. It was one of the worst disasters that the Japanese army suffered in the whole war.*

Total War: Guy Wint

With the blood of nearly 70,000 men soaking into the soil of northern Burma and more spilt as the combatants moved south, for once the code-name Operation *Dracula* seemed appropriate. But the actual occupation of Rangoon from a seaward assault, the objective of *Dracula*, would prove almost bloodless.

A favourite expression of the British East Indies Fleet's Commander-in-Chief, Admiral Sir Arthur Power, at pre-operation briefings in Colombo was about getting close to the enemy 'to see the whites of his eyes'. This may have inspired someone with the idea of providing Charlie Trusler and me with .45 revolvers to supplement his camera and my pen and notebook for our coverage of *Dracula*. In spite of every photographer's ambition to get close-ups, it is not impugning Charlie's valour to doubt whether he had any ambition to get a picture of the whites of any still-armed and belligerent Japanese. In any case, how was he supposed to wield a camera and a .45? Sensibly, he declined to be so equipped. Nobody in the European theatre had thought any more of arming ONPs and ONRs with revolvers than they had of giving us a tot before an assault. Although I had no idea under what circumstances I could possibly use it and unable to produce any reason to counter Charlie's scorn for what he considered to be Errol Flynn affectation, nevertheless I girded on my holster. This, combined with an item of clothing I would come by, would lead in the course of this op to a temporary rift in our normally amicable relations.

In some respects, the intended capture of the Burmese capital was a race to beat the monsoon and finish off the Burma campaign before SEAC was obliged to concede to the Americans who wanted to withdraw their transport aircraft for operations in China. They had all along considered the South East Asia campaign of secondary importance and were highly suspicious of British intentions: the restoration of the Union flag over its colonies. Also, Chiang Kai-shek was demanding the withdrawal of his Chinese troops from Burma. So the deadline for the retaking of Rangoon had been set for June 1945.

~~

We flew from Colombo to Calcutta, touching down in baking Madras in a Dakota in which comfort had been totally sacrificed to provide maximum space for personnel and equipment. There were several senior Army officers on board, one of whom, a lieutenant colonel, had curled up in the middle of the deck in the midst of his colleagues and was somehow managing to snatch forty winks. Somewhere south of the Himalayas we ran into a storm. Without any warning our plane plummeted and, after what seemed an eternity, it fetched up with a terrific jolt. Unforgettable is the expression of utter amazement on the colonel's face as he shot up from unconsciousness into a sitting position. Seconds later, we fell into another air pocket with the same plumb drop and shuddering arrest which made inexperienced aeronauts like myself marvel that the wings did not snap off.

We stayed overnight in Calcutta, time enough to note the appalling poverty and homeless thousands who slept in the streets. The next day we were airborne again and, via Chittagong and Akyab, eventually reached Ramree Island. Here we joined a flotilla of Light Coastal Forces which left Kyaukpu bound for the assembly point some twenty-five to thirty miles off the mouth of the Rangoon River, one of the drains of the Irrawaddy delta. Because of the rapid advance of the 14th Army, D-Day had been brought forward to 2 May, a fortnight before the monsoon was due—or so it was thought. In fact, it teemed with rain throughout the previous night.

This would be my fourth assault but the first one where there would be no preliminary heavy Naval bombardment. The river was too shallow for anything with more draft than MLs or MTBs to penetrate anywhere near the city twenty miles upstream. The bombardment, such as it was, would be by gun and rocket craft and bombing by aircraft. Indian infantry landed on the morning of 2 May, seven miles up-river on both sides, unopposed as at Akyab and other places on the Arakan coast. Only the Gurkha parachutists, dropped to capture the battery at Elephant Point, had a brief skirmish with the Japanese. There was a current unsubstantiated rumour that some troops were bombed by our own planes.

In the ML in which we proceeded cautiously up this tidal river or *chaung* we were unaware of the whereabouts of the enemy. On board were veterans of *chaung* warfare who had penetrated and fought the Japanese right down the Arakan coast. I knew why the crew was so alert and trigger-happy from interviews I had had with officers of a flotilla of MLs and from which I made this sketch for the *Ceylon Review*:

> Camouflaged, the Motor Launch, bristling with guns, nestles among the gaunt roots of the mangroves growing out of the soft ooze. To the commanding officer and his crew any movement other than the sluggish motion of this Burmese *chaung* means only one thing ... They are twenty miles from their natural element, the open sea. Many of them are veterans of engagements with their German counterparts in the English Channel, in 'E-Boat Alley' and in the Med. But this is a totally new type of warfare for Light Coastal Forces, stealthy and unpredictable. Everyone is tense and alert. Suddenly, a mangrove branch sways, almost imperceptibly. But the gunner has seen it. It might have been a breath of wind but the orders are 'open up' on anything in the jungle that moves. The gunner presses the trigger; the gun spits a short burst. The branch sways again; there is a snapping of twigs and a thud. That is all any of the crew see or hear but they know that another Japanese sniper will snipe no more. Over-dramatised? No, this incident actually happened—and was repeated a dozen times and more—when flotillas of Light Coastal Forces operating in the Arakan penetrated Burma's inland network of waterways

time and time again, disrupting Japanese lines of communication and supply and cutting their escape routes as they retreated before the 14th Army.

In fact, considerable numbers of Japanese troops managed to escape capture during the 1944–45 campaign and there were still 100,000 of them left in Burma after the fall of Rangoon.

This flotilla's CO also recalled the following incident:

> We were once patrolling up one of the *chaungs* when all seemed quiet and serene. A bullet out of the blue smashed through the for'ard window of the wheelhouse, missing my quartermaster by a hair's breadth. I immediately increased speed and brought all guns to bear on the spot where I thought the bullet had come from. I was not left in doubt for long. Other bullets followed, puncturing the hull and exhaust pipe and slashing through cushions in the wardroom, the First Lieutenant's suitcase with his Number Ones inside and two of the crew's overcoats. The snipers proved to be two machine-gun nests. We let them have it with everything we had and definitely knocked them out. We were sniped by rifle fire that same night as we came out of the river. But next day all was silent.

Illustrating the shallowness of these *chaungs* where the depth of water could change from eighteen to two fathoms within a short stretch, this CO described how his ML got stuck on an uncharted rock in the middle of a *chaung* and only got off after violent engine-produced oscillations and getting the ship's company to stand first on one side of the deck and then doubling over to the other. On another occasion he ordered a seaman to take a sounding. After some minutes he called to this man from the bridge, inquiring about the result of his findings. There was no answer; the seaman was still concentrating on his job. Further minutes elapsed before the CO, more impatiently, repeated his enquiry: 'What is the sounding?'

'I can still see the top, sir!' came the reply.

Despite learning that there were no Japanese in the city when we eventually tied up in Rangoon, our approach had been punctuated by short bursts of fire from one ML or another at suspect movements in the muddy undergrowth on the banks.

~~

The gilded glory of the Shwedagon pagoda, the men with hennaed beards and whiskers, the crones sitting on steps smoking pipes—these are fleeting impressions that remain of Rangoon, a city without motor traffic. Only gradually did cars appear from unlikely places where they had been hidden or even buried for years to avoid the Japanese commandeering them.

It was boots that made the most impact on my memory, on my appearance and on Lofty Trusler's threshold of tolerance. I found them in a market on a stall among brightly coloured vegetables and fly-blown meat. They were pigskin, boots of extraordinary suppleness which must have been Nipponese army issue. I was immediately seduced by their texture, in spite of their colour. They were yellow, not an unobtrusive ochre, nearer buttercup. Bright yellow boots, protruding from bottle-green battledress, which I had acquired since the Cheduba incident, I realised was not what would be expected of a properly dressed officer in His Majesty's Navy. But what the Hell, what harm could there be in a little sartorial unorthodoxy? I bought them with Indian rupees and at the first opportunity put them on.

When the courteous, shy and normally good-humoured Charlie saw his chum, not only accoutred with a revolver in a holster which was bad enough, but shod in Japanese yellow daisy-roots, that was the limit. Words were unnecessary. In no way would he be seen in the company of such an apparition. He turned on his heel and stalked out of my life—at least until we met up again in Colombo.

~~

This was 3 May, exactly five years since *Afridi* had steamed out of Namsen Fjord into the Norwegian Sea. It brought back memories of the other events of that memorable day. The thought came to me that night as I lay on a bare parquet floor in a spacious empty bungalow surrounded by lawns on the outskirts of the city. Before the occupation in March 1942 it had probably belonged to a British expatriate family who had either escaped or, more likely, spent years in detention or even perished. It would have been commandeered by the Japanese military. Where were they now? We had met no visible opposition coming up-river and there were certainly no enemy in the centre of the city. But how close were the Japanese? It was rather like that situation in Rouen when I was looking for the Green Berets and not knowing where the Germans were. Now, however, I was on my own. I had found the door of the bungalow open and walked in. Like the rest of Rangoon there was no electric light. I presumed the Japanese had sabotaged the power before departing. There did not seem to be any inhabitants in the vicinity from whom I could get a light of any kind. So I lay down early but with the faintly uneasy feeling, always accentuated at night, that unfamiliar sounds might herald a stealthy return of the last occupants. I was as ignorant of the fact that the Japanese had evacuated Rangoon six days earlier as I was that thousands of miles to the north-west, the Germans had capitulated in Italy the day before and the Russians had reached Berlin and raised the Red Flag over the Reichstag. On the *qui vive* and on an unyielding floor, I slept lightly.

~~

In the morning I became acquainted with the bungalow's last tenants. In a drawer of one of the few remaining pieces of furniture I found a number of snaps of Japanese soldiers, two on a motorcycle and a group posing with their truck. One of them could have been the prototype for the PoW camp commandant in *Bridge on the River Kwai*.

On the way back to the city centre, a White man in correspondent's uniform with a weeping Burmese woman at his side beckoned to me rather agitatedly. He turned out to be British, a news cameraman with a name that sounded like 'Bovril'. The woman was claiming that an Indian soldier had forced her to take off her bangles and hand them over. Sir Gallahad 'Bovril' insisted that all three of us search for the barracks where the Indian Infantry Brigade were billeted and contact an officer. A parade was duly ordered and the woman walked along the line peering into the face of each soldier until she spotted the man she claimed had been the robber. He confessed and produced the purloined bangles. I don't know how he was dealt with but I was gratified to see that an authenticated incident of pillage had been thwarted.

With 'Bovril' I hitched a passage on an ancient tramp, the *Salween*, which had formerly been commandeered as a trooper, and now crawled northwards the length of the Bay of Bengal. In Calcutta I discovered that my new companion lived in a well-furnished flat. He was greeted by his heavily-bejewelled Indian mistress. Several times, until I left to hitch another Dakota passage to Colombo, 'Bovril' tried to persuade me to part with the revolver for which he assured me he had much more need than I had: to protect his flat and its contents, including the bejewelled lady, from dacoits.

The yellow boots, which obviously could not be exposed within the precincts of the BEIF HQ, were stowed away for my eventual return to the UK—and I was reconciled with Lofty.

In the studio of Radio Colombo where I was waiting my cue to put over an account of Operation *Dracula*, the Sinhalese announcer-cum-disc jockey was playing music over the air from a gramophone which even for those days was patently of Steam Age vintage. Its motor, without warning, lost power but as the music started trailing towards a premature ending the jockey, in the best 'the show must go on' tradition, pushed the record around with his finger—an erratic prelude to the *Dracula* broadcast.

Chapter 17

Tribals Again

*No one killed them. It's the war, the whole bloody war. We've just got to do
these things and say our prayers at the end.*

[Spoken in remorse by the CO of the corvette *Compass Rose* after he had dropped
depth-charges on a U-boat contact knowing that they would also kill Allied seamen
swimming from their torpedoed freighter and expecting to be saved.]

The Cruel Sea: Nicholas Monsarrat

*The Allies learned in pain and sorrow that anti-aircraft guns alone were
insufficient defence against the bombers and that fighter cover was essential.
Without adequate defence against the dive-bomber, neither fleets nor armies
could operate.*

Narvik: Captain Donald Macintyre DSO and two Bars, DSC, RN

It was the long arm of coincidence that stretched out over a span of
five years and linked me with two Tribal class destroyers. My war at
sea had begun aboard *Afridi* and the last enemy action I would
witness was aboard *Tartar*.

By the end of the war there were over twenty classes of destroyers in
the Royal Navy, so there were at least nineteen chances to one against
serving again in the same class, odds which lengthened after taking into

consideration that eleven Tribals had been sunk.[81] I had been afloat in six different types of Naval craft. I could have served for the last time on any one of these or, for that matter, in some other kind of warship. As far as the British East Indies Fleet was concerned, the odds were thirty-six to one against me serving in a Tribal since there were only three of them in the BEIF's flotilla of thirty-nine RN destroyers (and those of four other nationalities). Furthermore, it was an incident which occurred when I was aboard *Tartar* similar to ones that happened five years before which would evoke a graphic recall of these and the other events of 3 May 1940.

Yet another link with the past was that all three of the BEIF Tribals had been in the Norwegian campaign. *Eskimo* had had the whole of her forepart blown off in the Second Battle of Narvik by a tin-fish fired from a German destroyer and at one time there had been so little hope of her surviving that her confidential books had been destroyed. Sufficient repairs were carried out when she was grounded in the fjord for her to steam stern-first to a safer anchorage and eventually to return to the UK to fight another day. *Nubian* had followed *Afridi* into Namsos for the evacuation.

Tartar had figured in the incident at the bombed and burning town of Molde when the courageous Norwegian General Ruge ordered his staff to disembark upon learning they were to be taken to the UK. The following day another of our ships landed him at Tromsö in the far north of Norway. *Tartar* had also had a successful brush with German destroyers off the Normandy beachhead three days after D-Day, though she herself sustained damage on that occasion. This, then, was the destroyer I was aboard when, in company with the other two BEIF Tribals, *Eskimo* and *Nubian*, we steamed out of Trincomalee on 5 June 1945 bound for yet another anti-shipping sweep, Operation *Irregular*, this time around the Nicobar Islands and off Sabang on the northern tip of Sumatra.

~~

The *Kuroshiyo Maru 2* was a large Japanese tank landing ship which had run the gauntlet of the BEIF when almost the entire fleet had put to sea after it was learned the cruiser *Haguro* was intending to evacuate troops from the Andaman Islands and transport them to Singapore. At the same

---

[81] Three bombed, including *Gurkha*, *Mashona* and *Zulu*. Five were torpedoed: *Cossack*, *Mohawk*, *Bedouin*, *Matebele* and *Somali*; *Sikh* was destroyed by Tobruk shore batteries; *Punjabi* was in a collision and *Maori* was scuttled in Malta.

time, the *Kuroshiyo*, escorted by Submarine-Chaser No. 57, was to evacuate 450 troops from the Nicobars, the islands due south of the Andamans. This she did, successfully eluding BEIF surface ships detached from the main force to look for her. They spotted the *Haguro* instead—and not only survived a bombing attack by an aircraft from one of our carriers but brought it down. The troops she carried appear to have been landed in Penang (Malaya). The *Kuroshiyo* and the same submarine-chaser escort (which had been repaired in Singapore after being damaged by a mine) had set forth again in June, probably intending to carry out further evacuations.

These two enemy vessels were first located by one of our submarines in the Makassar Strait between Borneo and the Celebes (today Sulawesi), about twenty miles north-east of Sabang, and in the early hours of 12 June, one week after we had left Trinco, our destroyers made contact. Within an hour both vessels were sent to the bottom by gunfire and torpedoes. As previously, survivors in the sea refused to be picked up. At least this was 'butchery' of warships, not another traumatic small-boat sweep like Operation *Sunfish*.

Perhaps an hour after these two ships had been sunk, I was standing on *Tartar*'s bridge as we sped westwards, Trinco-bound. The sea was as smooth as a plastic tablecloth, reflecting the grey, unbroken, high cloud ceiling. The only sounds were the deep hum of our turbines, the ping ... ping ... ping ... of the ASDIC and the barely audible swish of our bow wave as it curled back against the ship's sides. Suddenly, directly overhead there sounded the air-tearing swoosh that was instantly and unmistakably recognisable. Unlike when the rockets threatened annihilation at Walcheren, my reaction was instantaneous: the instinct of self-preservation took over before self-control had a chance. But even before I had gone halfway to hitting the deck, the bomb had dropped a few yards off our starboard bow with a comparatively subdued underwater explosion and I straightened up in time to see the fountain of displaced water falling back. Apart from slewing and heeling to port from the expanding wave impact, *Tartar* carried on slicing through the ocean. A few rounds were loosed off at the cloud layer but the enemy remained invisible and soundless. He could only have glimpsed us through a hole in the cloud and the bomb had been incredibly well aimed. According to John Winton in *Forgotten Fleet*, astern of us *Nubian* had a similar experience. This could only be accounted for if our hidden antagonist had released two bombs in quick succession; I was too preoccupied with

Tartar's near-miss to have glanced astern at *Nubian*. There was no further attack on either of us.

It was not until those elysian days in Ceylon between VJ-Day, the end of the Second World War, and returning to Blighty on HMT *Mooltan* when, idly reflecting on my good fortune at having survived the last six years unscathed, it struck me that, had the bomb aimed at *Tartar* hit its target, I might well have shared the fate of my uncle. He was a lieutenant in the North Staffs Regiment killed, like the poet Wilfred Owen, in Belgium only nine days before the armistice which had brought the First World War to an end. The *Tartar* near-miss did bring back vividly the last occasion, five years before, when I had been even closer not to one but to two exploding bombs and, within an hour, to another which had also near-missed a destroyer's bows ...

~~

Just after 08.30 on the morning of Friday 3 May 1940 the alarm rattlers sounded on *Afridi*. I had come off the middle watch at 04.00 and turned-in as we were still steaming through Namsen Fjord making for the open sea.[82]

What a contrast, I thought, as I harked back to that morning, between the warm Indian Ocean and the blue waters of the Norwegian fjord, icy under the clear canopy of an early spring morning, fed by the last snows from the tops of the distant mountains.

Breakfasts were abandoned as we clambered up the mess-deck ladder and made for our action stations. Mine was still the for'ard 4.7 guns' supply party. We were a mixed bunch: the NAAFI canteen manager's assistant, a supply branch rating, officers' stewards (who were Maltese) as well as off-watch seamen and stokers like me. Some of the thirty-five pongos, the very last soldiers to leave Central Norway, lent us a hand, passing up the shells and cordite to the guns' crews on the upper deck. The others sat on the seamen's mess-deck watching the Navy at work. Apparently, a seaplane had been shadowing the convoy since it left the fjord at 05.00. When the first attacks began around 08.45 and the guns started firing, some of the soldiers admitted to feeling uneasy at being in a confined space and made their way aft to the open deck in the waist of the ship where they had a chance of seeing what was going on.

---

[82] See pp. 117–118

The Navy, augmented by French and Polish ships, had embarked all 5,400 troops from Namsos undetected by the Germans in the short hours of darkness.[83] But it was obvious that we would be spotted in daylight, and so it was no surprise when the first waves of bombers came over. At first they seemed to pay most attention to the cruisers, especially *Devonshire*, in which Vice-Admiral Cunningham had been directing operations, and the French *Montcalm*. The anti-aircraft cruiser *Carlisle* put up a particularly effective barrage (almost expending her ammunition) and none of the cruisers was hit.

Some fifty bombers,[84] probably operating from Vaernes airport near Trondheim, had begun attacking the evacuation convoy at 08.50 and would continue to do so well into the afternoon and as far west as 200 miles from the Norwegian coast. Not only high-level JU 88s with which we were familiar but for the first time JU 87 Stukas which had been operating against our troops ashore were now going to try out their dive-bombing devilry against our ships. The French trooper *El Djezair* logged fifty attacks by more than forty bombers between 10.00 and 15.30 hours. The Luftwaffe was wheeling and diving in the cloudless sky [85] and the battle raged over the wide area occupied by the fleet. Sometimes *Afridi*'s guns would be silent as the attackers passed out of our range and concentrated on another part of the convoy. Then the gun supply parties would be able to stand easy and, since it was 'out pipes' on the mess-deck while the magazine was open, the men would slip out onto the upper for a smoke. This was also an opportunity for them to see what was going on.

Shortly after 10.00 there was a deep red flash followed by a billow of black smoke some miles ahead, away on our starboard beam—first blood to the dive-bombers.

An Aldis lamp flashed a message from *Devonshire*: the destroyers *Grenade* and *Imperial* were to go to the aid of the victim. Further messages flashed between us and the flagship and, ordered to provide anti-aircraft cover while a rescue operation was mounted, we also altered

---

[83] A total of 12,000 troops were evacuated from Central Norway; the others, from Åndalsnes, had already reached the UK safely. (See p. 114.) Rear-Admiral Cadart in command of the French troopships, in his secret report to his Admiral of the Fleet, claimed that because these *croiseurs auxiliaires* were seldom the bombers' targets 'the enemy cannot have known about the Namsos evacuation and presumed they were returning empty.'

[84] This is the estimate Rear-Admiral G. Vivien, in command of the anti-aircraft ships, and the figure Chamberlain gave the House of Commons; French sources and the American cinephotographer Bonney Powell somehow managed the precise figure of thirty-nine.

[85] Rear-Admiral Cadart's account reported: 'Weather very fine, wind NE, force 1 to 2, flat sea, clear sky, exceptional visibility.'

course some degrees to starboard. Able Seaman Jack Wearn from his action station by the low angle director abaft the bridge remembers hearing Captain Vian give the order: 'Signal *Kelly* I am going to assist *Bison*.' When we arrived on the scene, *Imperial* and *Grenade* were already alongside the stricken French destroyer.

French accounts of what happened vary slightly. One maintains that a bomb had exploded close to the bows of the French cruiser *Montcalm*, sending up a cascade of water which for seconds obscured her from the view of the other ships. Then, a little later, the *Montcalm* again became the principal target of the Stukas and one started to dive on the cruiser. In mid-descent, smoke started pouring from it and it seemed to the hundreds of pairs of eyes watching the contest that it had been hit. The elation of the crews was short-lived; it pulled out of the dive, evidently unharmed, altered course and started another dive, which became almost vertical, on the French destroyer *Bison*.

Another version described how the first wave of thirty-nine bombers came over, at first making repeated bombing runs from a comparatively high altitude. Then the tactics changed and the dive-bombing started, despite the barrage put up by the escorts. The *Montcalm* was picked on by one of these Stukas which dived on her, changed direction in the last seconds before releasing its bomb which hit the *Bison* instead. There was no mention in this account of smoke coming from the Stuka.

The *Bison* was a destroyer, first commissioned in 1930, which during night exercises off the coast of Brittany in February 1939 had her fo'c's'le sliced off as far as the bridge by the cruiser *Georges Leygues* with the loss of nineteen lives. Her refit in Lorient dockyard was not completed until a month after the outbreak of war. Now, thirteen months later, it was the *Bison*'s bridge which received a direct hit from the Stuka's bomb. She had already been 'sunk' over Radio Stuttgart by France's Lord Haw Haw, Paul Ferdonnet. Now, it was for real.

The Stuka's 600-lb. bomb tore through the *Bison*'s bridge, killing her CO, Captain Roger Bouan, and six other officers including the British liaison officer and exploded in the for'ard magazine. Observers on the troopers, *El-Mansour* and *El-Kantara*, afterwards described how *Bison*'s guns were blazing at the dive-bomber as it swooped almost vertically. Nothing seemed to happen for a few seconds, then a huge flame spurted from the forepart of the ship and there was an ear-splitting explosion which sent a 138-mm gun, platform and all, sky-high, followed by a gust of hot air. Telegraphist Bill Outram standing outside the galley of the destroyer *Imperial,* saw 'after an almighty bang, a huge cloud of debris, smoke and steam' and as it cleared he could see that 'there was nothing at all for'ard of the *Bison*'s bridge.'

The drama of the ensuing minutes was captured in the report of the *Montcalm*'s officer of the watch:

> First the stern then *Bison*'s funnels emerge as the smoke lifts. The whole ship for'ard of No. 1 funnel appears to be cut off. The after end is still afloat. A fire is spreading on the portside from the bows towards the stern. *Montcalm* makes a wide sweep to starboard, coming within a hundred metres of the *Bison*. Survivors, most of them in lifejackets, are lining up in good order on the stern and midships.

Boatswain's mate on *Bison,* Yves Rivoal, would recall how he had come off watch at 10.00 and was coming down from the bridge eight minutes later when the bomb struck, killing the man who had just relieved him. He himself suffered burns to the face, hands and forearms. He saw how the forepart of the vessel and sections of the bridge fell in burning fragments into the sea. In spite of his burns Rivoal was able to lower one of the whalers himself in stages, first by the stern then the bows until, a few feet from the water, he levelled it. Three other matelots dropped aboard. It was freed from the davits and cast off with Rivoal at the helm.

> We were in the middle of an oil slick though it had not yet caught alight. But rowing was made difficult by so many hammocks that had got stuck in the oil. Because the whaler was wooden we couldn't get close enough to the blazing navigation bridge to help those trapped inside all that red-hot ironmongery. But among those we were able to rescue were Fernand Taraud, who had been flung into the sea from the crow's-nest, and Master Gunner Louis Le Blais, my Côtes d'Armor (Breton) compatriot who was so badly burned about the head and his face so swollen that, in order to cut his chinstrap to get his helmet off, my jack-knife took away some of his skin. We rescued three more of my comrades who were unrecognisable and went alongside the *Imperial* where the wounded were taken on board. We cast off again and were able to fish out of the sea Chief Engine-room Artificer Louis

Nay who was hanging onto a raft, as well as four more sailors, their faces disfigured by the burning oil. When we came alongside *Afridi* an officer ordered us to leave the whaler and come on board. End of mission! We were given a very warm welcome by His Majesty's sailors.

The rest of the convoy sailed on, the ships disappearing one by one over the horizon.

Most of *Bison*'s visible survivors were clustered on the stern which was gradually lifting higher out of the water and listing to starboard the deeper her bows submerged. Through the black smoke every now and then flames flickered dull red. This much I saw before I had to double back to my for'ard guns' supply party as another air attack developed. What I did not personally witness during brief lulls in the firing I have since gathered from those who did.

Imperial Telegraphist, Bill Outram, recalls men jumping from *Bison* into the sea and *Imperial* lowering two boats to pick them up. With other destroyers, she went alongside *Bison*:

> We could smell and see an oil slick coming around *Bison*'s stern while we were taking off survivors. Then we became aware that the oil had ignited and we had to back off. One of our boats brought exhausted and badly burnt men aboard *Imperial*. But the crew of the other boat, which was closer to the *Afridi*, was ordered by Captain Vian to come aboard his ship and the boat itself was sunk.

Meanwhile the Luftwaffe kept up its attacks. There were several near-misses around *Grenade* which suffered superficial structural damage but one bomb burst close enough for its splinters to kill four men on one of the guns. She was also machine-gunned from the air and this may have been the genesis of a rumour on *Afridi* that the Germans had been firing on the Frenchmen in the water. For *Afridi* Signalman Harold Kirk, viewing the scene from the bridge, it was more than a rumour:

> Picking up survivors was made very difficult because the Stukas returned and machine-gunned them in the water as they swam towards us and lots of oil slicks were set on fire.

At least those aboard *Grenade* had the satisfaction of seeing one of the Junkers disappear trailing smoke from its engine. *Grenade*'s commanding officer, Cdr R. C. Boyle RN, was commended by Home Fleet Commander-in-Chief Admiral Sir Charles Forbes for 'gallantly securing the stern of his ship to the sinking *Bison*, despite burning oil and exploding ammunition and was responsible for saving the lives of many of the *Bison*'s ship's company by this act.' William Ridgewell, a young ordinary seaman at the time, remembered:

> We did secure to *Bison*, stern-to-stern, and several French personnel jumped aboard. Others who jumped from midships climbed up our scrambling nets or were pulled into our whaler. I believe our captain was awarded the DSC for this and several of our ship's company the DSM.

But seared into his memory while *Grenade* was alongside was what he saw when he managed to peer through one of the *Bison*'s scuttles onto a mess-deck:

> When the magazine exploded it must have wrought so much damage to bulkheads and deck-heads that the men I saw who were still alive on the mess-deck knew they were trapped. It was horrendous to see the terror on their faces. There was no escape for them and nothing we could do to help them. The oil-fuel from *Bison*'s fractured tanks had spewed into the sea and was alight. There was so much smoke it was making it impossible for our gunners to spot the attacking aircraft so we had to pull away.

For those who need to rationalise the fortuitous it was luck or Fate or the mysteriously selective whims of a deity which governed who was to escape and who to die. For the more pragmatic it was just pure chance. Stoker Petty Officer Eugène Thomas from the Morbihan district of Brittany, for instance, considered himself 'lucky' because he was the only one to survive out of the eight men who normally sat at his mess table. He was queuing up at the galley which was in the fo'c'sle waiting to be served his grub before going below for his watch in the engine-room. When the bomb exploded in the for'ard magazine the next thing he knew he was flying through the air and dropped into the sea.

I was in a state of shock and had swallowed a lot of oil-fuel by the time I was fished out of the freezing sea by a whaler after what seemed an age.

The most bizarre escape was probably that of Fernand Taraud, in peacetime a trawlerman from the Atlantic Ile d'Yer off the Vendée coast. Like so many fishermen, he was a non-swimmer. When he was hurled by the explosion from the crow's-nest, wearing his helmet, fur-lined donkey jacket and calf-length sea boots, his chances of survival would have been nil except for a 'trick of Fate' if you will. At that time in the French navy, seamen were not kitted out with rubber waders. Instead, their sea-boots were calf-length clogs which were, in fact, hollowed-out beech logs with a battleship-grey-painted cloth covering. When Taraud was thrown into the sea one of these *sabot-bottes* came off and floated upside-down. He was able to cling onto it until Rivoal and his lifeboat came to his rescue.

Like *Grenade* and *Imperial*, *Afridi* also went alongside briefly, to play hoses on the flames licking around a depth-charge. But it was evident that they were gaining control and *Bison* was in imminent danger, not only from exploding depth-charges which may not have been neutralised, but of blowing up if the flames reached her after magazine. Such an explosion would have been calamitous for any vessel alongside and further attempts at ship-to-ship rescue had to be abandoned. All three destroyers stood off.

Some of the Frenchmen were crawling up the sloping deck to join their comrades on the stern. Some had already slid over it or jumped over the side into the sea. This, however, was covered with a glutinous coating of oil-fuel from *Bison*'s ripped tanks. Through this the swimmers laboured towards the whalers which had been lowered from the destroyers.

A scrambling net had been hung over our side and I saw coughing, gasping men clinging to it as helping hands reached down to haul them inboard, exhausted and oil-sodden, their lungs choked with the foul fuel. Some men in the water were also swimming through flames. Oil-browned arms were flung upwards, fingers clutching at emptiness, and slid back beneath the surface, screams of terror and agony ending in choking gurgles. Those who were hauled over the sides of the whalers were blinded, their faces, necks, shoulders and arms a mess of blistered flesh. The boats' crews were in danger of being enveloped by the flames.

One of those pulled out of the sea and brought aboard *Afridi* was the *Bison*'s gunnery officer, Lieut de Vaisseau Oudin who, being the most senior of *Bison*'s surviving officers after she was hit, had taken command until, according to the French, he had been the last to leave the ship.

Once aboard *Afridi* the worst cases were carried to the wardroom,[86] the only part of the ship that had a carpet, and gently laid on it. Others crowded into the bath space to try and clean off the oil-fuel or huddled over the galley stove to restore their circulation.

Still others of the sixty-nine *Bison* survivors we managed to bring aboard refused to leave the upper deck: the shock of the recent experience of nearly being trapped aboard their sinking ship had given them a horror of being in a confined space. I would learn that *Grenade* had picked up thirty-six but by dawn next morning twenty of them were buried at sea, together with her own four casualties. Four of those rescued by *Imperial* would also die overnight.

When we pulled away from *Bison,* the men still on board the doomed ship were urged through a loudhailer from our bridge to jump into the water where the whalers could pick them up. This was communicated by our Jimmy the One, Lt Cdr Meyrick who was a qualified French interpreter. Either because they could not swim or, more likely, petrified into immobility by the horror they saw taking place in the water, a little knot of men clung like barnacles to the stern which was by now even higher out of the water. I saw one man had climbed part-way up a mast and was clinging to it in terror.

As I had learned from that '*Marie Celeste*' episode with the derelict Finnish freighter [87] it was a law of the sea that wrecks could not be left on the surface as they were a danger to other shipping. Yet this was not the time for three British destroyers, detached from the convoy beneath these Stuka-infested skies, to linger while *Bison* gradually submerged before taking the final plunge. The moment had arrived for a decision concerning the patient's assisted termination.

Captain Vian was faced with making a decision like that of the fictitious CO of the *Compass Rose* and no less painful because he had no choice. He received the order from Admiral Cunningham to sink the *Bison*. The request came to Cunningham from Rear-Admiral Derrien, in command of the French ships. Should he wait until the last visible survivor had left the stricken ship? It was one of those decisions war

---

[86] A subsequent report maintained twenty-five were 'seriously burnt'.
[87] See p. 54.

inexorably imposes on those in command. *Bison* would have to be sunk despite the remainder of her crew still clinging to what was left of her and undoubtedly with men trapped below decks. There could be no further delay. Those Frenchmen we had rescued who were capable of remaining on our upper deck would have to watch their comrades who, for whatever reason, were unable to plunge into the water, being blown to pieces by an ally.

Two torpedoes were fired but because *Bison* was wallowing in the swell, they missed. Our 4.7s then opened fire. The first salvoes straddled the target. The man up the mast and those on the stern waved frantically. Some of the Frenchmen on our deck were visibly shaking and as salvo after salvo tore into the hulk, some could stand it no longer and went for'ard under cover.

This episode must have been so traumatic for Vian that in his account of *Bison*'s fate in his memoirs he merely recorded: 'The hulk was sunk, and the destroyers proceeded to overtake the convoy.' But in his official report, written on board *Imperial* on 4 May, he did record that 'the majority of survivors'—not all, it should be noted, 'had been rescued by 11.30' and ten minutes later, after *Grenade* and *Imperial* had left the scene, 'the wreck was then sunk by *Afridi* and foundered at 12.07.' Nor is the fact that men were still on board mentioned in any of three French accounts, each of them maintaining, almost in the same words: 'On avait sauvé tous les survivants.'

The water must have poured into the rents we tore in *Bison* and pieces of superstructure on the stern flew in all directions. Her agony seemed like a bull that resists death to the last gasp after being pierced by scores of *baderilleros* and the final thrust of the matador's sword. Only very reluctantly did she settle lower and lower in the water. Ordinary Seaman Ridgewell recalls that as *Grenade* left the scene 'the fore-end of *Bison* was just beginning to drop below the surface.' At 12.07, with a final lurch, she rolled over and the agitated seas closed over her grave.

~~

With our normal complement supplemented by a colonel and thirty-five soldiers of the York and Lancaster Regiment from Namsos, and now the sixty-nine Frenchmen from *Bison*, there was a total of over 350 men on board *Afridi* as she turned her bows westwards and raced at full speed to catch up with *Grenade*, *Imperial* and the main force.[88]

The dancing gold of the sea and the blue sky were chopped out of sight when I closed the hatch of No. 3 boiler-room above my head for the afternoon watch. As I climbed down the near vertical ladder to the plates I could see Stoker Petty Officer Sam Hardy already darting a look into the furnace, giving a turn with a spanner on the oil-fuel pump, adjusting a valve. By the time I joined him he was wiping his hands with a piece of cotton waste. Then he began rolling a tickler—all the while muttering inaudibly. The fans were roaring: *Afridi*'s 45,000 horsepower was being strained to the full.

It was nearly two hours into the afternoon watch when the message came through from the engine-room that we had caught up with the convoy, were reducing speed and No. 1 boiler-room was shutting down; only two boilers were now necessary. The needle on the steam pressure gauge began to drop back. The fan speed was reduced but in place of its racket the guns suddenly started firing. Very shortly after the 4.7s barked, the pom-poms and point-fives joined in. To us down below, this could only mean another dive-bombing attack.

Sam, unable to make himself heard, started gesticulating, first pointing at the receding needle on the steam gauge, then stabbing the air with two fingers—his dumb language for me to put on two more sprayers to bring the pressure gauge needle back to the 350 lb. per square inch mark. If we were under attack we would probably need to increase speed, which meant making as much steam as possible, in spite of the order to close down No. 1 boiler.

I had just turned the valves of No. 6 and No. 8 sprayers at the side of the furnace front when there was a sudden tilt to starboard. We were making a very tight right turn. Then in quick succession came two dull detonations that made the plates shudder. Simultaneously, the lights went out. Sam leaped across the boiler-room and up the ladder, disappearing into the darkness above. There was a metallic clang as he closed the airlock door behind him.

---

[88] *Grenade* would herself be sunk three weeks later in the Dunkirk evacuation. *Imperial*'s end was similar to that of *Bison*: she had to be sunk by gunfire by a sister destroyer (*Hotspur*) in the Crete evacuation. After being near-missed by a bomb, her steering gear jammed and she nearly collided with our cruisers. Her crew and the soldiers on board her had been taken off first—many of them only to perish when *Hotspur* herself was then bombed and sunk.

Only the faintest glimmer of orange-yellow light came from behind the furnace flaps. Impressed on my mind was the image of the receding steam gauge needle and Sam's jabbing fingers. Whatever had happened, I decided the steam pressure must be maintained so that the ship was kept under way. Besides, 'obey the last order' is the Navy's rule, presumably even if it were not voiced but given with two upraised digits.

In the darkness I groped and fumbled with the sprayer valves: I had to twist them anti-clockwise to turn them on. I slithered like a boxer in the ring from one side of the boiler to the other, manipulating the sprayers, pushing the flaps in and out haphazardly, hoping they corresponded with the sprayers I was turning on. Handling sprayers in the dark was not something I was taught in my stokers' preliminary training in the Pompey Grammar School: nor since.

Suddenly, the airlock door opened far above me, and Sam appeared making urgent beckoning gestures. He shouted down: 'We've been hit, Nutty. For fuck's sake come up!' And as I climbed the ladder, he added: 'It's fucking awful up here.'

~~

The first thing I noticed up top was that the deck was tilting slightly for'ard and to port and that there were a lot of men either standing looking bewildered or hastening this way and that. It was not clear to me what had happened. By the tilt of the ship it was evident that we had been hit somewhere for'ard and must be taking in water. Before I could draw any other conclusion, an aircraft's engines were heard and a Junkers skimmed towards us flying low. It did not attack us, however. Perhaps it was taking pictures?

Then the safety valve lifted on the waste-steam pipe on the side of the funnel, adding a deafening din to the confusion. I wondered whether this was due to my efforts down No. 3 to keep the steam up; with Sam's frantic gestures to come up and without knowing what had happened, I had left the sprayers on, still making steam. I realised my good intentions had not only been in vain but, by producing this ear-splitting noise, were counterproductive.

Stoker PO Geordie Allen was handing out 'neck-breaker' life jackets from a locker. He thrust one into my hands, indicating that I should put it on although I was already wearing my blown-up Mae West. But a few moments later a soldier made hand signs to me—the noise of the blowing-off steam made speech useless—pointing out that, since I had a Mae West, could he have the lifejacket? I gave it to him, at which he wrung my hand—a well-intentioned if unnecessarily dramatic gesture. Geordie Allen passed a moment later, noticed me *sans* lifejacket, was mystified as to what had happened to the one he had just given me and evidently concluded that an imbecile who could lose it so quickly in such a situation was beyond further aid.

The engineer commander and Cock Kent got down on their knees and struggled to turn off the valve on the deck which controlled the oil-fuel supply to the boilers, the only way to stop making the steam that had lifted the safety valve. I wondered if the stoker down No. 2 boiler-room had turned off the sprayers or left them on. Cock Kent who had been down No. 2 would tell me later that he had only just missed injury by leaping several feet when the oil-fuel pump had toppled over.

On the starboard side of the upper deck there was a crowd of shouting seamen, some of them already standing in a whaler which had been slung outboard on its davits. They were just about to lower it into the sea when a stentorian voice from the bridge barked: 'Who ordered you to do that? Bring it inboard at once. *Griffin* is coming alongside.'

When *Griffin* did come alongside some jumped aboard her straight away as others had done already when *Imperial* had come alongside to port although up to now I had heard no order to abandon ship.

I moved for'ard to see what damage had been done. From what I learnt later, two JU 87 Stukas had dived on us and while the gunners were concentrating on these, a third had dived with the sun behind him, hence unnoticed by the gunners, and scored with two bombs. Dr Rowlands, a Gloucestershire GP, recalls how he saw this, as a young volunteer in the Friends Ambulance Unit on board the French troopship *El Djezair*. The unit, under the International Red Cross, had been tending Finnish wounded during the short war with the Soviet Union. When this ended, they got to Norway and were caught up in the retreat to Namsos. Two of their ambulances were riddled by machine-gun bullets from German aircraft but Rowlands was one of the twenty-five who managed to get on board the troops-packed *El Djezair* and to stay on the upper deck out of the 'atrocious conditions' below. 'As a passive observer—hoping that the next bomb was not for us—I witnessed the hits on *Afridi*. Two massive explosions were followed by a dense pall of smoke. The transports and escorts pressed on and the *Afridi* was lost from view. For almost sixty-three years I have carried a vision of men in the water and been troubled by not knowing the fate of the men on board.'

Rear-Admiral Vivien's report to Admiral Sir Charles Forbes, C-in-C Home Fleet, stated: ' ... after surviving four attacks, the fifth bomber hit her. HMS *Carlisle,*' (from which he was observing the scene) 'shot this Junkers down shortly after she had dropped her bomb.'[89] This is the only source where I have seen this claim. John Dunning OBE, at that time an RNVR Seaman Gunner aboard *Carlisle*, contends: 'Not one of our crew ever saw an aircraft brought down by our own gunfire. On our return to Scapa after Norway the captain told us that we had shot down at least two planes but at the time I remember none of us believed him and took his remarks to be a morale booster!'

According to Yves Rivoal, who it may be remembered had been ordered aboard *Afridi* from the *Bison*'s whaler, the Stukas had made yet another attack on the convoy. Two of them had aimed their bombs at the cruiser *Carlisle* and missed. The third dived on *Afridi* which was 'hit near the for'ard funnel like the *Bison* had been and half of the *Bison*'s survivors who were on the mess-deck in the fo'c'sle were killed.'

Afridi's Able Seaman Jack Wearn has a vivid memory from his position behind the bridge of those moments before and after the impact:

> We were steaming at high speed and slewing to port when there was a roar like an express train rushing through a station, then an instant's silence followed by a terrific 'Whoosh.' I must have been knocked out and when I came around I was on all fours. There was a lot of noise and shouting. The siren was wailing like a dying animal. The captain was shouting: 'Tow forward!' But there was no time to get the gear ready for that and a couple of minutes later he shouted: 'Clear the bridge!'[90] With others I climbed down onto the upper deck. By then the ship was down by the bows and obviously sinking. We moved aft taking with us some of the injured who had managed to crawl onto the upper deck.

---

[89] Rear-Admiral Vivien claimed in his report that *Carlisle* had 'almost certainly shot down one Heinkel III and four Junkers JU.87. Two were seen from the ship to crash and the other three were reported having crashed in the hills near Namsos'.

[90] In his report to Rear-Admiral (D) Halifax, Captain Vian recorded that preparations for *Afridi* to be taken in tow by *Imperial* were abandoned because 'the bows by this time [were] almost awash' and 'it became apparent that *Afridi* was about to founder.'

This differs in one respect from Vian's own report which said that *Afridi* continued to turn to starboard after one of the Stukas had dived on her from that side and another dived out of the sun to port and dropped two bombs from either wing from about 1,000 feet.

Radio-Telegraphist Jean Raoul aboard the French destroyer *Tartu* remembers intercepting the last messages from the *Bison* saying she was sinking and from *Afridi*, first that she was running out of ammunition, then that she had been hit and was also going down.

Another witness was Telegraphist Bill Outram who was on *Imperial*'s flagdeck after she had left *Bison* and had rejoined the convoy. Just as *Afridi* had also caught up there was a warning shout from one of *Imperial*'s lookouts giving an aircraft bearing.

> Looking astern from my elevated position I saw a Stuka. Then it dived. Next, there was a vivid flash as *Afridi* was hit, followed seconds later by the sound of an explosion. We immediately went to her assistance and went alongside her portside. Straight away *Afridi*'s crew started to come aboard. I noticed another ship, which I subsequently learned was *Griffin*, come alongside *Afridi*'s starboard side.

Whether he was the pilot of the Junkers 87 dive-bomber that aimed those bombs at *Afridi* I cannot be certain but Hauptmann (the Luftwaffe equivalent to the RAF's Flight Lieutenant) Paul Werner Hozzel was leader of the Stuka group which attacked both the *Bison* and *Afridi*. There were apparently from three to five planes making dives at *Afridi* and if, indeed, the plane that dropped the fatal two bombs was shot down as claimed by *Carlisle*, then Hozzel obviously could not have been the pilot. But five days later he received the Knight's Cross for his group's sinking of these two warships and a claimed 60,000 tons of merchant shipping. The thirty-year-old Hamburg-born son of a ship-broker had already been awarded an Iron Cross (2nd Class) for bombing Warsaw and, after Norway, would be in raids on England and on our troops in Crete and North Africa. Operations against Moscow, Stalingrad and in other parts of the Eastern Front followed. At the end of the war he was captured by the Russians and was not released until 1956. He ended his career as the equivalent of Brigadier General, in the army of the German Federal Republic. He died in 1997.

6 airoplanes in position 007 degrees 24 ~~miles from~~ 65°N 8°E
based on a fix taken at 0400

0835

My 0835 - Enemy aircraft bombing

0850

"BISON" foremost magazine exploded - "Grenade" "Imperial" standing by - "AFRIDI" reinforcing MONTCALM'S screen - "Carlisle" 1½ hours ammunition left. 39 A/c have attacked so far. My position 352° RJ CJ 48.-

"BISON" Sunk 1207-3

Signals, probably from *Devonshire*, recorded by a French radio-telegraphist and (below) French recordings of signals transmitted between Admiral Cunningham in *Devonshire* and Rear-Admiral Derrien in *Montcalm*. There is also one from Captain Vian in *Afridi* to Derrien. The body of Lieutenant-Commander Giraud, second-in-command of the *Bison*, was recovered from the sea and taken on board *Imperial*.
(Courtesy Service Historique de la Marine, Paris)

de "DEVONSHIRE" - BISON Hit bearing 275 degrees distant 5 miles in
in position 353 R J C U 44 X 04.

1010.

de C S 1   - Sink BISON. Send destroyers you can spare to screen.
My position ....
1010/3

de D. 4 (AFRIDI) - à C.S.1 et MONTCALM - BISON sunk.
1207/3

de "DEVONSHIRE" - H.M.S. AFRIDI hit.
1353/3

de C.S. 1   - Following received from IMPERIAL : request instructions wheter the late Capitaine de Corvette GIRAUD should be burried at sea. I would be grateful to know your wishes.
1913/3

de Al.MONTCALM - Your 1913. Burried at sea please.

One of the bombs had exploded beside or inside No. 1 boiler-room and destroyed the W/T (wireless telegraphy) office above it. The second had torn a gash on the port side of the fo'c'sle abreast the for'ard guns. Between those two bombs both the seamen's mess-deck (where many of the soldiers and *Bison* survivors had been) as well as the stokers' mess-deck were a shambles. My 4.7 supply party had been wiped out.

Those who had not been consumed by the fire which started immediately or asphyxiated by the fumes from the W/T department's batteries were also drowned by the inrush of water. No one in the stokers' mess could have stood a chance. The only officer killed was a Warrant Telegraphist, RN and thirteen telegraphist ratings.

I heard that Petty Officer L. T. ('Daisy') Bell had succeeded in rescuing some of those trapped in the seamen's mess by lying on the fo'c'sle deck, leaning over the side and pulling them through the gaping bomb-torn rent on the port side before the fore part of the ship settled further and the water rose and covered it.

After *Imperial* had come alongside us, Telegraphist Bill Outram, then twenty-four, had an experience which would haunt him for another six decades, particularly on emotional occasions like the Remembrance Day ceremony at the Cenotaph:

> I was on our flag-deck only about twenty feet distant from the portside of *Afridi*'s fo'c'sle. In a lower porthole I saw a face I instantly recognised as that of a particular friend of mine, *Imperial*'s quarter master/helmsman. He had been in the boat picking up the *Bison* men when its crew had been ordered aboard *Afridi*. The scuttle of course was secured so I couldn't hear anything, but my friend kept mouthing what I understood as 'Help me, Bill! Help me!' The signalman who was standing beside me agreed that that was what Jim was pleading. I went down into our empty communications mess-deck and said a prayer for Jim and for all the other men trapped in *Afridi*.

Vian recorded that six of *Afridi*'s ratings 'blown out of the ship by the explosion' were picked up by *Imperial*'s whaler.

Another gruesome incident which survivors remembered was of a soldier on the seamen's mess-deck who had tried desperately to squeeze through a porthole on the starboard side. Someone had shouted to him to withdraw his head and cross the deck so that he could pull him through the portside rent. But either because of terror or injury, the soldier persisted in trying to get through the scuttle. Sixty-two years later a Grantham man who said he was one of about ten soldiers of the Royal Lincolnshires aboard *Afridi* informed me that he had seen this incident but 'at the last few seconds I turned away.' Several men said the soldier was shot by an officer who considered this more humane than for the man to be beheaded or crushed by the *Griffin* which was just then coming alongside. With experience of similar tragedies, at least one scuttle on mess-decks was later made large enough for a man to get his shoulders through.

But it is testimony to human resilience that in recalling their traumatic experiences even those who were severely wounded remember certain humorous aspects of what happened.

Signalman Harold Kirk, who had been on watch on *Afridi*'s bridge since the early hours of the morning, was ordered by Vian to go below and rest. He went down to the communications mess-deck which was on the starboard side two decks below the for'ard guns. Utterly exhausted, he lay down in the middle of the mess-deck alongside the hammock netting (where all the bulky hammocks of the men who slept in the mess were stowed):

> I fell asleep to what I thought was Vera Lynn singing *Yours*.[91] It could have been coming over the radio or just a dream. The next thing I was conscious of was a massive bang on the portside aft of our mess and debris falling everywhere. The hammock netting had saved me. I jumped for the ladder to get up to the next deck but when I was half way up, the ship listed to port and I was thrown off. Fires had now started to blaze beneath my feet where the magazine and shell compartment was and the flames caught me and I was badly burnt. The amazing thing was that only my eyes were free of burns, so I must have automatically shut them. Once again I made a painful grab at the ladder which was now at an angle and pulled myself up to the next deck and then up to the fo'c'sle. I had my Mae West on but not inflated. Seeing 'Tiny' Ross, one of our yeomen of signals, I asked him to blow it up for me, which he did; then he rushed off. When we eventually met up again we had a good laugh over that because although he'd blown it up, in the stress of the moment he forgot to screw down the valve so all the air escaped immediately! I don't know how I got aboard *Griffin*—I suppose someone carried me.

---

[91] Dubbed 'The Forces' Favourite', the singer was made a Dame of the British Empire.

One of the first walking casualties I met being led along the deck was Stoker Petty Officer Chris ('Lofty') Coombes, the only survivor from No.1 boiler-room where, until recently, Cock Kent and I had kept watch. When the order had come to shut down No.1 boiler after *Afridi* had caught up with the convoy, Lofty had gone up the ladder to the platform at the top of the boiler to turn off the main steam valve. The bomb had ripped open the side; the sea had rushed in, immediately drowning the stokers on the plates below, including Jimmy Robertson (whose agility I had admired in my first boiler watch-keeping days in November). But it had swept Lofty Coombes, who had been on one of the upper rungs of the ladder, over to the other side of the boiler-room. Presumably it was the sea that had saved him from being scalded by the steam issuing from the fractured boiler. Although blinded (he recovered his sight in hospital, I learned later) he had swum across the boiler-room to where, through his eyelids, he sensed there was light—in fact it was coming through the rent made by the bomb. Once he had swum through this, he too was pulled to safety. Incredibly, though his eyes were shut and he was shaking from cold and shock, his long hair matted with oil-fuel, he was still smiling. When I asked him how he felt, he insisted he was 'all right'. We led him along the deck and lowered him onto the *Griffin*.

There is again the temptation to use commonplace phrases like 'bad luck' and 'fate' when one compares Lofty's escape with what happened to SPO Don Budgeon only yards away. Chai had been brewed in the Stoker POs' mess, and Budge in the goodness of his heart had been bringing a cuppa down to his chum, Lofty, on watch in No. 1 when the bombs hit *Afridi*. He was trapped in the tiny compartment between the hatch which he had closed behind him and the airlock door which he had just opened and was apparently fatally scalded when the bomb ripped open No. 1's boiler. Efforts to save him proved impossible and his would-be rescuers were haunted by his cries.

I soon realised that there was nothing more I could do for'ard and on returning I came across Ldg Stoker Jimmy Marden, the quiet engineer's writer from Horsham, limping along the upper deck. His face was blackened by blast and he was wounded in the leg. I put his arm around my neck and supported him around the waist. He, too, tried to smile and protested he could manage on his own since there were others far worse than himself who needed help. But he gave an involuntary wince of pain so I supported him until we reached the quarterdeck where he waited his turn to be helped aboard *Imperial*.

There were others, severely wounded, lying on the quarterdeck. One of them was my hammock neighbour, the hefty Ldg Stoker Roberts against whom I had bumped whenever there was a heavy roll. 'Morphia—for God's sake give me morphia,' he was pleading. The feet of the man whose hobby had been ballroom dancing with his wife in Pompey were hanging on by their tendons and resembled dollops of raw mincemeat. It was my first sight of serious injury. He was carried aboard *Griffin* where his feet were amputated but he died from shock.

Next, I recognised Stoker Frank Rattue lying on the deck, his face drained of colour. Still conscious, he was trying to say something. It was probably about his belt. Three years later, when I was in transit through Greenock, I met his brother. Being an unusual name, I had approached him when it had been called out over the Tannoy and he confirmed Frank had been his brother aboard *Afridi*. With a hint of suspicion he asked me whether I had any idea as to what had happened to Frank's belt which had contained his savings.[92] These should have gone to his mother but never reached her. I could only tell him that I helped to carry Frank on board *Imperial* but had then returned to *Afridi*. Frank had died before *Imperial* reached home waters.

Most of the badly wounded Frenchmen who had been placed in the wardroom had by now been removed to one or other of the two rescue ships alongside. But there remained a couple for whom there were no stretchers left. Two or three of us grabbed the corners of the carpet and lifted one of the wounded men in it and managed to carry him over the gangway to *Imperial*. We used the remaining rug for the other man and transported him in the same way. One of them had groaned as we picked him up and pleaded with us to leave him. The other just stared upwards in a state of shock after being bombed twice within four hours.

I had not noticed that someone[93] had been making a list of members of *Afridi*'s ship's company who had gone aboard *Imperial* in order to make a record of survivors and, by a process of elimination, of the missing. Whoever it was had failed to cross out my name when I returned to *Afridi* the last time. This would have unfortunate consequences.

~~

Everyone who could have been had now been rescued. *Afridi*'s bows

---

[92] The belt of a Naval rating in square rig had a purse in front. The flap was secured by a press-stud.
[93] It was the First Lieutenant assisted by Able Seaman 'Jock' Horsbrugh.

were steadily settling and the angle of the upper deck was growing steeper. I noticed Vian himself standing on the starboard side of the upper deck with another officer and a white-haired three-badge man, Chief Yeoman of Signals Bill Sweet, who was evidently trying to persuade the Captain to leave the ship. Vian was declining. Bill, recounting this episode later, said he believed the days were over when a captain felt honour-bound to go down with his stricken ship. The Navy needed men like Vian. 'I would only leave if he did and would have pushed him off if he'd tarried any longer,' he quipped. In fact, Bill was the last Lower Deck rating to leave the *Afridi*.

Because of our list, *Griffin*'s upper deck was below ours and it was from there that Cock Kent shouted up to me that there was nothing more to be done, that *Griffin* was shoving off any minute now and it was time I jumped aboard. I did just that. Whenever I am asked how long I spent in the icy waters of the Norwegian Sea I have had to admit I never even got my feet wet. The same could be said for three of the *Bison* men who had got into Rivoal's whaler except that for them it had been not once but twice in four hours. Unfortunately, the fourth man, Gunner René Coudron, who had gone to the help of several of his *Bison* shipmates before being one of the oarsmen in Rivoal's boat, was one of those who did not survive the second bombing.

My last sight from *Griffin*'s deck of Captain Vian was of his duffle-coated figure striding towards the other side of his stricken ship with Bill Sweet. They joined the other *Afridi* officers and *Bison*'s Gunnery Officer Oudin to take passage in *Imperial*.

Another curious omission in Admiral Vian's memoirs is that there is no mention that *Griffin*, commanded by Captain (later Rear-Admiral) John Lee-Barber DSO, came to our assistance. This could hardly have been a lapse of memory since in his report to Rear-Admiral (D) Halifax he had written: '*Griffin* proceeded alongside the starboard side of *Afridi* and *Imperial* the port; both ships were very well handled.' A quarter of an hour later, at 14.45—about forty-five minutes after being hit—we saw from about a mile away the Navy's biggest destroyer finally lurch into the depths, bows first, the eleventh RN destroyer to be sunk since the beginning of the war. It was two years to the very day since her first commissioning.

The old war horse, General Carton de Wiart, who had expressed disappointment at having to take passage in the cruiser *York* instead of with us, would record: 'I lost my chance of being sunk; I missed a great experience.'

There was still an hour and a quarter of the afternoon watch to go. Fishes were probably completing mine, far down below in *Afridi*'s No. 3 boiler-room.[94]

~~

Griffin's upper deck was a grim spectacle: the wounded were lying in the open, head to feet, head to head or side by side. A few were on stretchers, the rest just lying on the steel or corticene deck. Some had blood-soaked bandages, others had their wounds covered with bits of rag, several of those whose faces had not been blackened by the scorching breath of a bomb blast had the parchment pallor of the dying.

As the destroyer picked up speed and raced south-west through the Norwegian Sea, Shetlands-bound, she inevitably rolled in spite of the comparative calm and, as she did so, many of the wounded, too weak to steady themselves, slid inch by inch towards the edge of the deck where it seemed they could have been tilted into the sea. According to one estimate there were now 400 men aboard *Griffin*, more than double her own complement. Not only were there survivors from *Afridi*, thirty-four from the *Bison* and a few soldiers, but *Griffin* had already picked up survivors from the anti-submarine trawlers *Aston Villa* and *Gaul* which had been bombed in Namsen Fjord. Her flats and mess-decks were crammed with wounded. (*Afridi*'s badly-burned Signalman Harold Kirk found himself in *Griffin*'s drying room with no idea who had laid him there. He woke up to find his wounds had stuck to someone's blanket which had been put there after being dhobeyed.) The Breton Stoker Petty Officer Eugène Thomas, the 'lucky' eighth man at *Bison*'s mess table, also found himself on the *Griffin*; his luck had held through the *Afridi* crisis as well, though he would be ill enough to be taken aboard a hospital ship the following day and was eventually hospitalised in Brest. This overload of survivors and of the barely surviving was the reason why so many men who lay exposed on the upper-deck could not be brought under cover, at least for the time being. When we would reach safer waters and *Griffin*'s overtaxed crew could relax their efforts defending the ship, then perhaps they would have time to find space and shelter for them, I thought.

---

[94] An example of how literary condensation can give a distorted picture is an account an author gave his readers in a book published in 1973. He wrote *Afridi* 'engaged in this errand of mercy [going to *Bison*'s aid] was hit by several bombs, reared up and capsized.' Lord Lovat in his memoir, *March Past*, mentioned *Afridi* five times as being in the Lofoten Islands raid in March 1941, i.e. ten months after she had sunk.

It was getting colder as the horizon crept closer to the sun. I was still only in my boiler suit. Together with the uninjured survivors I tried to make our less fortunate comrades as comfortable as possible, above all to stop them from slipping over the side.

I held onto one Frenchman who was coughing and groaning without respite. He appeared to be in his mid-forties; his matted hair where it showed through a bloodstained bandage had streaks of grey. There were little rivulets of blood clotted on his ashen face which every now and then was contorted with pain. As I crouched beside him I stared out to sea searching the skies for some sign that the RAF would provide us with fighter cover. With the unreasonableness born of our vulnerability to the Stukas, some referred cynically to the 'Brylcreme boys', although they knew it was impossible to provide protection close to the Norwegian coast because the distance was too far to take-off from and return to the UK. But, I was thinking that surely *Griffin* and *Imperial* must be at least halfway to home waters with their cargo of broken bodies and shattered nerves. Yet, there were still no signs of friendly aircraft.

There was a flash aboard a destroyer away on *Griffin*'s starboard quarter followed a second later by a crack; her for'ard high-angle guns were firing. Above and between the two ships little grey puffs appeared. There were more flashes and reports and a string of puffs blossomed in the sky. A bomber was heading for us, cocking a snook at my musing.

In contrast to my passive role, preventing the Frenchman from sliding into the drink, one of *Afridi*'s survivors had found a practical way of relieving his feelings. I was surprised to see a seaman gunner, a swarthy lad with high cheekbones whom I recognised but had never spoken to (stokers had little contact with the rest of the ship's company) on a sponson above me manning *Griffin*'s starboard pom-pom. His eyes were mere slits beneath his cap, firmly kept in place by his chin stay, as he concentrated on the target. He swivelled around with the Bofors, keeping the bomber within the gun's 'spider web' sight. *Griffin*'s main armament was already firing. The bomber was almost overhead. *Afridi*'s gunner pressed the trigger and the eight barrels thrust forward and recoiled as each one in succession pumped its missiles skywards, the tracer arcing toward the plane. The noise was ear-splitting. But the shell bursts were wide of the mark. The bomber rolled and dived, screaming as it plummeted towards us. I heard the swoosh of the bomb—and leapt across the deck to flatten myself with my head under the gash-chute. There was a muffled explosion and *Griffin* jerked slightly out of the water. The bomb had missed, but only just. It had fallen within a few yards of the fo'c's'le and exploded just under the water. The JU87 sheered off, pursued by the little dirty-grey puffs, at first close to its tail, then the distance lengthening as it drew away and disappeared.

In Rear-Admiral Cadart's report it had been at 15.25 that *Montcalm* spotted in the distance seven or eight splashes from bombs aimed at *Imperial* and *Griffin*. Another report maintained nine enemy aircraft attacked the British destroyers, concentrating on *Griffin* (though I was only aware of one). Rear-Admiral Vivien would record that at about 15.15 *Carlisle*'s radar reported thirteen bombers to eastward, eight of which 'attacked a destroyer some ten miles astern.' A third French account estimated that one bomb fell twenty metres from *Griffin* (whose CO sent the terse signal to Admiral Cunningham: 'No hits.') A French officer on board *York* [95] was wondering: 'Is *Griffin* also going to die with all those passengers on board who have already been through two sinkings within a few hours?' For over seven hours there had been almost ceaseless attacks, he would recall later, and observers on *York* had counted forty-six bombing sorties by the Luftwaffe against our convoy CS 1.

A little self-conscious at having precipitated myself with such alacrity beneath, of all things, a gash-chute, through which garbage was shot into the sea, I resumed my place beside the groaning Frenchman. His lips were moving; he was trying to say something. I bent over to catch his words: 'Soif, à boire, à boire,' the dying man was repeating in a hoarse whisper and lifted his finger to his lips. I went to the galley and fetched a cup of water, held him around the shoulders and put the cup to his mouth. He took a few sips and, his eyes closed, nodded his thanks.

Before dark all the wounded had been removed under cover. The young RNVR surgeon [96] worked unceasingly under conditions he could never have imagined during his student days in Barts or St Thomas's. Rivoal recorded that a matelot from St Brieuc who had an arm amputated had died, as did others. 'My' Frenchman was one of them.

~~

It was cold on *Griffin*'s stokers' mess-deck. I looked around for something with which to cover myself before lying down on the iron deck which only had a canvas covering. Recently, *Griffin* had had prisoners on board from

---

[95] Lieut Olivier Nesque, in *L'Expédition de Namsos*.
[96] Two days before, ashore in Namsen Fjord, he had been operating on the wounded of the bombed HMTs *Aston Villa* and *Gaul*.

an intercepted German armed trawler which had been supplying U-boats. Although the crew had thrown her cipher apparatus overboard, I would learn after the war that from the papers seized and passed onto the Bletchley Park code-breakers, valuable information had been obtained. There were various souvenirs of the prisoners' sojourn and the stokers were still smoking their pungent German cigarettes, in spite of calling them 'camel-dung sweepings'. I made a valuable find: a pair of black leather German seaman's trousers with a grey cotton lining which had elastic around the ankles.[97] Since I only had a singlet and pants under my boiler suit, I drew on these trousers, curled up on the deck and fell asleep.

At about 05.00 the alarm rattlers sounded-off and, once more, there was the familiar rush up the ladder. No one had allocated 'passengers' like me an action station but, with the fate of my comrades on *Afridi*'s mess-decks fresh in mind, I followed the others up top. Outside, the air was crisp though already the sun was shining from a clear blue sky. An unidentified object had been spotted on the surface of the sea by a lookout. As *Griffin* drew alongside it turned out to be a submerged RAF fighter, one wing-tip protruding above the surface. It was gently swaying with the restless motion of the sea. We stared through the pellucid greenness at the cockpit. It was empty. Had the pilot bailed out and, if so, had he been picked up? Or had his body been washed away?

It was yet another wreck to be sent full fathoms five. Round after round of point-five shells were pumped into the fighter before it sank. The only requiem I heard was from a Geordie seaman: 'Bye, that's the first fookin' fighter we've seen and the booger 'as to be a fookin' wreck!'

~~

Within a few hours the welcoming green hills of the Shetlands hove in sight and *Griffin* was soon steaming up Yell Sound into a wide bay, Sullom Voe.[98] Signals had been sent for hospital ships to rendezvous with *Griffin* and *Imperial*. But there was no hospital ship. We dropped anchor alongside *Imperial* and the badly wounded as well as the dead were transferred. Then it was the turn of the *Afridi* survivors. As we stepped aboard *Imperial* each man's name was ticked off on a list by *Afridi*'s First Lieutenant. When I stood in front of him, saluted and gave my name, he exclaimed: 'That's strange. We had you down as missing.' I would

---

[97] See plate 27, xii.
[98] It would become Europe's largest oil terminal.

subsequently learn I was in good company: the same thing had happened to Colonel Peter Fleming and, by coincidence, when he too was in Sullom Voe. A Swedish radio broadcast had announced that it believed he had been killed in the raids on Namsos on 20 April. The agencies had picked it up and 'AUTHOR KILLED IN NORWAY' was the way the *Daily Sketch* headlined the story. Naturally, it caused considerable distress to Fleming's actress wife, Celia Johnson (the heroine in the often revived film *Brief Encounter*) and to his other relatives. As for mine, I learned when I got home on survivor's leave that my parents had received the dreaded 'missing' telegram, a severe shock to a frail mother and an already ailing father turned seventy. The error had evidently occurred when I went aboard *Imperial* more than once, each time returning to *Afridi*.

It was several hours before a white hospital ship marked with a huge red cross, the French *Sphinx*, entered the bay. The wounded, strapped to stretchers, were hauled aboard.

~~

Imperial's Lower Deck was cleared and officers and men crowded onto the quarterdeck. A padre was standing in the stern. At his feet lay the bodies of some of those who had died from their wounds, wrapped in coarse, brown sacking. Those who were wearing them removed their caps while the padre intoned the service for burial at sea. His surplice, like the White Ens'n at half-mast, flapped in the keen breeze from the north-east. It also ruffled the hair of the men who gently lifted their comrades one by one onto a plank.

Which of those anonymous bundles, I was wondering as they slid into the deeps of Sullom Voe, is Roberts or Rattue, Jimmy Robertson or another of my messmates with whom I had lived in such close proximity during the last six months or, perhaps, the Frenchman who had craved water. Only much later did I learn about those who had died on *Imperial* and *Grenade* and had already been buried at sea.

As the last shell-weighted bundle splashed into the green waters close to *Imperial*'s stern the wind carried across to the island of North Roe the untrained voices of Jock and Mick, Cock and Geordie, Taff, Skouse and Brummy, pronouncing each in his own way the words of the hymn which they and their shipmates, believers and sceptics alike, had sung many times before but probably never with such genuine emotion: 'Our shelter from the stormy blast, and our eternal home.'

~~

After the emotion, the impersonal statistics, but since figures for the ships' companies on board *Bison* and *Afridi* at the time either differ according to the various sources or are unavailable, the exact numbers of survivors also vary. For *Bison,* the figures for her complement differ from 209 to 268. Of these, 120 men are believed to have been picked up by the three British destroyers, including seventy wounded of whom twenty died on *Grenade* and four on *Imperial. Afridi* certainly picked up sixty-nine Frenchmen of whom thirty-five did not survive after we were bombed.[99] This makes a total of fifty-nine who died on British ships. Yves Rivoal in one part of his account of the 3 May events wrote that there were 112 *Bison* survivors out of a complement of 268 but in another place he recorded that 148 went missing out of 256 'officiers, officiers mariniers, quartier maîtres et marins'. On calculations based on these varying figures, there was anything between twenty-five and eighty-four men either killed outright when she was hit or were drowned or died on board, trapped below decks, or were in the stern when she was given *Afridi*'s *coup de grâce.*

In addition, Commander Robert Graham DSO, RN, who had been on the cruiser *Exeter* in the River Plate encounter with the *Graf Spee* and who was the British liaison officer on board *Bison,* together with two RN ratings, a telegraphist and a quartermaster, as well as the Norwegian Namsos pilot, were killed.

Afridi's peacetime complement had been approximately 220 and it was 256 in 1940. A French source maintained that there were 210 survivors of her ship's company. On the basis of Commonwealth War Graves Commission data we can be certain that one officer, forty-nine ratings and two NAAFI canteen staff were killed outright or later died of their wounds: a total of fifty-two. Of these, sixteen were in the engine room branch— 'Pusser' Reid was a survivor—and fourteen were telegraphists. Their branches suffered the heaviest casualties. There were in addition thirty-one of *Afridi*'s crew who were wounded but survived, of whom nine were stokers. Of the thirty-six soldiers who embarked at Namsos, thirteen were killed and eleven wounded. Thus at least one hundred definitely perished of 350 or more men who were aboard *Afridi* when she was bombed.

Mountbatten claimed *Kelly* destroyed at least one dive-bomber in the course of this action. Rear-Admiral Vivien, commanding the anti-aircraft ships, wrote that in operations in the Namsos area between 25 April and 3 May, *Carlisle* 'almost certainly shot down one Heinkel III and four

---

[99] One of them was Premier Maître Mécanicien Louis Nay who was one of the men whom Yves Rivoal and his mates in the whaler rescued. See p. 277.

Junkers JU 87. Two were seen from the ship to crash and the other three were reported having crashed in the hills near Namsos.'[100] The official Admiralty communiqué stated:

> Following upon the withdrawal of our troops from Norway, HM ships, of which the destroyer *Afridi* (Captain P. L. Vian DSO, RN) was one, provided defence for the troop convoy against aircraft and submarine attack. With the arrival of daylight, repeated waves of enemy aircraft kept up incessant attacks upon the convoy, but the barrage maintained by the anti-aircraft guns of the escort was so effective that the troop transports were untouched. It was in the course of this operation that HMS *Afridi* was struck by bombs and subsequently sank. Two enemy aircraft were shot down. The next of kin of casualties have been informed.

~~

That was the Allies' first 'Dunkirk'. In the House of Commons debate of 7 and 8 May on the 'Conduct of the War' which would lead within days to the demise of the Chamberlain administration and Churchill becoming Prime Minister, the Labour MP for Leeds, South East, Major James Milner, declared that the withdrawal from Central Norway was a notable military feat 'but you cannot win a war by repeated withdrawals and retreats.' This truism was echoed by the Deputy Leader of the Opposition Arthur Greenwood: 'Wars are not won on masterly evacuations.' Yet, as they were speaking, the panzers were rolling towards the Belgian frontier and in another twenty-two days the drama of the Dunkirk evacuation would be played out.

Three days after the remnants of the British Expeditionary Force were rescued from the beaches and mole of Dunkirk, the remainder of the Allied Expeditionary Force in Norway—Poles, French and the multi-national Foreign Legion—left Narvik, some 500 miles to the north of Namsos. They had captured the port from the Germans at considerable cost (not least in Norwegian civilian lives and property) including the loss of an aircraft carrier and two destroyers[101] only to be pulled out again almost immediately. Norway would be under the thrall of Nazi Germany for the next five years.

---

[100] See a *Carlisle* rating's comment on p. 286.
[101] See p. 115.

Postscript

The people of Namsos had to rebuild their broken town; no help was forthcoming from the invaders who had destroyed it. By February 1941 Harbour Master Henrik Andersen had rebuilt the family home. Only the main road out of the ruined town separated it from the cemetery where British and French servicemen were buried. On Christmas Eve 1940, the Andersens did something for which there was no tradition in Norway: between three and four o'clock—it was dark in this northern latitude—they placed candles on these men's graves and lit them, under the noses of the Germans. Henrik's son, Jens-Anton, recalls:

> We did it in remembrance of those who gave their lives so that one day we could live again in freedom. It was a token of resistance to the invaders and every year of the Occupation since then, except one, we and our friends lit the candles at the same time on Christmas Eve so that the people going to church later would be sure to see them. The Quislings and Gestapo didn't like it but if they had tried to stop us that would have strengthened the resistance and given the Nazis more problems.
>
> On Christmas Eve 1943 I remember some Russian prisoners-of-war were digging up the ground across the road from the cemetery in preparation for the construction of a German bunker. When they saw us lighting the candles they understood what we were doing and stopped work. That evening the German guards were more easy-going than usual and did nothing to stop us as we exchanged greetings with the prisoners and gave them food parcels. That was solidarity in practice!
>
> The following year, 1944, my father was already in prison in Trondheim when my mother and I were thrown out of our house by the Gestapo and police on 19 December. We had to

leave town with nothing and stay in a little cabin in a valley near the Namsen River about twenty kilometres away. So the candles weren't lit on that Christmas Eve 1944. But on New Year's Eve I had to go down into town and, together with a friend, we managed to place the candles on the Allies' graves. And we have done it on every Christmas Eve since then. Now it is my father's second and third generation which is keeping up the tradition, keeping alive the memories of these men.

A strong liaison was forged with the French veterans and in 1957 a monument was erected in Namsos cemetery for their fallen comrades. Since then a ceremony attended by a delegation from France, and often by representatives from the French embassy in Oslo, has been held beside it on every 17 May, Norwegian Constitution Day. In 1999 the French ambassador presented Jens-Anton Andersen with a gold medal in recognition of his efforts on behalf of Franco-Norwegian *entente cordiale*. But his gratification at being so honoured was tempered by one regret: although British losses were heavier than those of their allies, yet there had been no British representatives at any of these ceremonies in Namsos and no British memorial there. In the campaign's land operations over 1,800 British were dead, missing or severely wounded; 1,300 Norwegians; 530 French and Poles. Lost at sea were 2,500 Royal Navy and Merchant Navy men as well as eleven Royal Navy warships sunk and more casualties in several others.

It was no consolation to Jens-Anton and his friends that the Commonwealth War Graves Commission had well-tended graves of British servicemen in several Norwegian civil cemeteries, the nearest to Namsos being in Trondheim's Stavne cemetery a hundred miles distant, as well as imposing war memorials in the UK where they are honoured.

Namsos is where the Allies' Central Norway campaign ended, where in the fjord or off the Namdal coast, six Royal Navy ships were sunk and eleven sustained casualties. Why should post-war generations of Namsos citizens and visitors not have something tangible to remind them that, at the very least, there was British participation in the Allies' attempt, brief and forlorn though it was, to stem the conquest of their country?

In Hyde Park, north of the Serpentine, there is a boulder with an inscription recording that it was 'brought here from Norway where it was worn and shaped for thousands of years by forces of nature—frost, running water, rock, sand and ice—until it obtained its present shape.' It is the memorial from the men of the Royal Norwegian Navy and the Norwegian Merchant Fleet thanking the British people 'for friendship and hospitality during the Second World War.' On a visit to London in January 1999, Mr Andersen, on being shown this stone expressed his 'sincere regret that there is no memorial in Namsos for all the British sailors and soldiers who were killed in the evacuation. We in Namsos have not forgotten them and their families. There *must* be something, one of these days, to record the losses borne by the British.'

That day came sooner than certainly anyone this side of the Norwegian Sea expected. A Namsos Memorial appeal was launched by Friends of War Memorials whose patron is the Countess Mountbatten of Burma, eldest daughter of the captain of HMS *Kelly* which led the ships up Namsen Fjord for the evacuation. Generous donations were given by the Foreign and Commonwealth Office; the York and Lancaster Regiment (whose thirteen Hallamshire men died when *Afridi* was bombed); by the King's Own Yorkshire Light Infantry; corporate bodies such as Enterprise Oil and even in Namsos itself by Forestia, a Norwegian firm which exports timber to Britain, and by individuals including the daughter of author Peter Fleming. Namsos Town Council contributed to the cost of lifting an Ice Age boulder from a moraine, after it had been buried under two metres of that winter's snow, and transporting it to the site it had prepared in a prominent position in the town near the Norwegians' own war memorial.

All was ready in Namsos for the unveiling of the town's own British war memorial on 17 May 2000. The day before the ceremony, a little group, including two *Afridi* survivors, two Hallamshire veterans and the widow of another who had died when *Afridi* was bombed, were taken by their Norwegian hosts to a spot on the rocky Namsen Fjord seashore. Here, the ship's bell recovered from the wreck of HMT *Gaul*[102] was tolled and Jens-Anton Andersen quoted John Donne as we threw roses on the sea opposite where this anti-submarine trawler had been bombed and sunk on 1 May 1940:

'... for whom the bell tolls, it tolls for thee.'

At the unveiling itself by our ambassador, the ship's bell of another bombed anti-submarine trawler, HMT *Aston Villa*, was tolled by a

---

[102] See pp. 103 and 113.

Norwegian veteran who had escaped via neutral Sweden to Britain where he had joined a ship of the Royal Norwegian Navy at Harwich to carry on the fight. With the British group mingled some of the forty French men and women who had earlier that day gathered around their own memorial when a plaque was unveiled to those who died after the *Bison* was bombed. Among them was Jean Raoul, the radio telegraphist on board the French destroyer *Tartu* who had heard the last messages from the *Bison* and *Afridi*.[103]

For those at the unveiling who had taken part in these events and for the widow, its symbolism was palpable and emotive. But it was the significance of something expressed by someone who was not himself present which showed that among the 21st century's teenage generation there are some who do link what happened in the past with the present and future, significant because of its vindication of such little ceremonies 'keeping the events of the Second World War intact in the communal memory'. A sixteen-year-old Sheffield student, on learning why his father and grandfather, a Hallamshire veteran, were going to Namsos, unsolicited and quite spontaneously penned a message which his father read out at the unveiling:

> When I think of the war I can only see images in black and white. Young men in their uniforms waiting to go away from their homes, not knowing when or if they will be coming back. The more I think about it, the more I think what life may have been for me. Without their courage and bravery I would not be so fortunate as to have the life I have, one without constant fear or the threat of violence. These men and women fought so that I could have the freedom to say what I want and the freedom to determine my own future. This is ours today because of people like my Granddad who risked everything, including, most importantly their life, for me.

The inscription in English on the British memorial faces down to the harbour where the first Allied landings took place and only a fortnight later the last Allied troops in Central Norway were withdrawn in the brief hours of darkness of 3 May 1940:

---

[103] See p. 286.

IN MEMORY OF THE BRITISH CASUALTIES SUFFERED IN H.M. SHIPS *AFRIDI, MAORI, GRENADE, BITTERN, CARLISLE, ASTON VILLA, ARAB, GAUL, RUTLANDSHIRE & ST. GORAN,* AND IN THE HALLAMSHIRE BN., YORK & LANCASTER REGT., THE KING'S OWN YORKSHIRE LIGHT INFANTRY AND THE ROYAL LINCOLNSHIRE REGT. IN THE APRIL–MAY 1940 BLITZ AND EVACUATION FROM NAMSOS, AS WELL AS THE UNKNOWN ROYAL AIR FORCE PILOT WHO DIED IN 1942.

On the other side, facing the church (which had to be completely rebuilt after the blitz) is inscribed in Norwegian:

IN MEMORY OF THE BRITISH ARMY AND NAVY FORCES WHO DIED DURING THE NAMSOS CAMPAIGN APRIL–MAY 1940. THEY DIED SO WE CAN LIVE IN PEACE, FREEDOM AND DEMOCRACY.

In the words of the British Ambassador, Richard Dales: 'An anomaly has been repaired at last.'

Each year since the unveiling, to make up for the years when there was no British memorial at Namsos, its townsfolk have given a warm welcome to the party of 1940 veterans, their families and friends from the UK and even from Australia and the USA who have come together in the days around 17 May to keep alive the memory not only of their own countrymen but of the Norwegians, French and Russians who died here in the struggle against tyranny. They also join their hosts in the colourful, musical and above all youthful celebrations of Norway's National Day.

Just as Jens-Anton Andersen and his friends have kept up the tradition for over six decades of lighting candles to kindle remembrance of their Allies, these annual visits from the UK are also contributing to the 'communal memory' of this early phase of the Second World War.

ACKNOWLEDGEMENTS AND SOURCES

My sincere thanks to everyone who helped in the production of *Full Circle*, foremost to the publisher for scrupulous editing and assiduous attention to the illustrations, nearly all of them between fifty-eight and sixty-four years old and showing their age. My thanks also to all those who were in any way involved in researching or providing data including: the staffs of the Imperial War Museum Library and Photographic Archive; the Royal Naval Museum, Portsmouth; the Ministry of Defence Naval Historical Branch; the Commonwealth War Graves Commission; the Middlesex Regimental Association for the tracing of my counterpart in the Army (the No. 10000001 militiaman); the Royal British Legion and the ten ex-servicemen who answered my appeal in *Legion*, and to the RAF Personnel Management Agency for tracing Aircraftsman No. 701000 and to Mr Wallace Weatherall himself.

I would particularly like to express my gratitude to Mr Jens-Anton Andersen for answering my myriad questions, for his patient and indefatigable researching in his own Namsos archives and for allowing me to browse through some of them and to choose pictures from his extensive collection. Thanks too to Mr John Connor for sending me Robin Sadler's translation of Mr Andersen's *Årbok for Namdalen*.
I was privileged to be given access to Peter Fleming's Namsos notes by his daughter Mrs Kate Grimond.

I am grateful to those former members of the ships' companies of HM Ships *Afridi*, *Imperial*, *Grenade* and *Nubian:* Harold Kirk; Jack Wearn; Fred Aris; William Ridgewell; Daniel Kington; Bill Outram and Captain M. D. Rahilly, RN (rtd.); as well as those who wrote to me about comrades who did not survive. I am also grateful to others like John Connor of the Royal Artillery light anti-aircraft batteries set up in Namsen Fjord and to Forbes Wilson for his invaluable PRO research and his conscientiously and beautifully produced 'individual website' dedicated to his grandfather, CO of HMT *Rutlandshire*. They all supplemented my account of the events of April/May1940 with graphic details.

I was fortunate to receive unexpected aid from two French sources: first from the late M. Eugène Thomas who sent me the fascinating *Contre Torpilleur Bison 22 Mai 1930–3 Mai 1940* by Yves Rivoal, the boatswain's mate on *Bison* (and my sincere thanks to the Naval Attaché at the French Embassy in London for responding to my SOS for translations of French naval ranks into their RN equivalents); second, from M. Jean Raoul who obtained through his relative, Amiral le Berre, important documents concerning the loss of *Bison* and *Afridi* from the Paris Service Historique de la Marine. This is also an opportunity to thank again my friend Marielle Dunand in Paris for so kindly making inquiries concerning an article and a book about the *Bison* published so many years ago.

I am indebted to the late Captain Stephen Roskill DSC, RN for his three-volume *War at Sea 1939–1945* (HMSO); to Dr Kingston Derry for *The Campaign In Norway* in the UK Military Series of HMSO's *History of the Second World War* and to *Naval Operations of the Campaign in Norway April–June 1940* edited by David Brown (Frank Cass Publishers), all of which were invaluable for fixing precise dates, the chronology of events and for innumerable details which could not possibly have been known to servicemen at the time.

For quotations from speeches in the House of Commons I was lucky to have my father's copy of *Hansard*: *Official Report Fifth Series Parliamentary Debates 1939–40 Vol 360 23 April–13 May*. For enlightenment on the origins of many of the words and phrases that were/are common currency on the Lower Deck, I would thank Surgeon Commander Rick Jolly, RN for his *Jackspeak, A Guide to Royal Navy Slanguage* (Palamanando Publications, PO Box 42 Torpoint, Cornwall PL11 2YR) which he explains is 'a dictionary and reference to slang, euphemisms, idiom and usage—past and current—of the Royal Navy and Royal Marines.' (Its numerous cartoons by Tugg are sure to appeal to the Rabelaisian in most of us, service and lay alike.)

I am also grateful to the authors, many of whom are no longer with us, whose books I either consulted or to which I have referred in the body of the text: to Peter Calvocoressi and Guy Wint for *Total War* (Allen Lane, the Penguin Press); Admiral of the Fleet Sir Philip Vian, GCB, KBE, DSO, RN for *Action This Day* (Frederick Muller); Captain Donald Macintyre DSO and two Bars, DSC, RN for *Narvik* (Evan Bros.); Lt-General Sir Adrian Carton de Wiart VC, KBE, CB, CMG, DSO for *Happy Odyssey*

(Jonathan Cape); Jack Adams for *The Doomed Expedition—The Campaign in Norway* (Leo Cooper); *Norway:* Christopher Buckley for *The Commandos Dieppe* (HMSO); Major-General J. L. Moulton for *The Norwegian Campaign of 1940* (Eyre & Spottiswoode); Sir Cecil Parrott for *The Tightrope* (Faber & Faber); François Kersaudy for *Norway 1940* (Collins); Theodor Brock for *The Mountains Wait* (Michael Joseph); Raymond du Pavillon for *Les Dessous de l'Expédition de Norvège 1940* (Artaud); Olivier Nesque for *L'Expédition de Namsos* (limited edition, 300 copies); Philip Ziegler for *Mountbatten: the official biography* (Collins); Richard Hough for *Mountbatten, Hero of Our Time* (Weidenfeld & Nicolson); Duff Hart-Davis for *Peter Fleming: A Biography* (Jonathan Cape); Peter Fleming for *Invasion 1940* (Ruper Hart-Davis); *Churchill and The Admirals* (Collins) and *Naval Policy Between The Wars*; Tom Harrison for *Living Through the Blitz* (Collins); William Griffiths for *My Darling Children—War From The Lower Deck* (Leo Cooper); Frederick Wigby for *Stoker—Royal Navy* (Blackwood); Sydney Greenwood for *Stoker Greenwood's Navy* (Midas); Tristan Jones for *Heart of Oak* (The Bodley Head); Max Hastings for *Overlord, D-Day and the Battle for Normandy* (Michael Joseph); David Holbrook for *Flesh Wounds* (Methuen); Freedman Ashe-Lincoln for *Secret Naval Investigator* (Kimber); Lord Lovat for *March Past: A Memoir* (Weidenfeld & Nicolson); Ian Ousby for *Occupation: The Ordeal of France 1940–1944* (Pimlico); Cornelius Ryan for *A Bridge Too Far,* (Coronet Books/Hamish Hamilton); Edgar J. March for *British Destroyers 1892–1953* (Sealey, Service & Co.); T. D. Manning for *The British Destroyer* (Godfrey Cave Associates); John Costello & Terry Hughes for *The Battle of the Atlantic* (Collins); Nicholas Monsarrat for *The Cruel Sea* (Cassell) and for *Life Is A Four-Letter Word Part II: Breaking Out* (Cassell); John Winton for *The Forgotten Fleet* (Michael Joseph); Laurens Van Der Post for *Yet Being Someone Other* (Hogarth); John Fletcher-Cooke for *The Emperor's Guest* (Hutchinson); Lord Hill-Norton for *Sea Power* (Faber & Faber), and to Patrick Beesly for *Very Special Intelligence* (Hamish Hamilton).

Wherever possible, where quotations from books have been made, permission has been obtained from the publishers or copyright-holders.
Thanks to my sons, Roderick and Andrew, for reading through the manuscript and my wife's good-humoured patience during *Full Circle*'s long gestation.

Finally, my apologies to anyone who has been overlooked; I assure them it was inadvertent. J.G.

GLOSSARY

Terms used in the Second World War Royal Navy

Andrew, Merry Andrew: Slang name for the Royal Navy. In rhyming slang: Peas and Gravy.

Bootnecks, Leathernecks: Royal Marines.

Bunting tosser, Bunts: Signals rating.

Chief Petty Officer: Highest non-commissioned rank (equivalent to Sergeant-Major). In the Engine Room Branch, Chief Stoker sometimes referred to as Chief Boiler-buster.

Chief ERA: Chief Engine Room Artificer or Chief Tiffy, highest non-commissioned rank in the Engine Room Branch. In the commissioned ranks: Senior Engineer (usually with the rank of Lieutenant Commander) and Commander (E).

Commissioned ranks (with Army equivalents): Sub-Lieutenant (2nd lieut); Lieutenant (Captain); Lieutenant Commander (Major); Commander (Colonel); Captain (Brigadier); Captain (D) in command of a flotilla of destroyers; Commodore ranks above Captain, usually in command of a squadron or other unit of the fleet; Rear-Admiral, Vice-Admiral, Admiral, Admiral of the Fleet (Major-General, Lieutenant-General, General, Marshal, Field Marshal).

Dab-toe or **Sand-scratcher**: Stokers' terms for Seamen.

ERA: Engine Room Artificer.

First-Lieutenant: 'Jimmy-the-One'. The second-in-command to the Captain on board a destroyer, responsible for the 'ship-shape and Bristol-fashion' cleanliness and appearance of the ship.

Flat: On a warship, an internal deck space not within a mess, e.g. canteen flat or sickbay flat.

Galley buzz: A rumour circulating through the ship, traditionally supposed to originate in the galley (ship's kitchen).

Gongs: Medals.

Grog: See Tot.

Jack: Generic name for a sailor but ratings usually refer to themselves as 'matlows' (matelots).

Jaunty: Jack's name for the Master-at-Arms, the chief regulating petty officer responsible (under the First Lieutenant) for organising the ship's routine.

Jenny Wrens: Jack's name for members of the Women's Royal Naval Service (equivalent to the Army's WRACs and RAF's WAAFs).

'Jimmy-the One': See First Lieutenant.

Killick: Originally, a certain type of anchor. A leading hand (equivalent to a corporal) because he wears an anchor emblem on his right arm, red on his shipboard uniform, gold on his 'tiddley suit' for going ashore.

Leathernecks: Royal Marines.

Mess: living quarters on a warship (or in a Naval barracks) e.g. seamens' or stokers' mess.

MTB: Motor Torpedo Boat.

Muck-sticks: Rifles.

Ordinary Seaman (abbreviation = **OD**): the lowest rank in the Seamen's Branch (equivalent to a Private).

Petty Officer: A non-commissioned rank (equivalent to sergeant). In the Engine Room Branch, Stoker Petty Officer (SPO).

Pigs: Jack's collective name for officers; can be expressed conversationally, but with increasing vehemence according to the degree he feels he has been wronged by one particular individual.

PO: Petty Officer, equivalent to a sergeant.

Pompey: Portsmouth.

Pusser: Derivation from purser, the paymaster in the old Navy. A stickler for keeping to Navy routine and traditional way of doing things. The Army equivalent to 'regimental'. A full description in *Jackspeak* (See Acknowledgements and Sources).

SPO: Stoker Petty Officer.

Rating: Any non-commissioned rank.

(The) Smoke: London.

Sprog: A novice.

Tot: Daily measure of rum that was issued to ratings, diluted to ranks below POs.

Ullage: In a barrel the empty space between the top of the beer (wine) and the lid. Hence used by Jack to denote somebody he considers worthless, as in the phrase 'a useless piece of ullage'.

INDEX